Dr. Bhim Rao Ambedkar

Dr. Bhim Rao Ambedkar

Dr. C.P. Raj
Dr. Ved Prakash

AMIGA PRESS. INC
Delhi -110051

AMIGA PRESS. INC
H.O :- 28-A, Indra Park, Chander Nagar
Delhi :- 110051 (India)
Tel :- 011-22504028, +91-98736-57000
Email :- amigapress@gmail.com
amigaeditorial@gmail.com
Website :- www.amigapress@co.in

This edition is published by Amiga Press.Inc

ISBN : 978-93-84533-28-1

First Published 2018

PRINTED : THOMSON PRESS INDIA

Preface

Bhimrao Ramji Ambedkar (14 April 1891 — 6 December 1956), also known as Babasaheb, was an Indian jurist, political leader, Buddhist activist, philosopher, thinker, anthropologist, historian, orator, prolific writer, economist, scholar, editor, revolutionary and a revivalist for Buddhism in India. He was also the chief architect of the Indian Constitution. Born into a poor Mahar, then Untouchable, family, Ambedkar spent his whole life fighting against social discrimination, the system of Chaturvarna — the categorization of Hindu society into four varnas — and the Hindu caste system. He is also credited with providing a spark for the conversion of hundreds of thousands of Dalits with his Ambedkar (ite) Buddhism. Ambedkar has been honoured with the Bharat Ratna, India's highest civilian award.

Overcoming numerous social and financial obstacles, Ambedkar became one of the first "Dalit" to obtain a college education in India. Eventually earning law degrees and multiple doctorates for his study and research in law, economics and political science from Columbia University and the London School of Economics, Ambedkar returned home as a famous scholar and practiced law for a few years before publishing journals advocating political rights and social freedom for India's untouchables. He is regarded as a Bodhisattva by Indian Buddhists even though he never claimed himself to be a Bodhisattva.

Dr. B.R. Ambedkar educated himself as a the most qualified person of his time, inspired untouchable castes to reject Brahmanical Social Order (BSO) that kept them socially degraded, economically poor, culturally despised, economically poor, culturally despised, politically powerless, and denied them the basic human rights. Overcoming numerous social and financial obstacles, Ambedkar became one of the first "Dalit" to obtain a college education in India. Eventually earning law degrees and multiple doctorates for his study and research in law, economics and political science from Columbia University and the London School of Economics, Ambedkar returned home as a famous scholar and practiced law for a few years before publishing journals advocating political rights and social freedom for India's untouchables. He is regarded as a Bodhisattva by Indian Buddhists even though he never claimed himself to be a Bodhisattva.

Ambedkar was one of the most prominent political figures of his time. He was critical of mainstream Indian Political parties for their lack of emphasis for elimination of the caste system. He accused Gandhi for reducing the untouchable community to a figure of pathos. At a depressed classes conference on August 8, 1930 Ambedkar outlined his political vision insisting that the safety of the depressed classes hinged on their being Independent of Government and the Congress.

The emergence of the Ambedkarite movement has been one of the most significant developments in Rajasthan since 1930s. The present study examines the emergence, ideology and programme, mobilisational strategies and spread of the Ambedkarite movement, against the backdrop of two important changes witnessed in the state since the early 1930s: a wave of Dalit assertion and grass-roots activism. It is based upon extensive field work and interviews with the initiators of the movement and generation of post-independence educated, upwardly mobile, socially aware and politically conscious Dalits.

Since 1948, Ambedkar had been suffering from diabetes. He was bedridden from June to October in 1954 owing to clinical depression and failing eyesight. He had been increasingly embittered by political issues, which took a toll on his health. His health worsened as he furiously worked through 1955. Just three days after completing his final manuscript 'Buddha And His Dhamma', it is said that Ambedkar died in his sleep on December 6, 1956 at his home in Delhi.

The book, which provides a rare opportunity to debate and discuss the contribution of Dr. Ambedkar in nation-building, will be great interest to all sections of people.

—*Editor*

Contents

1

Biography

Bhimrao Ramji Ambedkar (14 April 1891 — 6 December 1956), also known as *Babasaheb*, was an Indian jurist, political leader, Buddhist activist, philosopher, thinker, anthropologist, historian, orator, prolific writer, economist, scholar, editor, revolutionary and a revivalist for Buddhism in India. He was also the chief architect of the Indian Constitution. Born into a poor Mahar, then Untouchable, family, Ambedkar spent his whole life fighting against social discrimination, the system of *Chaturvarna* — the categorization of Hindu society into four *varnas* — and the Hindu caste system. He is also credited with providing a spark for the conversion of hundreds of thousands of Dalits with his Ambedkar (ite) Buddhism. Ambedkar has been honoured with the Bharat Ratna, India's highest civilian award.

Overcoming numerous social and financial obstacles, Ambedkar became one of the first "Dalit" to obtain a college education in India. Eventually earning law degrees and multiple doctorates for his study and research in law, economics and political science from Columbia University and the London School of Economics, Ambedkar returned home as a famous scholar and practiced law for a few years before publishing journals advocating political rights and social freedom for India's untouchables. He is regarded as a Bodhisattva by Indian Buddhists even though he never claimed himself to be a Bodhisattva.

EARLY LIFE

Bhimrao Ramji Ambedkar was born in the British-founded town and military cantonment of Mhow in the Central Provinces (now in Madhya Pradesh). He was the 14th and last child of Ramji Maloji Sakpal and Bhimabai. His family was of Marathi background from the town of Ambavade in the Ratnagiri district of modern-day Maharashtra. They belonged to the Hindu, Mahar caste, who were treated as untouchables and subjected to intense socio-economic discrimination. Ambedkar's ancestors had for long been in the employment of the army of the British East India Company, and his father Ramji Sakpal served in the Indian Army at the Mhow cantonment. He had received a degree of formal education in Marathi and English, and encouraged his children to learn and work hard at school.

Belonging to the Kabir Panth, Ramji Sakpal encouraged his children to read the Hindu classics. He used his position in the army to lobby for his children to study at the government school, as they faced resistance owing to their caste. Although able to attend school, Ambedkar and other untouchable children were segregated and given no attention or assistance by the teachers. They were not allowed to sit inside the class. Even if they needed to drink water somebody from a higher caste would have to pour that water from a height as they were not allowed to touch either the water or the vessel that contained it. This task was usually performed for the young Ambedkar by the school peon, and if he could not be found Ambedkar went without water. Ramji Sakpal retired in 1894 and the family moved to Satara two years later. Shortly after their move, Ambedkar's mother died. The children were cared for by their paternal aunt, and lived in difficult circumstances. Only three sons — Balaram, Anandrao and Bhimrao — and two daughters — Manjula and Tulasa — of the Ambedkars would go on to survive them. Of his brothers and sisters, only Ambedkar succeeded in passing his examinations and graduating to a higher school. His native village name was "Ambavade" in Ratnagiri District so he changed his name from "Sakpal" to "Ambedkar" with the recommendation and faith of Mahadev Ambedkar, his Deshastha Brahmin teacher who believed in him.

Ramji Sakpal remarried in 1898, and the family moved to Mumbai (then Bombay), where Ambedkar became the first untouchable student at the Government High School near Elphinstone Road. Although excelling in his studies, Ambedkar was increasingly disturbed by the segregation and discrimination that he faced. In 1907, he passed his matriculation examination and entered the University of Bombay, becoming one of the first persons of untouchable origin to enter a college in India. This success provoked celebrations in his community, and after a public ceremony he was presented with a biography of the Buddha by his teacher Krishnaji Arjun Keluskar also known as Dada Keluskar, a Maratha caste scholar. Ambedkar's marriage had been arranged the previous year as per Hindu custom, to Ramabai, a nine-year old girl from Dapoli. In 1908, he entered Elphinstone College and obtained a scholarship of twenty five rupees a month from the Gayakwad ruler of Baroda, Sahyaji Rao III for higher studies in the USA. By 1912, he obtained his degree in economics and political science, and prepared to take up employment with the Baroda state government. His wife gave birth to his first son, Yashwant, in the same year. Ambedkar had just moved his young family and started work, when he dashed back to Mumbai to see his ailing father, who died on February 2, 1913.

POLITICAL CAREER

In 1935, Ambedkar was appointed principal of the Government Law College, Mumbai, a position he held for two years. Settling in Mumbai, Ambedkar oversaw the construction of a house, and stocked his personal library with more than 50,000 books. His wife Ramabai died after a long illness in the same year. It had been her long-standing wish to go on a pilgrimage to Pandharpur, but Ambedkar had refused to let her go, telling her that he would create a new Pandharpur for her instead of Hinduism's Pandharpur which treated them as untouchables. Speaking at the Yeola Conversion Conference on October 13 near Nasik, Ambedkar announced his intention to convert to a different religion and exhorted his followers to leave Hinduism. He would repeat his message at numerous public meetings across India

In 1936, Ambedkar founded the Independent Labour Party, which won 15 seats in the 1937 elections to the Central Legislative Assembly. He published his book *The Annihilation of Caste* in the same year, based on the thesis he had written in New York. Attaining immense popular success, Ambedkar's work strongly criticized Hindu orthodox religious leaders and the caste system in general. Ambedkar served on the Defence Advisory Committee and the Viceroy's Executive Council as minister for labour. With *What Congress and Gandhi Have Done to the Untouchables*, Ambedkar intensified his attacks on Gandhi and the Congress, hypocrisy. In his work *Who Were the Shudras?*, Ambedkar attempted to explain the formation of the Shudras i.e. the lowest caste in hierarchy of Hindu caste system. He also emphasised how Shudras are separate from Untouchables. Ambedkar oversaw the transformation of his political party into the All India Scheduled Castes Federation, although it performed poorly in the elections held in 1946 for the Constituent Assembly of India. In writing a sequel to *Who Were the Shudras?* in 1948, Ambedkar lambasted Hinduism in the *The Untouchables: A Thesis on the Origins of Untouchability*:

The Hindu Civilisation.... is a diabolical contrivance to suppress and enslave humanity. Its proper name would be infamy. What else can be said of a civilisation which has produced a mass of people... who are treated as an entity beyond human intercourse and whose mere touch is enough to cause pollution?

In a "communal malaise", both groups [Hindus and Muslims] ignore the urgent claims of social justice.

PAKISTAN OR THE PARTITION OF INDIA

Between 1941 and 1945, he published a number of books and pamphlets, including *Thoughts on Pakistan,* in which he criticized the Muslim League's demand for a separate Muslim state of Pakistan but considered its concession if Muslims demanded so as expedient. In the above book Ambedkar wrote a sub-chapter titled *If Muslims truly and deeply desire Pakistan, their choice ought to be accepted*. He wrote that if the Muslims are bent on Pakistan, then it must be conceded to them. He asked whether Muslims in the army could be trusted to defend India. In the event of Muslims invading India or in the case of a Muslim rebellion, with whom would the Indian Muslims in the army side? He concluded that, in the interests of the safety of India, Pakistan should be acceded to, should the Muslims demand it. According to Ambedkar, the Hindu assumption that though Hindus and Muslims were two nations, they could live together under one state, was but a empty sermon, a mad project, to which no sane man would agree.

THE SIGNIFICANCE OF AMBEDKAR

In the grounds of the parliament building in Delhi stands a statue of a stout, elderly man clad in a business suit and wearing spectacles. The statue is about fifteen feet high, and stands with right foot slightly advanced on the square top of a pedestal of much the same height. Underneath the left arm of the statue is a large book, while its right arm is outstretched practically to its full extent, index finger pointing in the direction of the parliament building. The statue represents Bhimrao Ramji Ambedkar, Law Minister in the Government of India from 1947 to 1951; the book underneath his arm is the Indian Constitution, and his finger points to the parliament building because it was there that in 1948 he presented his draft Constitution to the Constituent Assembly, there that it was accepted a year later, and there that the legislation based on its provisions has ever since been passed.

Bhimrao Ramji Ambedkar was one of the most remarkable men of his time, and the story of his life is the story of how exceptional talent and outstanding force of character succeeded in overcoming some of the most formidable obstacles that an unjust and oppressive society has ever placed in the way of the individual. Born in Mhow in central India in 1891, he was the fourteenth child of parents who belonged to the very lowest stratum of Hindu society. According to orthodox Hindu tradition, he was not entitled to receive education or to acquire property, he could engage only in the most menial and degrading work, and he could not come into physical contact with members of the higher castes. In short, Bhimrao Ramji Ambedkar was born an outcaste or Untouchable. He was expected to wear cast-off clothes, to eat the leavings of his higher caste masters, to be humble and obedient, and to accept his lot as the well-deserved punishment for sins committed in a former existence.

Fortunately for him, however, his father had served in the Indian Army and there acquired a certain amount of formal education in both Marathi and English. This enabled him to teach his children, especially Bhimrao Ramji, and to encourage them in their own pursuit of knowledge. In 1908 the young Ambedkar passed the matriculation examination of Bombay University, and so uncommon was such an achievement on the part of an Untouchable boy that the event was celebrated with a public meeting. Four years later he graduated from the same university with Politics and Economics as subjects and soon afterwards entered the service of the Baroda State, the ruler of which had awarded him a scholarship. At this point his father died (his mother had died when he was five) and four months later the bereaved son left India to continue his studies at Columbia University (USA) on a further scholarship from the same liberal-minded ruler. Though he had climbed higher up the ladder of academic achievement than any other Untouchable, Ambedkar was far from being satisfied. Convinced as he was that knowledge is power, he knew that without that power in full measure he had little hope of breaking the bonds that kept millions of Untouchables in a state of virtual slavery – and how strong those bonds were his own bitter personal experience had already taught him.

From 1913 to 1917, and again from 1920 to 1923, Ambedkar was in the West, and when at the age of thirty-two he finally returned to the country of his birth it was as one of the most highly qualified men in public life. During his three years at Columbia University he studied Economics, Sociology, History, Philosophy, Anthropology, and Politics, and was awarded a Ph.D. for the thesis which he eventually published in book form as *The Evolution of Provincial Finance in British India*. His first published work, however, was a paper on 'Castes in India: Their Mechanism, Genesis and Development' which he had originally read at an Anthropology seminar conducted by one of his professors. After completing his studies in America, Ambedkar left New York for London, where he was admitted to the London School of Economics and Political Science and to Gray's Inn. A year later his scholarship came to an end and it was only in 1920 that, having taught in a Bombay college and started a Marathi weekly called Mooknayak or 'Leader of the Dumb', he was able to return to London and resume his studies there. In the course of the next three years he completed his thesis on *The Problem of the Rupee*, for which the University of London awarded him a D.Sc., and was called to the Bar. Before leaving England he spent three months in Germany, where he engaged in further studies in Economics at the University of Bonn.

Thus the man who returned to India in April 1923 to continue his fight on behalf of the Untouchables and, indeed, all the Depressed Classes, was uniquely well equipped for the task, and from this time onwards it becomes increasingly difficult to separate the biography of Bhimrao Ramji Ambedkar from the history of modern India. During his three year absence in London the Indian political scene had changed dramatically. The demand for independence from Britain had grown louder than ever: Mahatma Gandhi had started advocating a policy of non-cooperation with the Government and only a year before Ambedkar's return had launched the first of his campaigns for mass civil disobedience.

But though Ambedkar was a staunch patriot, and though initially he was of the opinion that only political independence would bring social equality within the reach of the Depressed Classes, he was emphatic that if – as Gandhi and the Congress Party maintained – no country was good enough to rule over another it was equally true that no class was good enough to rule over another class. Certainly the Caste Hindus were not good enough to lord it over the Depressed Classes, and while Ambedkar remained sharply critical of British rule it was to the removal of the social, economic, educational, and legal disabilities of the Depressed Classes that he devoted the major part of his energies. As early as 1920 he had realized, however, that the interests of the Depressed Classes would have to be safeguarded by means of separate electorates, at least for a period, and it was his increasing insistence on this point that eventually brought him into open conflict with Mahatma Gandhi and the Congress Party, as well as with practically the whole of orthodox Hindu India.

This conflict did not come to a head until 1932. In the meantime Ambedkar established himself in Bombay, built up his legal practice, taught in college, gave evidence before various official bodies, started a newspaper, and was nominated to the Bombay Legislative Council, in whose proceedings he at once took a leading part. He also attended the three Round Table Conferences that were held in London to enable representatives of the various Indian communities and the three British political parties to consider proposals for the future constitution of India. One of his most significant achievements during the years immediately following his return to India in 1923 was the formation of the Bahishkrit Hitakarini Sabha or Depressed Classes Welfare Association, the objects of which were to promote the spread of education and culture among the Depressed Classes, to improve their economic condition, and to represent their grievances.

These grievances were serious enough. Untouchables were not allowed to enter Hindu temples, they could not draw water from public tanks or wells, they were denied admittance to schools, and prevented from moving about freely in public places – and so on. Between 1927 and 1932 Ambedkar therefore led his followers in a series of non-violent campaigns to assert the right of the Untouchables to enter Hindu places of worship and to draw water from public tanks and wells. Two of these campaigns were of special importance. These were the campaigns against the exclusion of Untouchables from the Kalaram Temple, Nasik, and from the Chowdar Tank, Mahad, both of which involved tens of thousands of Untouchable satyagrahis or 'passive resisters', provoked a violently hostile reaction from the Caste Hindus and, in the case of the Chowdar Tank campaign, resulted in a legal as well as a moral victory for the Depressed Classes only after years of litigation. The Chowdar Tank campaign also saw the ceremonial burning of the *Manusmriti* or 'Institutes of Manu', the ancient Hindu law book that bore much of the responsibility for the cruel and degrading treatment that the Untouchables had hitherto suffered at the hands of the Caste Hindus. By committing the much-revered volume to the flames the Depressed Classes were serving notice to the orthodox Hindu community that in future they intended to be treated as human beings.

Unpopular as Ambedkar's activities had already made him with the Caste Hindus, during 1931 and 1932 he became more unpopular still. In his own words, he became the most hated man in India – hated, that is, by the Caste Hindus and by the Congress Party, which they dominated. The cause of the trouble was Ambedkar's continued insistence on the necessity of separate electorates for the Depressed Classes. Mahatma Gandhi and the Congress Party were opposed to separate electorates for the Depressed Classes (though not for the Muslims, Sikhs, Christians, and Europeans), and Ambedkar and Gandhi had clashed on the subject at the Second Round Table Conference, when the Mahatma went so far as to challenge the right of Ambedkar to represent the Untouchables.

Ambedkar's arguments did, however, convince the British Government, and when Ramsay MacDonald published his Communal Award the following year the Depressed Classes were given the separate electorates for which they had asked. Gandhi's response was to go on a fast to the death for the abolition of separate electorates for the Depressed Classes.

Since he was the acknowledged leader of the independence movement his action created consternation throughout India. Ambedkar was reviled as a traitor and threats were made against his life. But though unmoved by the pressure that was brought to bear on him Ambedkar was not unwilling to negotiate and eventually agreed to exchange separate electorates for joint electorates and a greatly increased number of reserved seats.

This agreement was embodied in a document that became known as the Poona Pact, the signing of which by Ambedkar marked his emergence as the undisputed leader of the Depressed Classes.

In the mood of relief that swept the country when the weak and ailing Mahatma ended his fast there was even a little sympathy to spare for the wretched Untouchables, but it did not last long, and soon Ambedkar was as much hated as ever. Partly as a result of the opposition he had encountered over the question of separate electorates, partly because of the continued exclusion of Untouchables from Hindu temples, Ambedkar now began to think that the Caste Hindus were not going to mend their ways.

He therefore changed his tactics – though not his strategy – and started exhorting his followers to concentrate on raising their standard of living and gaining political power. He also began to think that there was no future for the Untouchables within Hinduism and that they should change their religion. These thoughts found dramatic expression at the 1935 Depressed Classes Conference, when he made his famous declaration that though he had been born a Hindu he did not intend to die one – a declaration that sent shock waves through Hindu India. In the same year Ambedkar was appointed principal of the Government Law College, Bombay, built a house for himself and his books, and lost his wife Ramabai. They had been married in 1908, when he was sixteen and she was nine and she had borne him five children, of whom only one survived. Though the demands of public life had left him with little time for his own domestic affairs, Ambedkar was deeply attached to the gentle and self-effacing woman and mourned her bitterly.

When he had recovered from his grief he plunged back into his customary activities and soon was busier than ever. In the course of the next few years he founded the Independent Labour Party, took part in the provincial elections that were held under the Government of India Act, 1935, was elected to the Bombay Legislative Assembly, pressed for the abolition of agricultural serfdom, defended the right of industrial workers to strike, advocated the promotion of birth control, and addressed meetings and conferences all over the Bombay Presidency.

In 1939 World War II broke out in Europe and the fact that Britain was locked in a life-and-death struggle with Nazi Germany soon had its effect on the political situation in India. According to Gandhi and the Congress Party, Britain's difficulty was India's opportunity, and from 1940 they adopted a policy of non-cooperation with the Government war effort.

Ambedkar did not agree with this attitude. Not only was he not a pacifist but he regarded Nazi ideology as a direct threat to the liberties of the Indian people. He therefore exhorted them to help defeat Nazism by supporting the Government, and himself encouraged the Untouchables to join the Indian Army. In 1941 he was appointed to the Defence Advisory Committee and in the following year joined the Viceroy's Executive Council as Labour Member, a post he occupied for the next four years. During the same period he transformed the Independent Labour Party into the All-India Scheduled Caste Federation, founded the People's Education Society, and published a number of highly controversial books and pamphlets. Among the latter were *Thoughts on Pakistan*, *What Congress and Gandhi have Done to the Untouchables*, and *Who Were the Shudras?*

In 1947 India achieved independence and Ambedkar, who had already been elected a member of the Constituent Assembly, was invited by Pandit Nehru, the first prime minister of the country, to join the Cabinet as Minister for Law. A few weeks later the Assembly entrusted the task of framing the Constitution to a Draft Committee, and this committee elected Ambedkar as its chairman. For the next two years he was hard at work on the Draft Constitution, hammering it out article by article and clause by clause practically single-handedly.

While he was thus engaged the country was passing through a period of turmoil. Independence had been won only at the cost of partition, partition had led to the wholesale slaughter of Hindus by Muslims and Muslims by Hindus, and at the beginning of 1948 Mahatma Gandhi was assassinated. Besides being deeply concerned about the fate of the Untouchables living in what was now Pakistan Ambedkar had troubles of his own to face. His health had been deteriorating for some time, and now gave him cause for such grave concern that on the day following his fifty-eighth birthday he married a Brahmin woman doctor whom he had met in hospital and who would, he hoped, be able to provide him with the care he needed. Despite his ill health Ambedkar managed to complete the Draft Constitution by the beginning of 1948 and later that year, when it had been before the country for six months, had the satisfaction of introducing it in the Constituent Assembly. Thereafter he piloted it through its three readings with his usual competence and in November 1949 it was adopted by the Assembly with very few amendments. The new Constitution gave general satisfaction and Ambedkar was warmly congratulated by friend and foe alike. Never had he been so popular.

The press hailed him as the Modern Manu, and the irony of the fact that it was an Untouchable who had given Free India its Constitution was widely commented upon. Though he lived for seven more years, it was as the Architect of the Constitution and the Modern Manu that he was destined to pass into official history. When his statue came to be erected outside the parliament building after his death it was therefore as the Modern Manu that he was depicted, holding the Constitution underneath his arm and pointing in the direction of the parliament building.

But though by 1948 Ambedkar had achieved so much, and though today he is most widely remembered as the author of the Indian Constitution, his greatest achievement was in fact still to come. This achievement was an essentially spiritual one, and it came only at the very end of his life, when he had spent several years in the political wilderness after failing to secure the passage of the Hindu Code Bill. The Bill represented a putting into shape by Ambedkar of work accomplished during the previous decade by a number of eminent Hindu lawyers and dealt with such matters as marriage and divorce, adoption, joint family property, women's property, and succession.

Though it was a reforming rather than a revolutionary measure, the Bill met with violent opposition both inside and outside the Assembly, and even within the Cabinet. Ambedkar was accused of trying to destroy Hinduism and there were angry exchanges on the Assembly floor between him and his orthodox opponents. In the end the Bill was dropped after only four clauses had been passed and in September 1951, tired and disgusted, Ambedkar resigned from the Cabinet.

In his resignation statement (which he was prevented from making in the Assembly itself) he explained that he had left the Cabinet for five reasons. The second of these was that it was apathetic to the uplift of the Scheduled Castes, the fifth that Pandit Nehru had failed to give adequate support to the Hindu Code Bill.

Ambedkar's resignation from the Cabinet marked the virtual end of his political career. In the general elections of January 1952 he failed to win a seat in the Lok Sabha or House of Representatives, and was equally unsuccessful when he contested a by-election the following year.

Towards the end of March 1952 he was, however, elected to the Rajya Sabha or Council of States as one of the seventeen representatives of the State of Bombay, and was soon vigorously attacking the Government. But while he continued to participate in the proceedings of the Rajya Sabha, and was to do so until the end of his life, from now onwards Ambedkar's energies were increasingly devoted to more important things. Ever since the 1935 Depressed Classes Conference, when he had shocked Hindu India with the declaration that though he had been born a Hindu he did not intend to die one, he had been giving earnest consideration to the question of conversion. The longer he thought about it the more he was convinced that there was no future for the Untouchables within Hinduism, that they would have to adopt another religion, and that the best religion for them to adopt was Buddhism.

During his years in office it had been hardly possible for him to bring about so momentous a change, but he had lost no opportunity of educating his followers in the issues involved, and it became increasingly apparent in which direction he – and they – were moving. In 1950 he not only praised the Buddha at the expense of Krishna, Christ, and Muhammad but also visited Ceylon at the invitation of the Young Men's Buddhist Association, Colombo, addressed a meeting of the World Fellowship of Buddhists in Kandy, and appealed to the Untouchables of Ceylon to embrace Buddhism.

In 1951 he defended the Buddha against the charge that he had been responsible for the downfall of the Indian woman and compiled the *Bauddha Upasana Patha*, a small collection of Buddhist devotional texts. Thus when his resignation from the Cabinet, and his failure to secure election to the Lok Sabha, finally left Ambedkar with the time and energy for his greatest achievement, the ground was already well prepared.

In 1954 he twice visited Burma, the second time in order to attend the third conference of the World Fellowship of Buddhists in Rangoon. In 1955 he founded the Bharatiya Bauddha Mahasabha or Indian Buddhist Society and installed an image of the Buddha in a temple that had been built at Dehu Road, near Poona. Addressing the thousands of Untouchables who had assembled for the occasion, he declared that henceforth he would devote himself to the propagation of Buddhism in India.

He also announced that he was writing a book explaining the tenets of Buddhism in simple language for the benefit of the common man. It might take him a year to complete the book, but when it was finished he would embrace Buddhism. The work in question was *The Buddha and His Dhamma*, on which he had been working since November 1951 and which he completed in February 1956. Not long afterwards Ambedkar, true to his word, announced that he would be embracing Buddhism in October of that year. Arrangements were accordingly made for the ceremony to be held in Nagpur, and on 14 October 1956 the Untouchable leader took the Three Refuges and Five Precepts from a Buddhist monk in the traditional manner and then in his turn administered them to the 380,000 men, women, and children who had come to Nagpur in response to his call.

After further conversion ceremonies in Nagpur and Chanda Ambedkar returned to Delhi knowing that the Wheel of the Dharma had again been set in motion in India. A few weeks later he travelled to Kathmandu in Nepal for the fourth conference of the World Fellowship of Buddhists and addressed the delegates on 'The Buddha and Karl Marx'. On his way back to Delhi he made two speeches in Benares and visited Kusinara, where the Buddha had died.

In Delhi he took part in various Buddhist functions, attended the Rajya Sabha, and completed the last chapter of his book *The Buddha and Karl Marx*. On the evening of 5 December he asked for the Preface and Introduction to *The Buddha and His Dhamma* to be brought to his bedside, so that he could work on them during the night, and the following morning he was found dead. It was 6 December, he was 64 years and 7 months old, and he had been a Buddhist for only seven weeks.

But though Bhimrao Ramji Ambedkar had been a Buddhist for only seven weeks, during that period he had probably done more for the promotion of Buddhism than any other Indian since Ashoka. At the time of his death three quarters of a million Untouchables had become Buddhists, and in the months that followed hundreds of thousands more took the same step – despite the uncertainty and confusion that had been created by the sudden loss of their great leader.

So much was this the case that when the results of the 1961 census were published it was found that in the course of the previous decade the number of Buddhists in India had risen by a staggering 1,671 per cent and that they now numbered 3,250,227, more than three quarters of whom lived in the State of Maharashtra. This was Ambedkar's last and greatest achievement, so that even though it was as the Architect of the Constitution of Free India and the Modern Manu that he passed into official history and is today most widely remembered, his real significance consists in the fact that it was he who established a revived Indian Buddhism on a firm foundation.

It is therefore as the Modern Ashoka that he really deserves to be known, and the statue standing outside the parliament building in Delhi should really depict him holding *The Buddha and His Dhamma* underneath his arm and pointing – not for the benefit of the Untouchables only, but for the benefit of all mankind – in the direction of the Three Jewels.

In order to appreciate the nature of Ambedkar's achievement, and thus the real significance of the man himself, it will however be necessary for us to take a look at the diabolical system from which he sought to deliver the Untouchables, as well as to trace the successive stages of the road by which he – and his followers – travelled from Hinduism to Buddhism.

We shall also have to see the way in which Ambedkar discovered his spiritual roots, explore his thoughts on the subject of the Buddha and the future of his religion, survey the historic occasion on which he and 380,000

Untouchables were spiritually reborn, study his posthumously published magnum opus and, finally, see what happened after his death.

But before that, a few personal recollections may not be out of place.

MAN OF THE HOUR

BRA now decided to practice law that would provide him with opportunities, means & leisure to devote himself to the aim of his life, the uplift of the Untouchables. With the help of Naval Bathena he started his life as a Barrister in June 1923. The thorns of untouchability, the color of his skin, the inexperienced legal mind & unhelpful surroundings in courts turned his path into an uphill task. But BRA knew that excellence in pursuit is achieved by laborious application.

BRA joined the Appellate side of the Bombay Bar as success in practice on the Original side depended more upon one's influence with the solicitors than upon one's ability. The Solicitors would not have anything to do with him on account of his untouchability and thus he had to be happy with whatever work came his way. Whats new, all famous legal luminaries had to start their early career cooling their heels.

By now outer influences and inner forces had brought about a visible change in the mental & moral outlook of the DC. The spread of education, development of communications, mode of traveling & spirit of nationalism had gradually begun to act as an effective correctness to the prejudicial ideas of untouchability. The rise of the textile industry during World War I helped the DC too since they had to work with other classes & stimulated them to better their own condition. On the top of it was the impetus to democratic ideals generated by the inevitable forces of World War I that gave an impetus to social reformation the world over.

About this time D Gholap, the first nominated member of the DC in the Bombay Legislative Council, moved a resolution in order to make primary education compulsory in order to bring it within the reach of the DC. But the most important resolution was one moved by S K Bole which the Bombay Legislative Council adopted on 4/8/1923. Moving the resolution he said that untouchability was a stigma on the good name of India: 'It is in the interests of the country that the DC should be given better treatment. The Council recommends that that the Untouchable Classes be allowed to use all public watering places, wells & dharamshalas which are built & maintained out of public funds'. Bole's work was widely appreciated by the DC of Bombay.

Another notable proclamation was made concerning the DC at the end of 1923. Stimulated by Gandhi's support to the Indian Muslims on the issue of Khilafat, presiding at a meeting called to present an address to Gandhi at Madras, Yakub Hussein once openly enjoined upon the Muslims the duty of converting all the Untouchables of India to Islam.

1924, Savarkar, Gandhi, BRA – this was one of most eventful years in Indian history. After undergoing a hellish life for 12 years in Andaman Savarkar was released & interned in Ratnagiri. Gandhi too was released on health grounds after suffering for nearly two years consequent to the debacle of his Khilafat-Swaraj Movement.

Savarkar worked for the consolidation of Hindu society & for the upliftment of the DC. Gandhi too did the same. BRA prepared himself for the same. He convened a meeting in March 1924 to consider establishing a central institution for removing difficulties of the untouchables & placing their grievances before the Government. So in July was formed 'Bahishkrit Hitakarini Sabha, activities confined to Bombay. Its aim was to promote the spread of education – culture among DC, advance & improve their economic condition, to represent their grievances.

Why was BRA chartering a different path? BRA was looking at social reforms in the sense of the reorganization & reconstruction of Hindu society on the basis of equality and not at issues like widow remarriage, education of women etc. Despite the good work by the Prarthana / Brahmo Samaj / princes none could stir in the heart of these suppressed people an emotion of confidence, hope & aspiration for their own salvation. Self-help is the best help. The conservative feeling in the country at this juncture was unmoved as a rock. Only the conscience of the more political minded Hindus was tweaked when they were reminded by the rival Muslim politicians that more than one-third of the Hindu population was not accepted by the Hindus as part & parcel of the community. That is why the Hindu Mahasabha & the Arya Samajists could not succeed much in their work of consolidation of Hindu society.

To be fair to the Hindu Mahasabha it must be said that they undertook a mission, which the conservative minds looked upon disfavor. Now when they were fighting foreign rule by raising the issue of social reform they ran the risk of alienating the conservative Hindu whose support they needed. But more than that the reason for their failure was that some of their first rate leaders were orthodox at heart, resolutions / intent were good but execution bad. Their apathy & indifference was so much that even Swami Shraddhananda had to resign from their camp. No wonder the Mahasabha was described by the World Press as reactionary instead of having great leaders like Shraddhananda & Savarkar. Congress leaders were concerned only with Muslim sentiments, did not care about the disabilities of the DC or note their conversion to Islam & Christianity. They did follow Gandhi's movement for uplift of the Untouchables.

Gandhi believed in the caste system & the four varnas. He wanted to raise the DC to the status of the fifth class, improve their lot but cared not to hurt the sentiments of his orthodox capitalist admirers who were the prop of his movement. His was more propaganda than effective change while Savarkar / BRA were social revolutionaries. Savarkar stand was nationalistic, realistic & revolutionary in outlook & action in as much at molding different castes into a casteless society in which all Hindus would be socially, economically & political equal. But as he was interned in Ratnagiri district the impact could not be seen outside that district.

BRA was one amongst the DC. He knew what it meant to be born & live the life of an untouchable. He gave vent to their passions, mind & stifled self. A man of great knowledge & boundless energy he was a man who regarded the woes & miseries of those classes as a personal humiliation, and thus had taken a vow to make self-respecting citizens out of those virtual slaves. He urged the Untouchables to fight for self-elevation. He cried out excerpts 'You have been groaning from time immemorial & yet you are not ashamed to hug your helplessness as an inevitability'. The spate of his burning speeches began to have a telling effect upon their minds & to rouse them against their slavery.

BRA did not join the movement for the political independence of India. Those who were deprived of their political rights by foreign rulers were busy fighting them since they would rule India once the foreigners left. BRA's aim was liberation of the DC for which he knew he would have to fight with caste Hindus & to deal with the British govt in respect of political rights. He however realized that hatred of British rule would be inviting double enmity of his people. So he thought it prudent to cooperate with the British so far as that cooperation would be able to secure rights for the DC.

With the birth of the Bahishkrit Hitkarini Sabha dawned a new age of self-respect. It started in 1925 a hostel at Sholpaur, a monthly magazine named Saraswati Vilas. The DC were now being attracted to BRA's personality. He provided over the first conference of Untouchables at Malwan in Ratnagiri district in April 1925. But the most o/s event of the year was the satyagraha sponsored by Ramaswami Naicker, a non-Brahmin leader at Vaikam in the Travancore State for vindicating the rights of Untouchables to use a certain road to which they were forbidden entry. Another important incident took place when an untouchable by name Murgesan entered a Hindu temple in Madras despite a ban on Untouchables. BRA was watching these events closely, his message of self-elevation was gathering force in its appeals. He was also gaining foothold as a lawyer. The spasms of social resolution were stirring the society. Inspite of the Bole resolution a number of Local Boards & Municipalities had not granted DC their civic rights. Bole moved another resolution on 5/8/1926 recommending to the govt not to give grant to those Municipalities etc which refused to give effect to the resolution passed by the Council three years ago.

BRA continued to live in these B.I.T Chawls; three storied buildings each containing about 80 one-room tenements, common baths. Men of authority came to see him at home. At times he was without his full dress when people came to see him without appointments. Although he was best qualified to fill the position of the Principal of Sydenham College he was not appointed inspite of the best efforts of Dr R P Paranjpye, then the Member for Education. He accepted a part time post of a lecturer in the Batliboy's Accounting Training institute where he taught Mercantile Law.

It was during this time that his wife gave birth to a son Rajratna. Before that his wife gave birth to a daughter who passed away in infancy. However BRA lost Rajratna in July 1926. He was very grieved & depressed because of the death. He had acquired strength of mind, knowledge of all most all the scriptures. Like a yogin he was now spending his days in penance & austerities, immersed in silent contemplation. Men of DC came to him for help, legal advice, he fought their cases free, treated them with care & love. BRA was an expert at cooking. The most important attribute of a great leader, next to spotless sincerity, is the possession of an ever flowing heard towards his men who are ready to do or die at his command.

UP AGAINST SLAVERY

1927 opened with a meeting at the Koregaon War Memorial held by the DC. BRA addressed them and said that although hundreds of fighters from their community had fought on the side of the British they ungratefully later dubbed them a non-military community. About this time the Governor of Bombay nominated BRA to the Bombay Legislative Council. The DC Teachers felicitated him on his nomination. The DC had begun to look up to BRA now. And now we come to a momentous event in the life of BRA, the march to Mahad. Based on resolutions moved by Bole in the Bombay Legislative Council, years 1923 – 1926, the Mahad municipality had thrown open the Chowdar Tank to the Untouchables. However, the resolution was a mere gesture in that the Untouchables had not exercised their right due to the hostility of the caste Hindus. The Kolaba DC decided to hold a conference at Mahad on 19-20/3/1927.

BRA delivered his presidential address. He said that demilitarization was one of the causes of their downfall. Excerpts 'The military offered us unique opportunities of raising our standard of life & proving our merit & intellect. It is nothing less than a treachery on the part of the British to have closed the doors of the army to the Untouchables who had helped them establish the Indian empire while their home govt was at grips with the French during the Napoleon War'.

'No lasting progress can be achieved unless we put ourselves through a three fold process of purification. We must improve the general tone of our demeanor, re-tone our pronunciations and revitalize our thoughts. It is high time we rooted out from our mind the ideas of highness & lowness among ourselves. We will attain self-elevation only if we learn self-help, regain our self-respect and gain self-knowledge'. He impressed upon them the importance of entering government services & of education.

On the first day, a few caste Hindu spokesmen, local + outsiders, made speeches justifying the rights of DC & promised them help. The Subjects Committee, decided after taking the sense of the upper classes who attended the Conference, that the Conference should go in a body to the Chowdar Tank & help the DC to establish their right to take the water.

In pursuance of the resolution of the Mahad Municipality in 1924 throwing open the tank to the DC; BRA & thousands of other delegates began marching towards the tank. BRA took water from the Tank & now drank it, so did his followers. Having done so they returned peacefully to the pandal. Two hours after the event, some evil-minded caste Hindus raised a false rumor that the Untouchables were also planning to enter the temple of Veereshwar. All of orthodox Mahad was up in arms & the whole town at once became a surging mass of rowdies. These men did not field lowered in the scale of life, when Muslims who condemned them as kafirs, broke their idols took water. Their bravadoes died off in their throats when the Christians, who believed the religious truth outside the Bibiblical revelation was a work of the devil, took water from the same tank but when Untouchables who worshipped the same God as they did took water there was a furor.

Enraged at this misconstrued outrage on their religion & at the thought of defilement of the temple of Veereshwar, the caste Hindus dashed into the pandal of the DC. Majority of the delegates had dispersed by then, there was confusion in the pandal. Not knowing what to do delegates – women/children included ran into Muslim houses for shelter. Now the DC were enraged, all set to take revenge but BRA appealed for peace & discipline. Later five caste Hindus were sentenced to four months rigorous imprisonment by the District Magistrate.

Thus ended the first big, open Conference of the DC in Maharashtra & their first public attempt to assert their civic rights. It was as significant an event in Indian history as the partition of Bengal, the first bonfire of foreign cloth made by Savarkar & Bose's war of liberation of 1943. It is very interesting to note that both the Indian political & socio-religious revolution had their origin in Maharashtra.

Now DC applied their mind to self-improvement & self-culture as never before. They realized the importance of organization & active struggle. The struggle of Mahad pushed ahead the destiny of the DC ahead by fifty years. However, offended orthodox Hindus now sharpened the claws of social boycott of the DC. They refused to sell them corn, picked quarrels under any pretext and had a number of them jailed. For months the wave of protest against the unjust, inhuman conduct of the Mahad caste Hindus swept India.

One leader who fearlessly & whole-heartedly supported BRA's struggle was Savarkar. He said that untouchability must be condemned & abolished. He upheld the satyagraha of the untouchables at Mahad and declared that the pious & bounden duty of the Hindu world at large to restore full human rights to their co-religionists. The caste Hindus of Mahad conducted a purification ceremony of the Chowdar Tank. Few caste leaders like Bapurao Joshi stood the wrath of the orthodox for years supported the DC while others helplessly simmered at the perverse attitude of the orthodox.

BRA had now to face a flood of criticism. So he felt the need for a mouthpiece as never before. He started his fortnightly Marathi paper, Bahishkrit Bharat in 1927. Justifying the need for a mouthpiece for the DC, BRA said that in the ensuing political reforms, which he expected to be affected by 1930, if the Untouchables failed to secure representation in proportion to their population, they would be doomed. To guard against this the DC need to be kept fully informed about the happenings in the land & their grievances, views / reactions must be placed before before Govt & people. Through the paper he said that temples & watercourses should be open to the Untouchables because they were Hindus.

Some people criticized BRA by saying that people were not prepared for the radical change of society as advocated by him. BRA threw back the argument at them by asking why they clamored for independence when the people as a whole neither deserved nor were prepared for it. One in a hundred, he said, understood the significance of national independence & even then Tilak rose for their deliverance. They criticized BRA because he drove the Untouchables to adopt a militant policy. If Tilak were born an untouchable he would not have said 'Swaraj is my birthright' but he would have said 'Annihilation of Untouchability is my birth right'. BRA's reading of Tilak is unchallengeable. A man of Tilak's cast, volcanic force, iron will would have surely applied his brains to shell the strongholds of orthodoxy had he been born an Untouchable. 'Lost rights are never regained', said BRA, 'by begging and by appeals to the conscious of the usurpers, but by relentless struggle'. 'Goats are used for sacrificial offerings and not lions,' he concluded.

The proceedings of the new Legislative Council commended in February 1927. In his maiden speech BRA pointed out that out of its total revenue of 15.5 crores, about 9.9 crores was being levied by the Executive without the consent of the Council. BRA also explained how the difference in the method of levying land revenue & income-tax worsened the lot of the poor farmer who was required to pay the tax at the same rate whether he was a owner of one acre of land or a Jagirdar, whether there was a failure or abundance of crops. Said he 'holders of income below a certain minimum are exempt from levy. But under the land revenue the tax is collected from everyone rich or poor'. He raised a number of other issues relating to prohibition, education etc. Inspite of being BRA's first speech it was impressive, illuminating and stimulating.

On prohibition he said, 'I feel Sir, the success of prohibition entirely depends upon the financial solution of the question, upon how we will manage to make good the loss we are bound to incur as a result of our new excise policy'. True & practical observations! On Education he appealed to the Govt to give favored treatment to the backward classes.

Just then Maharashtra was celebrating the tercentenary birthday of Shivaji in 1927. BRA was invited to preside over a meeting at Badlapur near Bombay. Cordially received by a Brahmin host, BRA ably & vigorously dwelt upon Shivaji's different facets of life such as his achievements, character & policy. Then he asked his 5,000 strong audiences to think over the causes that led to the downfall of the empire founded to the invidious inequality in the social field & to the hatred for the Peshwa rule.

In the third week of July 1927, BRA addressed an important meeting in Poona. A part of the meeting was the refutal by BRA of charged leveled against him of partiality. He sought to dispel such claims by detailing upon his work in the hostels at Nasik & Jalgaon, which were open to all Untouchable students.

He asked the Chamars why they did not send able representatives to the Legislative Council to defend their interests. He said that he was willing to give his place to the worthiest leader from their community of one came forward to serve the cause. He warned them not to be stooges in the hands of interested groups. Nothing could be achieved said he if they did not adopt an aggressive attitude and prove by their thought, words & deeds that they would not now tolerate insult & disabilities any further. He urged the DC to wrest the right of drinking water in public places & force their entry into public temples.

In the Council, with regard to the Composition of the Senate, he supported the view that the Backward & Depressed Classes should have representation on the Senate of Bombay University. Besides showing interest in the major legislation affecting the whole Province, BRA was very watchful about the welfare of the DC. Even at the news of the faintest injustice done to them he took up cudgels on their behalf.

POONA PACT

By now Ambedkar had become one of the most prominent untouchable political figures of the time. He had grown increasingly critical of mainstream Indian political parties for their perceived lack of emphasis for the elimination of the caste system. Ambedkar criticized the Indian National Congress and its leader Mohandas Gandhi, whom he accused of reducing the untouchable community to a figure of pathos. Ambedkar was also dissatisfied with the failures of British rule, and advocated a political identity for untouchables separate from both the Congress and the British. At a Depressed Classes Conference on August 8, 1930 Ambedkar outlined his political vision, insisting that the safety of the Depressed Classes hinged on their being independent of the Government and the Congress both:

We must shape our course ourselves and by ourselves... Political power cannot be a panacea for the ills of the Depressed Classes. Their salvation lies in their social elevation. They must cleanse their evil habits. They must improve their bad ways of living.... They must be educated.... There is a great necessity to disturb their pathetic contentment and to instill into them that divine discontent which is the spring of all elevation. Ambedkar's political work had made him very unpopular with orthodox Hindus, as well as with many Congress politicians who had earlier condemned untouchability. This was largely because these "liberal" politicians usually stopped short of advocating full equality for untouchables.

In 1932, M. C. Rajah concluded a pact with two right-wingers in the Indian National Congress, Dr. B. S. Moonje and Jadhav. According to this pact, Moonje offered reserved seats to scheduled castes in return for Rajah's support. This demand prompted Ambedkar to make an official demand for Separate Electorate System on an all-India basis. Ambedkar's prominence and popular support amongst the untouchable community had increased, and he was invited to attend the Second Round Table Conference in London in 1932. Gandhi fiercely opposed separate electorate for untouchables, Gandhi believed in Chaturvarna system, but accepted separate electorate for all other minority groups like Muslims, sikhs...etc. Gandhi feared that separate electorates for untouchables would divide Hindu society for future generations.

When the British agreed with Ambedkar and announced the awarding of separate electorates, Gandhi began a *fast-unto-death* while imprisoned in the Yerwada Central Jail of Pune in 1932 against the separate electorate for untouchables only. , Gandhi asked for the political unity of Hindus. Gandhi's fast provoked great public support across India, and orthodox Hindu leaders, Congress politicians and activists such as Madan Mohan Malaviya and Palwankar Baloo organized joint meetings with Ambedkar and his supporters at Yeravada. Fearing a communal reprisal and killings of untouchables in the event of Gandhi's death, Ambedkar agreed under massive coercion from the supporters of Gandhi . This agreement, which saw Gandhi end his fast, while dropping the demand for separate electorates that was promised through the British Communal Award prior to Ambedkar's meeting with Gandhi. Ambedkar was to later criticise this fast of Gandhi as a gimmick to deny political rights to the untouchables and increase the coercion he had faced to give up the demand for separate electorates.

IMPORTANT EVENTS IN HIS LIFE

- Birth, 14th April 1891
- Witness in South Barrow Commission, 1917
- Untouchables' conference, Nagpur, 1918
- Bahishkrit Hitkarini Sabha Formed 20th July 1924
- Nominated as MLC, Bombay Province, 1926
- Mahad Satyagraha, December 1927
- Witness in Simon Commission, May 1928
- Nashik Kala Ram temple Satyagraha, 2nd March 1930
- Representative at Round Table Conference, 1930-32
- British Communal Award, 20th August 1932
- Poona Pact, 20th September 1932
- Yewale District, Nasik Conference, 23rd October 1935
- Mahar Parishad, Bombay Province, 31st May 1936
- Independent Labout Party Formed, August 1936
- Elected MLA, Bombay Province, January 1937
- All India Scheduled Caste Federation Formed at Nagpur, April 1942
- Appointed as Labour Minister in the Viceroy's Executive Council, July 1942
- People's Education Society Formed, July 1945
- Elected to Constituent Assembly from Bengal, November 1946
- Law Minister in Independent India, 15th August 1947
- Appointed as Chairman, Drafting Committee of the Constitution of India, 29th August 1947

- Resigned from Union Cabinet, September 1951
- Elected to Rajya Sabha, March 1952
- Buddhist Society of India Formed, May 1955
- Embraced Buddhism, 14th October 1956
- Parinirvan (Death), 6th December 1956

Dr. Babasaheb Ambedkar and his Writings

- The National Dividend of India, 1916
- Small Holdings in India and Their Remedies, 1917
- Weekly 'Mook Nayak', Started 31st January 1920
- Provincial Decentralisation of Imperial Finance in British India, June 1921
- The Problem of a Rupee—Its Origin & Its Solution, March 1923
- The Evolution of Provincial Finance in British India, 1925
- Weekly 'Bahishkrit Bharat', Started 13th April 1927
- Weekly 'Janata', Started December 1930
- Annihilation of Caste, December 1935
- Federation Vs Freedom, January 1939
- Thoughts on Pakistan, December 1940
- Mr. Gandhi & the Emancipation of the Untouchables, December 1942
- Ranade, Gandhi & Jinnah, January 1943
- What Congress & Gandhi have done to the Untouchables, June 1945
- Who Were the Sudras?, October 1946
- States & Minorities, March 1947
- The Untouchable, October 1948
- Maharashtra as Linguistic Province, October 1948
- Thoughts on Linguistic States, December 1955
- Buddha & His Dhamma, Published 1957

22 VOWS OF DR. AMBEDKAR

Dr. B.R. Ambedkar prescribed 22 vows to his followers during the historic religious conversion to Buddhism on 15 October 1956 at Deeksha Bhoomi, Nagpur in India. The conversion to Buddhism by 800,000 people was historic because it was the largest religious conversion, the world has ever witnessed. He prescribed these oaths so that there may be complete severance of bond with Hinduism. These 22 vows struck a blow at the roots of Hindu beliefs and practices. These vows could serve as a bulwark to protect Buddhism from confusion and contradictions. These vows could liberate converts from superstitions, wasteful and meaningless rituals, which have led to popularisation of masses and enrichment of upper castes of Hindus.

The famous 22 vows are:

- I shall have no faith in Brahma, Vishnu and Mahesh nor shall I worship them.
- I shall have no faith in Rama and Krishna who are believed to be incarnation of God nor shall I worship them.
- I shall have no faith in 'Gauri', Ganapati and other gods and goddesses of Hindus nor shall I worship them.
- I do not believe in the incarnation of God.
- I do not and shall not believe that Lord Buddha was the incarnation of Vishnu. I believe this to be sheer madness and false propaganda.
- I shall not perform 'Shraddha' nor shall I give 'pind-dan'.
- I shall not act in a manner violating the principles and teachings of the Buddha.
- I shall not allow any ceremonies to be performed by Brahmins.
- I shall believe in the equality of man.
- I shall endeavour to establish equality.
- I shall follow the 'noble eightfold path' of the Buddha.
- I shall follow the 'paramitas' prescribed by the Buddha.
- I shall have compassion and loving kindness for all living beings and protect them.
- I shall not steal.
- I shall not tell lies.
- I shall not commit carnal sins.
- I shall not take intoxicants like liquor, drugs etc.
- I shall endeavour to follow the noble eightfold path and practise compassion and loving kindness in every day life.
- I renounce Hinduism which is harmful for humanity and impedes the advancement and development of humanity because it is based on inequality, and adopt Buddhism as my religion.
- I firmly believe the Dhamma of the Buddha is the only true religion.
- I believe that I am having a rebirth.
- I solemnly declare and affirm that I shall hereafter lead my life according to the principles and teachings of the Buddha and his Dhamma.

DEATH

Since 1948, Ambedkar had been suffering from diabetes. He was bedridden from June to October in 1954 owing to clinical depression and failing eyesight. He had been increasingly embittered by political issues, which took a toll on his health. His health worsened as he furiously worked through 1955. Just three days after completing his final manuscript 'Buddha And His Dhamma', it is said that Ambedkar died in his sleep on December 6, 1956 at his home in Delhi.

Some of his supporters doubt his natural death and think death may not have been natural and put forward different theories. Try to draw parallel between his and Gandhi's death and blame Caste Brahmins. A Buddhist-style cremation was organised for him at Chowpatty beach on December 7, attended by hundreds of thousands of supporters, activists and admirers.

Ambedkar was survived by his second wife Savita Ambedkar, born as a Caste Brahmin and converted to Buddhism with him. His wife's name before marriage was Sharda Kabir. Savita Ambedkar died as Buddhist in 2002. Ambedkar's grandson, Prakash Yaswant Ambedkar leads the Bharipa Bahujan Mahasangha and has served in both houses of the Indian Parliament.

A number of unfinished typescripts and handwritten drafts were found among Ambedkar's notes and papers and gradually made available. Among these were *Waiting for a Visa*, which probably dates from 1935-36 and is an autobiographical work, and the *Untouchables, or the Children of India's Ghetto*, which refers to the census of 1951.

A memorial for Ambedkar was established in his Delhi house at 26 Alipur Road. His birthdate is celebrated as a public holiday known as Ambedkar Jayanti. He was posthumously awarded India's highest civilian honour, the Bharat Ratna in 1990. He is the namesake of many public institutions, such as the Dr. Babasaheb Ambedkar Open University in Ahmedabad, Gujarat.

A large official portrait of Ambedkar is on display in the Parliament building. Jabbar Patel directed the Hindi-language movie "Dr. Babasaheb Ambedkar" about the life of Ambedkar, released in 2000, starring South Indian actor Mammootty as Ambedkar.

Sponsored by India's National Film Development Corporation and Ministry of Social Justice, the film was released after a long and controversial gestation period. Dr. Ambedkar was the main architect of the Indian Constitution. He was born in a very poor low caste family of Madhya Pradesh. In U.S.A., he did his M.A. in 1915 and Ph.D. in 1916. From 1918 to 1920, he worked as a Professor of Law. Dr. Ambedkar set up his legal practice at the Mumbai High Court.

A number of unfinished typescripts and handwritten drafts were found among Ambedkar's notes and papers and gradually made available. Among these were Waiting for a Visa, which probably dates from 1935-36 and is an autobiographical work, and the Untouchables, or the Children of India's Ghetto, which refers to the census of 1951. A memorial for Ambedkar was established in his Delhi house at 26 Alipur Road.

His birthdate is celebrated as a public holiday known as Ambedkar Jayanti. He was posthumously awarded India's highest civilian honour, the Bharat Ratna in 1990. He is the namesake of many public institutions, such as the Dr. Babasaheb Ambedkar Open University in Ahmedabad, Gujarat. A large official portrait of Ambedkar is on display in the Parliament building. Jabbar Patel directed the Hindi-language movie "Dr. Baba Saheb Ambedkar" about the life of Ambedkar, released in 2000, starring South Indian actor Mammootty as Ambedkar. Sponsored by India's National Film Development Corporation and Ministry of Social Justice, the film was released after a long and controversial gestation period.

2

Ambedkar and Untouchability

UNTOUCHABLES

Before one tries to know what it is to be an Untouchable one would like to know what is the total population of the Untouchables of India. For this one must go to the Census Report. The first general census of India was taken in the year 1881. Beyond listing the different castes and creeds and adding up their numbers so as to arrive at the total figure of the population of India the Census of 1881 did nothing. It made no attempt to classify the different Hindu castes either into higher and lower or touchable and untouchable. The second general census of India was taken in the year 1891. It was at this census that an attempt to classify the population on the basis of caste and race and grade was made by the Census Commissioner for the first time. But it was only an attempt.

The third general census of India was taken in 1901. At this census a new principle of classification was adopted namely "Classification by Social precedence as recognised by native public opinion". To this serious opposition was raised by high caste Hindus to the enumeration by caste in the Census Report. They insisted on the omission of the question regarding caste.

This objection did not have any effect on the Census Commissioner. In the opinion of the Census Commissioner enumeration by caste was important and necessary. It was argued by the Census Commissioner that "whatever view may be taken of the advantages or disadvantages of caste as a social institution, it is impossible to conceive of any useful discussion of the population questions in India in which caste would not be an important element.

Caste is still 'the foundation of the Indian social fabric' and the record of caste is still 'the best guide to the changes in the various social strata in the Indian Society' Every Hindu (using the term in its most elastic sense) is born into a caste and his caste determines his religious, social, economic and domestic life from the cradle to the grave. In western countries the major factors which determine the different strata of society *viz.* wealth, education and vocation are fluid and catholic and tend to modify the rigidity of birth and hereditary position.

In India spiritual and social community and traditional occupation override all other factors. Thus where in censuses of western countries an economic or occupational grouping of the population affords a basis for the combination of demographic statistics, the corresponding basis in the case of the Indian population is the distinction of religion and caste. Whatever view may be taken of caste as a national and social institution it is useless to ignore it, and so long as caste continues to be used as one of the distinguishing features of an individual's official and social identity it cannot be claimed that a decinnial enumeration helps to perpetuate an undesirable institution.

This Census of 1901 did not result in fixing the total population of the Untouchables at any exact figure. This was due to two reasons. In the first place no exact tests were applied to determine who is an Untouchable. Secondly a class of the population which was economically and educationally backward but not Untouchable was mixed up with those who were actually Untouchables.

The Census of 1911 went a step further and actually laid down ten tests to mark off the Untouchables from those who were Touchable. Under these tests the Census Superintendents made a separate enumeration of castes and tribes who (1) denied the supremacy of the Brahmins; (2) did not receive the Mantra from Brahmana or other recognised Hindu Guru; (3) denied the authority of the Vedas; (4) did not worship the great Hindu Gods; (5) were not served by good Brahmanas; (6) have no Brahmin priests at all; (7) have no access to the interior of the ordinary Hindu temple; (8) cause pollution; (9) bury their dead and (10) eat beef and do not reverence the cow.

The separation of the Untouchables from the Hindus was insisted upon by the Muslims in a memorial to the Government dated 27th January 1910 in which they claimed that their representation in the political bodies of the country should be in proportion to the population of Touchable Hindus and not Hindus as a whole because they contended that the Untouchables were not Hindus.

Be that as it may the Census of 1911 marks the beginning of the ascertainment of the population of the Untouchables. Efforts in the same direction were continued at the Census of 1921 and 1931. As a result of these efforts the Simon Commission which came to India in 1930 was able to state with some degree of surety that total population of Untouchables in British India was 44.5 millions.

Suddenly, however, in 1932 when the Lothian Committee came to India to investigate the question of franchise for the reformed Legislatures and began its investigation, the Hindus adopted a challenging mood and refused to accept the figure given by the Simon Committee as a true figure of the Untouchables of India. In some provinces the Hindus went to the length of denying that there were any Untouchables at all. This is due to the fact that the Hindus had by now realised the danger of admitting the existence of the Untouchables. For it meant that a part of the representation enjoyed by the Hindus will have to be given up by them to the Untouchables.

The Census of 1941 must be left out of consideration. It was taken during the war and it was a sort of a rough measure. The latest Census is that of 1951. The following figures are taken from the statement issued by the Census Commissioner. The Census Commissioner gives the population of the Scheduled Castes in India as 513 lakhs. The total population of India, as shown by the 1951 census is 3,567 lakhs, excluding 1.35 lakhs, the enumeration records in whose case were destroyed by fire in the Census Tabulation Office at Jullundur. Out of the total population of 3,567 lakhs, 2,949 lakhs live in rural areas and 618 lakhs in the urban areas.

The Scheduled Castes in rural areas total 462 lakhs and in urban areas their figures are 51 lakhs. Non-agricultural classes for the whole population total 1,076 lakhs, the Scheduled Castes 132 lakhs. Cultivators of land, wholly or mainly owned, and their dependants total 1,674 lakhs for the whole population, 174 lakhs for the Scheduled Castes. Cultivators of land, wholly or mainly unowned and their dependants are 316 lakhs for the whole of India, 56 lakhs for the Scheduled Castes. Cultivating labourers and their dependants are 448 lakhs for the whole of India, 148 lakhs for the Scheduled Castes. Figures for non-agricultural classes are as follows:

Production other than Cultivation: Total 377 lakhs. Scheduled Castes 53 lakhs.

Commerce: Total 213 lakhs. Scheduled Castes 9 lakhs. Transport: Total 56 lakhs. Scheduled Castes 6 lakhs. Other services and miscellaneous sources: Total 430 lakhs, Scheduled Castes 64 lakhs.

Out of a total Scheduled Caste population of over 513 lakhs, 114 lakhs live in North India (Uttar Pradesh); 128 lakhs in East India (Bihar, Orissa, West Bengal, Assam, Manipur and Tripura); 110 lakhs in South India (Madras, Mysore, Travancore-Cochin and Coorg); 31 lakhs in West India (Bombay, Saurashtra and Kutch); 76 lakhs in Central India (Madhya Pradesh, Madhya Bharat, Hyderabad, Bhopal and Vindhya Pradesh); and 52 lakhs in North-West India (Rajasthan, Punjab, Patiala and East Punjab States Union, Ajmer, Delhi, Bilaspur and Himachal Pradesh).

WHAT ABOUT THE UNTOUCHABLES?

Caste and Untouchability are the two great social evils in India. Caste has disabled the whole Hindu Society. Untouchability has suppressed a large class of people. And yet the British Government has completely ignored the two evils. One may search in vain the Indian Code to find any law dealing with Caste or with Untouchability. It is true that caste and untouchability are social matters.

They will vanish when people will begin to interdine and intermarry. Law cannot compel a person to dine with another. It is true, law cannot compel a person to marry with another. But it is also true that Law can prohibit a Caste from preventing a person from marrying a person outside his caste. Caste continues because a Caste can conspire to punish its members if they break the rules of caste by declaring a social boycott against him. It would have been perfectly possible to have enacted a law declaring such social boycott to be a crime. Again in the matter of Untouchability the disabilities are not merely social. They are fundamentally civic. Inability to I get admission to school, to be able to take water from a public well, to be able to get into a public conveyance, to be able to get into public service, are all civic disabilities. It was the duty of the British Government to legislate at least to the extent necessary to protect their civic rights. It was possible to do so. A short Enactment on the lines of Caste Disabilities Removal Act would have been sufficient. Yet the British Government has gone on as though these two evils did not exist at all. Indeed it is most extraordinary thing to note that although Legislative Bodies were established in India in 1861 and have been passing laws on every social questions and discussing public questions, yet except on two occasions the Untouchables were not even mentioned. The first "occasion on which they were mentioned was in 1916, when one Parsi gentleman Sir Maneckji Dadabhoy moved the following Resolution in the Central Legislature:

> *"That this Council recommends to the Governor General in Council that measures be devised with the help, if necessary, of a small representative committee of officials and non-officials for an amelioration in the moral, material and educational condition of what are known as the Depressed Classes, and that, as a preliminary step the Local Government and Administrations be invited to formulate schemes with due regard to local conditions."*

There was no sympathy to this resolution. The Hindu members of the Legislature were angry with the mover for his having brought such a subject before the Legislature.

Pandit Madan Mohan Malviya said: "Sir, it seems rather ungracious to say so, but a sense of the dignity of the proceedings of this Council compels me to utter a protest against the manner in which sometimes subjects are brought before it for consideration............. "In moving the Resolution the object of which I may at once say, has my wholehearted support, my friend, the Hon'ble Mr. Dadabhoy, went out of his way to make remarks against the Hindu community which, I think, he ought to have avoided............I am not here to defend everything Hindu that exists. I am not here to apologise for the many prejudices or superstitions, which I am sadly conscious are to be found among one portion or another of our community.

But it is not the Hindu community alone which finds it difficult to get rid of prejudices....... Without meaning the smallest disrespect, I would instance the case of the marriage with a Deceased Wife's Sister Bill......... We Hindus have got some much worse prejudices to fight against.......... But I do not think it is within the province of a member of this Council either to lecture to the Hindus present here or to those outside as to the socio-religious disabilities among themselves which they might fight against and remove. I think the province of Members of this Council is limited to dealing with matters of legislation or other administrative matters which may properly be taken up by the Government.

As has been already pointed out, the Government have, in pursuance of a wise and liberal policy, laid it down that they shall not interfere in matters of a religious or socio-religious character, and accusations of the character in question ought, therefore, to be avoided there............... I do not wish to descend into a disputation as to the merits of the imputations or the justification for the general observations that have been made......... And yet, if I do not, I am left in the position that I have heard without protest remarks showing that the Hindu Community from one end of the country to the other was guilty of all that my friend, the Hon'ble Mover of the Resolution, has suggested............ I am conscious that we Hindus have many prejudices to fight against and conquer; but I submit that this is not the place to tell us of them."

Even a social Reformer like Sir Surendranath Bannerjee was not happy. He said:

I regret very much that my Hon'ble friend the Mover of this Resolution went somewhat out of his way to level (I do not think he did it intentionally) an attack against the Hindu Community. He must bear in mind that we are the inheritors of past traditions, of a civilization as ancient as the world. That civilization undoubtedly had its defects,' but that civilization in the morning of the world was the guarantee for law and order and social stability. In the past it afforded consolation to millions. We are trying to evolve a national system in conformity with our present environments, but we cannot push aside all those things which have come down to us from the past.

We reverence the venerable fabric which has been built up by our ancestors. We notice their defects, and we are anxious to get rid of them gradually and steadily, not by any revolutionary movement, but the slow, steady process of evolution. My friend must have a little sympathy with us; he must extend to us the hand of generosity in our efforts to deal with the problems. My Hon'ble friend suggests that Government should take measures........ We welcome the action of Government in a matter of this kind, but after all, if you analyse the situation, it is a social problem, and the British Government, very properly, as I think, in conformity with its ancient traditions, holds aloof from all interference with social questions.

"Government can do a great by way of education, a great deal by helping forward the industrial movement among the Depressed Classes. But the vital problem, the problem of problems, is one of social uplifting, and there the Government can only afford to be a benevolent spectator. It may sympathize with our efforts, but it cannot actively participate in them........"

The Hon'ble Mr. Dadabhoy had to defend himself. In his reply he said:

"Sir, I find myself in a very peculiar and unfortunate position. There are two parties in this Council, and they are both on the defensive on this occasion. My justification for bringing in this Resolution, if any justification were needed, is to be found in the unenthusiastic and half-hearted support which I have received from my non-official colleagues. It was no pleasure, I assure you. Sir, to me to bring in this Resolution. If I could possibly have avoided it, I would have very cheerfully and very willingly done so. This is the sixth year of the life of this Reformed Council, as Hon'ble Members are aware, and the second term is now approaching expiration. During the major portion of that time—the five years that I have been on this Council—1 anticipated that the champions of public liberty, public spirit and public enterprise and culture—men like my friends the Hon'ble Surendra Nath Bannerjee or the Honourable Pandit Madan Mohan Malaviya—would take the trouble of moving a Resolution to this effect. I waited all this time to see if one of these enthusiastic members would bring in a Resolution for the amelioration of the Depressed Classes, but when I found that none of them had taken up the matter—though at times this matter is discussed even in the Congress Pandal in a certain manner; when I found that it was not taken up in this Council— .... I, as a Parsee, representing a Hindu constituency thought it my duty to bring this matter for public discussion in this Council."

The Government naturally felt relieved by this quarrel. Resting behind the moral support of the Hindu members of the Legislature for covering up their delinquency Sir Reginald Crad-dock speaking on behalf of the Government disposed off the Resolution in the following terms:

"Sir, we sympathize with the objects of the Hon'ble Mr. Dadabhoy's Resolution. We are willing to go so far as to ask Local Governments to put on record what they have done, are doing, and what further they can do, to improve the condition of these people. But we can place no faith in special committees. Have I not indicated to the Council how wide are the problems, and how impossible it would be to deal with them by means of Committees? The problems extend over the whole range of Government from top to bottom. What I say is that, while extending our sympathy to the objects aimed at by the Hon'ble Mr. Dadabhoy, we can go no further than promise to refer the question to Local Governments, and ask them whether they can do more than they are doing. That is as far as we can go, and with that assurance, I will ask the Hon'ble Member to withdraw his Resolution."

The second time the Untouchables are mentioned in the proceedings of the Legislature was in 1928 when Mr. M. R. Jayakar moved the following Resolution:

"This Assembly recommends to the Governor-General in Council to issue directions to all Local Governments to provide special facilities for the education of the Untouchables and other depressed classes, and also for opening all public services to them, specially the Police."

On this occasion the Government of India was no more enthusiastic than it was in 1916. Mr. G. S. Bajpai, speaking on behalf of the Government of India said:

"The Local Governments are alive to their responsibility, they are doing what they can. It is not my privilege to claim for them that they have achieved the ideal, but I do claim that there is an awakening and an awakened and roused sense of responsibility and a roused sense of endeavour for improving the position of these depressed classes. That being so, it is no function to interfere by direction or by demand. They (i.e. the Government) can, if the House wishes, communicate to them the views of the House on this very national problem."

For this speech, Mr. Bajpai, according to the official report of the proceedings, was cheered!

Such is the record of the British Government in the matter of social Reform. What a miserable record it is? How meager a record it is; Six social Laws in sixty years of legislative activity!! From the very beginning, its attitude to social reform has been of a very halting character. It kept on some mask of a responsible Government up to 1860. After 1860 it threw off the mask. The Government would not move and reform came to a dead stop. In 1881 a great agitation was started in favour of legislation prohibiting child marriage. Rather than be pestered with social reform, it took courage to announce publicly and once for all its policy of opposition to reform. In a Government Resolution of that year, the British Government proclaimed:

"In dealing with such subjects as those raised in Mr. Malabari's Notes, the British Government in India has usually been guided by certain general principles. For instance, when caste or custom enjoins a practice which involves a breach of the ordinary criminal law, the State will enforce the law. When caste or, custom lays down a rule which is of its nature enforceable in the Civil Courts, but is clearly opposed to morality or public policy, the State will decline to enforce it. When caste or custom lays down a rule which deals with such matters as are usually left to the option of citizens, and which does not need the aid of Civil or Criminal Courts for its enforcement. State interference is not considered either desirable or expedient."

In the application of such general principles to particular cases, there is doubtless room for differences of opinion; but there is one common-sense test which may often be applied with advantage in considering whether the State should or should not interfere in its legislative or executive capacity with social or religious questions of the land now under notice. The test is, ' Can the State give effect to its commands by the ordinary machinery at its disposal? ' If not, it is desirable that the State should abstain from making a rule which it cannot enforce without a departure from its usual practice or procedure.

If this test be applied in the present case, the reasons will be apparent why His Excellency in Council considers that interference by the State is undesirable, and that the reforms advocated by Mr. Malabari, which affect the social customs of many races with probably as many points of difference as of agreement, must be left to the improving influence of time and to the gradual operation of the mental and moral development of the people by the spread of education.

It is true that the British Government in India has by its legislation set up a standard of morality independent of, and in some material respects differing from, the standard set up by caste; and it may be that the former standard has had some beneficial effect in influencing native customs, practices, and modes of thought. But legislation, though it may be didactic purposes; and in the competition of influence between legislation on the one hand, and caste or custom on the other, the condition of success on the part of the former is that the Legislature should keep within its natural boundaries, and should not, by overstepping those boundaries, place itself in direct antagonism to social opinion. The policy laid down in this Resolution has ever since remained the policy of the British Government in the matter of Social Reform.

Why did the British Government leave the Untouchables in the cold without any care or attention?

The explanation for so criminal a neglect was furnished by Sir Reginald Craddock. In replying on behalf of the Government of India on the Resolution moved by Sir Maneckji Dadabhoy in the Imperial Legislative Council in 1916, he stated what the position of the British Government took with regard to the Untouchables in the following terms:

> *"With regard to them (i.e. the Untouchables) the difficulty is not that Government does not recognize them, but that, until the habits and prejudices of centuries are removed, the hands of their neighbours must necessarily press upon them............ you must remember that these people live mostly in villages and very often in the back lane of towns, and that their neighbours have not yet come under these broad and liberal minded influences. Therefore, as many speakers have indicated, the problem in dealing with this question is more social and religious than purely administrative."*

I know myself of many difficulties in the matter of schools. There are many places where the Maharboys will not be allowed into the school; they may be allowed in the Verandah and get only a small part of the master's attention there, or they may be entirely excluded. But it is only gradually that the difficulty can be met. I have constantly dealt with this very problem on the spot. I have reasoned with people; I have said to them. There are tax payers like yourselves, either let them come into the school, or if you wish to indulge in your own prejudices—they may be reasonable prejudices, as you consider them—but if you wish to indulge them, should you not contribute something in order that these boys may have a school of their own?

In that what some of the better people have come forward to help in the matter of wells, and schools for the low castes; they have assisted, and the difficulties have been got over. But of course if is a matter which must take time, and Government itself cannot use compulsion. They go rather near to it sometimes, for example, in travelling by railway: and when petitions are presented in Court. But they cannot ensure that these people shall always be well treated in their offices. Very often, I think, some of these classes refrain from seeking service they might otherwise wish to secure, because their neighbours are not likely to treat them warmly. Although the Hon'ble mover described the statement made by the Government of Bombay as a ' magnificent *non-possumus*', I think that it very accurately describes that the real difficulties of the situation are. Even though Government is willing to help in every way these unfortunate people, yet it remains true that ' the position of these castes and tribes in the future depends partly on their own selves, and partly those more favoured Indian Communities, which by extending the hand of human comradeship or hardening their hearts and averting their faces, have it in their power to elevate or to degrade them.'

"That Sir, I think, represents very truly and accurately the position of affairs as regards these Depressed Classes."

The same attitude was reiterated in 1928 when the resolution of Mr. Jayakar was discussed in the Central Legislative Assembly. Mr. Bajpai speaking on behalf of the Government said:

"It is not by increasing the number of special schools or by providing special facilities that you are going to solve this problem (of the Untouchables). You will solve this problem only by a quickening and broadening the spirit of all sections of the community towards the so called depressed classes."

Leaving the problem to be solved by the quickening of the consciences of the Hindus, the British Government just neglected the Untouchables and believed that as a Government they were I not called upon to do anything to help to improve the lot of the Untouchables. How did the British justify this neglect of so helpless and so downtrodden a class of their subjects as the Untouchables? The answer is very clear. They did it by taking the view that the evil of Untouchability was not of their making. They argued that if they did not deal with the evil of untouchability, they are not to be blamed for it because the system did not originate with them. This was clearly enunciated by the Government of Bombay in 1856. In June 1856 a petition was submitted on behalf of a Mahar boy to the Government of Bombay complaining that though willing to pay the usual Schooling fee, he had been denied admission to the Dharwar Government School. In disposing of the application, the Government of Bombay thought the matter so important that it issued a Resolution dated 21st July 1856 of which the following is the full text:

1. The question discussed in the correspondence is one of very great practical difficulty.
2. There can be no doubt that the Mahar petitioner has abstract justice on his side; and Government trust that the prejudices which at present prevent him from availing himself of existing means of education in Dharwar may be ere long removed.
3. But Government are obliged to keep in mind that to interfere with the prejudices of ages in a summary manner, for the sake of one or few individuals, would probably do a great damage to the cause of education. *The disadvantage under which the petitioner is not one which I has originated with the Government,* and it is one which Government cannot summarily remove by interfering in his favour, as he begs them to do."

This is of course an easy view of the duties of a Government. It is not a responsible view. It is certainly not a view which a civilized Government would take. A Government which is afraid to govern is not a Government.

It is only a corporation formed to collect taxes. The British Government undoubtedly meant to be more than a mere tax gathering machinery. It claimed to be a civilized Government. Then why did it not act to prevent wrong and injustice? Was it because it had no power or was it because it was afraid to use them or was it because it felt that there was nothing wrong in the social and religious system of India?

The answer is that it had the power, the amplest power. It did not use it because for a part of the period it did not think that there was anything wrong in the social system of the Hindus and during the period when it became convinced that things were wrong it was overpowered by sense of fear. It is notorious that the beginning of its career the British had a dread and a horror of the consequences of permitting the diffusion of "Christian truth". But it is not quite as notorious that the British at the same time were showing a corresponding respect for native prejudices. Mr. Ward, a Missionary in Calcutta records in his journal for 1802 the following fact:

> *"Last week a deputation from the Government went in procession to Kali Ghat, and made a thank offering to this Goddess of the Hindus, in the name of the Company, for the success which the English have lately obtained in this country. Five thousand rupees were offered. Several thousand natives witnessed the English presenting their offerings to this idol. We have been much grieved at this act, in which the natives exult over us."*

Another illustration of the same is furnished by Mr. Robert Lindsay who was a civilian in the employment of the East India Company in the time of Warren Hastings. Describing his initiation into his new office of Resident at Sylhet he says:

> *"I was now told that it was customary for the new Resident to pay his respects to the shrine of the tutelary saint, Shaw Jullol. Pilgrims of the Islam faith flock to this shrine from every part of India, and afterwards found that the fanatics attending the tomb were not a little dangerous. It was not my business to combat religious prejudices, and I therefore went in state, as others had done before me, left my shoes on the threshold, and deposited on the tomb five gold mohurs as an offering. Being thus purified I returned to my dwelling and received the homage of my subjects."*

How much the British Government had become associated with and interested in supporting native prejudices can be seen from the following memorial which was submitted to the Government of Madras by Bishop Corrie in 1833. The instances cited in the Memorial were these:

> *"First, that it is now required of Christian servants of the Government, both civil and military, to attend to Heathen and Mohammedan religious festivals, with the view of showing them respect Second, that in some instances they*

are called upon to present offerings, and to do homage to idols. Third, that the impure and degrading services of the pagodas are now carried on under the supervision and control of the principal European, and therefore, Christian officers of the Government, and the management and regulation of the revenues and endowments, both of these pagodas and mosques, so vested in them, under the provision of regulation vii of 1817, that no important idolatrous ceremony can be performed, no attendant of the various idols, not even the prostitutes of the temple, be entertained or discharged, nor the least expense incurred, without the official concurrence and orders of the Christian functionary. Fourth, that British officers, with the troops of the Government, are also now employed in firing salutes and in otherwise rendering homage to Mohammedan and idolatrous ceremonies, even on the Sabbath day; and Christians are thus not unfrequently compelled by the authority of Government to desecrate their own most sacred institutions and to take part in unholy and degrading superstitions."

This is enough to show that the British Government in India "not content with their exertions to suppress the diffusion of the saving truths of the Gospel was openly and authoritatively aiding and abetting the worst forms of devil-worship; that they were taking all the hideous indecencies and revolting cruelties of Hinduism under their especial patronage; sending their own masters-of-the-ceremonies to preside over the hellish orgies; and with paternal tenderness managing the property of the idol temples pampering the priests, cherishing the dancing girls, and doing such honour to heathen is generally as was best calculated to maintain it in a high state of exultant obesity.

It was not till 1841 that Government dissociated itself from actual participation in the Hindu and Mohammedan religions I ceremonies and that too after a great deal of agitation by the Missionaries.

"In a circular letter signed by the Military Secretary to the Government of Fort St. George, and addressed to the Commander-in-Chief, under date of July 6, 1841, it is intimated," under instructions from the Court of Directors, conveyed through the Government of India ", that "the attendance of troops or of military bands at native festivals or ceremonies, and the firing of salutes on occasions of that nature," were "in future to be discontinued, with the object of separating the Government and its officers, as far as possible, from all connection with the ceremonies of the Hindu and Mohammedan religions. "The ordinary marks of respect paid to native princes on the occasions of their going forth or returning from such festivals or religious observances were, however, to be paid; and the change was to be effected "in a manner calculated not to alarm the minds of the natives or to offend their feelings. "These orders were circulated by the Commander in Chief to the Generals commanding divisions, and by them to the regiments under their several commands."

What reform could be expected from a Government which had become so steeped in native prejudices and which wasted such official resources to tend them and keep them up?

It was stricken and paralysed by sympathy. When it ceased to sympathise with the prejudices it was overtaken by fear. This fear arose out of two considerations. The first consideration related to the promises it had made to the people of India.

On assuming the Government of any new territory, previously under native rule, it was the practice of the British Government to announce to the people that they would be protected in the free exercise of their religions and that neither their institutions nor their usages would be assailed.

Thus in 1801 a solemn declaration was made, in the following terms to the people of the Carnatic:

"Although the Right Honourable the Governor in Council trusts that the experience which the inhabitants of the Carnatic have already had, will have rendered it unnecessary for His Lordship to explain the general principles of moderation, justice, protection, and security, which form the characteristic features of the British Government, yet His Lordship in accepting the sacred trust transferred to the Company by the present engagements, invites the people of the Camatic to already and cheerful obedience to the authority of the Company, in a confident assurance of enjoying, under the protection of public and defined laws, every just and ascertained civil right, with a free exercise of the religious institutions and domestic usages of their ancestors".

In may 1834 the following proclamation was issued to the people of Coorg when it was conquered:

"Whereas it is the unanimous wish of the inhabitants of Coorg to be taken under the protection of the British Government, His Excellency the Right Honourable the Governor-General has been pleased to resolve that the territory heretofore governed by Veer Rajunder Woodyer shall be transferred to the Honourable Company. The inhabitants are hereby assured that they shall not again be subjected to native rule; that their civil rights and religious usages, will be respected, and the greatest desire will invariably be shown by the British Government to augment their security, comfort, and happiness."

In 1849, on the annexation of the Punjab, the following assurance was given to the people:

"The British Government will leave to all the people whether Mussulman, Hindu, or Sikh, the free exercise of their own religions; but it will not permit any man to interfere with the other in the observance of such forms and customs as their respective religions may either enjoin or permit."

Other similar proclamations may be cited. They were treated as pledges. Whether it was just and politic that such pledges should have been given, it was felt that it was impolitic to ignore them once they were given. This was the general view. But there were always some who construed them literally and whose point of view was not to draw any distinction and make any reservations and who wished to interpret the pledges as amounting to saying to the Indians, "You have enjoyed it undisturbedly under the new "and who argued that "any departure from this would be a breach of faith. "Fear of breach of faith was one consideration. Fear of open rebellion was another. Fear of rebellion so far as the British Government in India was concerned was not a fear of the unknown. It was a fact of experience. There was one rebellion in 1801 which was known as the Vellore Mutiny. There was another rebellion in 1857.

It was known as I the Sepoy Mutiny. The Vellore Mutiny was a small flame. But I the Sepoy Mutiny was a conflagration. In both cases the cause alleged was an interference with the religious practices of the Hindus. Two rebellions are enough to teach a lesson and the lesson of these two rebellions was not lost upon the British Government. The Vellore Mutiny of 1801 had made the British Government cautious in the matter of social innovations. The Sepoy Mutiny of 1857 made hostile to any kind of social reform. The British did not want to take any risk and from their point of view the risk was very great. The Mutiny made them so panicky that they felt that loss of India was the surest consequence of social reform and as they were anxious to keep India they refused to look at any project of Social Reform. This attitude of the British Government to Social reform is quite understandable. However sovereign a Government may be its authority as pointed out by Prof. Dicey is circumscribed by two limitations:

> *"There is first of all the internal limitation which arises from the character, motives and interests of those who are in power. If the Sultan does not abolish Mahomedanism, Pope ban Catholicism, the Brahmin condemn caste, or the British Parliament declare the preservation of blue-eyed babies illegal, it is not because they "cannot" do things, but it is because they "will "not do those things. In the same way if the Executive in India did not do certain things most conducive to progress, it I was because by reason of its being imperial and also by reason of its character, motives and interests, it could not sympathize with the living forces operating in the Indian Society, was not charged with its wants, its pains, its carvings and its desires, was inimical to its aspirations, did not advance Education, disfavoured Swadeshi or snapped at anything that Smacked of nationalism, it was because all these things went against its grain. But an irresponsible government is powerless to do even*

such things as it may like to do. For its authority is limited by the possibility of external resistance. There are things which it would do but dare not do for the fear of provoking thereby resistance to its authority. Ceaser dare not subvert the worship of the Roman people, a modern parliament dare not tax the Colonies, however much they would. For the same reason the Government of India dared not abolish the caste system, prescribe monogamy, alter the laws of succession, legalize intermarriage or venture to tax the tea planters. Progress involves interference with the existing code of social life and interference is likely to cause resistance. None the less a Government which is of the people and is not detached from them can venture on the path of progress, because it is in a position to know where the obedience will end and resistance will begin. But the Indian Executive, not being of the people, could not feel the pulse of the people. The gist of the matter is that the irresponsible Executive which had been in power in India was paralysed between these two limitations on its authority and much of what to make life good was held up. Part of the programme it would not undertake and the other part it could not undertake. That there was some advancement in material progress is not to be denied. But no people in the world can long remain contented with the benefits of peace and order, for they are not dumb brutes. It is foolish to suppose that a people will indefinitely favour a bureaucracy because it has improved their roads, constructed canals on more scientific principles, effected their transportation by rail, carried their letters by penny post, flashed their messages by lightening, improved their currency, regulated their weights and measures, corrected their notion of geography, astronomy and medicine and stopped their internal quarrels. 'Any people, however patient, will sooner or later demand a Government that will be more than a mere engine of efficiency."

People wanted freedom political, economic and social. This the British Government declined to create:

"As a result of this, so far as the moral and social life of the people was concerned, the change of Government by the Mughals to a Government by the British was only a change of rulers rather than a change of system. Owing to the adoption of the principle of non-interference partly by preference and partly by necessity by the British ' the natives of India found themselves under a Government distinguished in no vital respect from those under which they had toiled and worshipped, lived and died through all their weary and forgotten history. From a political standpoint, the change was but the replacement of one despotism by_ "another. It accepted the arrangements as it found them and preserved them faithfully in the manner of the Chinese tailor who, when given an old coat as a pattern, produced with pride an exact replica, rents, patches and all.'"

This policy of nonintervention though understandable, was so far as the Untouchables were concerned, mistaken in its conception and disastrous in its consequences. It may be granted that Untouchables can only be lifted up by the Hindus recognizing his human rights and him as a human being as correct. But that does not dispose of the matter. Question remains how is this recognition of his rights as a human being to be secured. There are only two ways of helping to realize this object. One way is to make him worthy of respect and the other is to punish those who disrespect him and to deny him his rights. The first way involves the duty to educate him and to place him in positions of authority. The other way involves social reform by making recognition of Untouchability a penal office. Neither of this the British Government was prepared to do.

It would not give the Untouchables any preferential treatment in public service. It I would not undertake to reform Hindu Society. The result was that _ Untouchable has remained what he was before the British, namely an Untouchable. He was a citizen but he was not given the rights of a citizen. He paid taxes out of which schools were maintained but his children could not be admitted into those schools. He paid taxes out of which wells were built but he had no right to take water from them. He paid taxes out of which roads were built. But he has no right to use them. He paid taxes for the upkeep of the State. But he himself was not entitled to hold offices in the state. He was a subject but not a citizen.

The Untouchable stood most in need of education and supply of water. He stood mostly in need of office to protect himself. Owing to his poverty he should have been exempted from all taxes. All this was reversed. The Untouchable was taxed to pay for the education of the touchable. The Untouchable was taxed to pay for the water supply of the touchable. The Untouchable was taxed to pay for the salary of the touchables in office.

What good has British conquest done to the Untouchables? In education, nothing; in service, nothing; in status, nothing. There is one thing in which they have gained and that is equality in the eye of the law. There is of course nothing special in it because equality before law is common to all. There is of course nothing tangible in it because those who hold office often prostitute their position and deny to the Untouchables the benefit of this rule. With all this, the principle of equality before law has been of special benefit to the Untouchables for the simple reason that they never had it before the days of the British.

The Law of Manu did not recognize the principle of equality. Inequality was the soul of the Law of Manu. It pervaded all walks of life, all social relationships and all departments of state. It had fouled the air and the

Untouchables were simply smothered. The principle of equality before law has served as a great disinfectant. It has cleansed the air and the Untouchable is permitted to breath the air of freedom. This is a real gain to the Untouchables and having regard to the ancient past it is no small gain.

SLAVES AND UNTOUCHABLES

Far from being ashamed of untouchability, the Hindus try to defend it. The line of their defence is that the Hindus have never upheld slavery as other nations have done and that in any case, untouchability is not worse than slavery. This argument was used by no less a person than the late Lala Lajpat Rai in his book called 'Unhappy India'. It would have been unnecessary to waste one's time in refuting this countercharge had it not been that on account of its plausibility the world at large not having witnessed anything worse than slavery is likely to believe that untouchability cannot be worse than slavery.

The first reply to the countercharge is that it is quite untrue that slavery was not recognised by the Hindus. Slavery is a very ancient institution of the Hindus. It is recognised by Manu, the Hindu lawgiver and has been elaborated and systematised by the other Smriti writers who followed Manu. Slavery among the Hindus was never merely ancient institution, which functioned, only in some hoary past. It was an institution which continued throughout Indian history down to the year 1843 and if it had not been abolished by the British Government by law in that year, it might have continued even today.

As to the relative merits of slavery and untouchability, the best way to meet the countercharge is to compare and contrast untouchability with slavery as it existed in ancient Rome and in modern America. What was the *de facto* condition of the slaves in the Roman Empire? The best description I know of is to be found in Mr. Barrow's *Slavery in the Roman Empire*. Says' Mr. Barrow:

> *"Hitherto, it is the repulsive side of household slavery that has been sketched. There is also another aspect. The literature reveals the vast household as normal. It is, of course, the exception. Large slave staffs undoubtedly existed, and they are generally to be found in Rome. In Italy and the Provinces there was less need of display; many of the staff of the Villa were engaged in productive work connected with land and its produce. The old-fashioned relationship between foreman and slave remained there; the slave was often a fellow worker. The kindliness of Pliny towards his staff is well known. It is in no spirit of self-righteousness, and in no wish to appear in a favourable light in the eyes of the future generations which he hoped would read his letters that he tells of his distress at the illness and death of his slaves. The household (or Pliny) is the slaves' republic. Pliny's account of his treatment of his slaves is sometimes regarded as so much in advance of general or even*

> *occasional practice as to be valueless as evidence. There is no reason for this attitude.*
>
> *From reasons both of display and genuine literary interest, the rich families attached to their households, slaves trained in literature and art. Clavisices Sabinus is said by Seneda to have had eleven slaves taught to recite Homer, Hesioid, and nine lyric poets by heart. 'Book cases would be cheaper', said a rude friend. 'No, what the household knows the master knows' was the answer. But, apart from such abuses, educated slaves must have been a necessity in the absence of printing;.... The busy lawyer, the dilettante poet, the philosopher and educated gentlemen of literary tastes and need of copyists and readers and secretaries. Such men were naturally linguistic also; a* librarius *who dies at the age of twenty boasts that he was 'literatus Graecis Latinis'.* Amanuenses *were common enough; librarians are to be found in public and private libraries.... Shorthand writing was in common use under the Empire, and slave* Notarii *were regularly employed. Many freemen, rhetoricians and grammarians are collected by Snetonius in a special treatise. Verrius Flaccus was tutor to Austus's grandsons, and at death was publicly honoured by a statue. Scribonius Aphrodisius was the slave and disciple of Orbilius and was afterwards freed by Scribenia. Hyginus was librarian of the Palatine Library, in which office he was followed by Julius Modestus, his own freeman. We hear of freemen historians of a slave philosopher who was encouraged to argue with his master, friends of slaves and freed architects. Freemen as doctors occur frequently in the inscriptions, some of them specialists, they had been trained in big households as slaves, as is shown by one or two examples; after Manumission they rose to eminence and became notorious for their high fees."' The tastes of some section of society demanded that dancer, singers, musicians, mountebanks, variety artists, athletic trainers and messieurs should be forthcoming. All these are to be found in slavery often trained by teachers who had acquired some reputation."*

The age of Augustus was the beginning of a period of commercial and industrial expansion.... Slaves had indeed been employed (in arts and crafts) before, but the sudden growth of trade.... their employment in numbers that would otherwise have been unnecessary. Romans engaged more freely and more openly in various forms of commercial and industrial venture. Yet, even so, the agent became more important, for commercial activities became more widespread; and such agents were almost necessarily slaves.... (this is so) because the bonds of slavery (are elastic). (They could be) so relaxed as to offer an incentive to the slave to work by the prospect of wealth and freedom, and so tightened as to provide a guarantee to the master against loss from the misconduct of his slave.

In business contracts between slave and master or third person seem to have been common, and the work thus done, and no doubt, the profits were considerable.... Renting of land to the slave has already been noticed.... and in industry much the same system was used in various forms; the master might lease a bank, or a business of the use of a ship, the terms being a fixed return or the slave being paid on a commission basis.

The earnings of the slave became in law his peculium was saved it might be used to a variety of purpose. No doubt in many cases this fund was expended in providing food or pleasure. But peculium must not be regarded merely as petty savings, casually earned and idly spent. The slave who made his master's business yield profits, to his own profit too, very often, had a keen sense of the best use to make up his own money. Often he reinvested it in his master's business or in enterprises entirely unrelated to it. He could enter into business relations with his master, from whom he came to be regarded as entirely distinct, or he could make contracts with a third person. He could even have procurators to manage his own property and interests. And so with the peculium may be found not only land, houses, shops, but rights and claims.

The activities of slaves in commerce are innumerable; numbers of them are shopkeepers selling every variety of food, bread, meat, salt, fish, wine, vegetables, beans, lupine-seed, honey, curd, ham, ducks and fresh fish; others deal in clothing—sandals, shoes, gowns and mantles. In Rome, they plied their trade in the neighbourhood of the Circus Mamimus, or the Porticus Trigemimus; or the Esquiline Market, or the Great Mart (on the Caolian Hill) or the Suburra .... The extent to which slave secretaries and agents acted for their masters is shown very clearly in the receipts found in the house of Caecillius Jucundus at Pompei.

That the State should possess slaves is not surprising; war, after all, was the affair of the State and the captive might well be State-property. What is surprising is the remarkable use made of public slaves under the Empire and the extraordinary social position occupied by them....

"'Public slave' came to mean before the Empire a slave of the State employed in its many offices, and the term implied a given occupation and often social position. The work of slaves of the State, slaves of the townships, and slaves of Caesar comprises much of what would now fall to parts of the higher and the whole of the lower branches of the civil services and of the servants of Municipal Corporations, working both with head and hands.... In the subordinate levels (of the Treasury) there worked numbers of clerks and financial officers, all freedmen and slaves. The business dealt with must have been of vast range.... The Mint.... the immediate head was a knight, in charge

of the minting processes.... a freedman was placed; under him served freedmen and slaves.... From one branch of State service, at any rate, slaves were rigorously excluded, except on one or two occasions of exceptional stress. They were not allowed to fight in the Army because not thought worthy of honour. Doubtless other motives were present also; it would be dangerous experiment to train too many slaves systematically in the use of Arms. If, however, slaves served rarely in the fighting line, they are regularly to be found in great numbers behind it employed as servants, and in the commissariat and transport. In the fleet slaves were common enough."

Let us turn to the *de facto* position of the Negro in the United States during the period in which he was slave in the eye of the law. Here are some facts which shed a good deal of light on his position:

"Lafayette himself had observed that white and black seamen and soldiers had fought and messed together in the Revolution without bitter difference. Down in Granville County, North Carolina, a full blooded Negro, John Chavis, educated in Princeton University, was conducting a private school for white students and was a licentiate under the local Presbytery, preaching to white congregations in the State. One of his pupils became Governor of North Carolina, another the State's most prominent Whig senator. Two of his pupils were sons of the Chief Justice of North Carolina. The father of the founder of the greatest military Academy of the State attended his school and boarded in his home..... Slave labour was used for all kinds of work and the more intelligent of the Negro slaves were trained as artisans to be used and leased. Slave artisans would bring twice as much as an ordinary field hand in the market. Master craftsmen owned their staff. Some masters, as the system became more involved, hired slaves to their slave artisans. Many slave artisans purchased their freedom by the savings allowed them above the normal labour expected."

"The advertisements for runaways and sales are an index to this skill. They received the same or better wages than the poor white labourer and with the influence of the master got the best jobs. The Contractors for masons' and carpenters' work in Athens, Georgia in 1838 were petitioned to stop showing preference to Negro labourers. "The white man is the only real, legal, moral, and civil proprietor of this country and state. The right of his proprietorship reached from the date of the studies of those whitemen, Copernicus and Galileo, who indicated the sphericity of the earth; which sphericity hinted to another white man, Columbus, the possibility by a westerly course of sailing, of finding land. Hence by whitemen alone was this continent discovered, the whitemen alone, aye, those to whom you decline to give money for bread or clothes for their famishing families, in the logical manner of withholding work

from them defending Negroes too in the bargain." In Atlanta in 1858 a petition signed by 2 white mechanics and labourers sought protection against the black slave artisans of masters who resided in other sections. The very next year sundry white citizens were aggrieved that the City Council tolerated a Negro dentist to remain and operate in their midst. 'In justice to ourselves and the community it ought to be abated. We, the residents of Atlanta, appeal to you for justice'. A Census of free Negroes in Richmond County, Georgia, in 1819 showed carpenters, barbers, boatcorkers, saddlers, spinners, millwrights, holsters, weavers, harness makers, sawmill attendants and steamboat pilots. A Negro shoemaker made by hand the boots in which President Munrow was inaugurated. Harriet Martineau marvelled at the slave workmanship in the delicately tiled floors of Thomas Jefferson's home at Monticello. There still stands in the big house of the old plantation, heavy marks of the hands of these Negro craftsmen, strong mansions built of timber hewn from the original oak and pinned together by wooden pins. Negro women skilled in spinning and weaving worked in the mills. Buckingham in 1839 found them in Athens, Georgia, working alongside with white girls without apparent repugnance or objection. Negro craftsmen in the South, slave and free fared better than their brothers in the North. In 1856 in Philadelphia, of 1637 Negro craftsmen recorded, less than two-thirds could use their trades; 'because of hostile prejudice'. The Irish who were pouring into America from the very beginning of the nineteenth century were being used in the North on approximately the same motives of preference, which governed Negro slavery. 'An Irish Catholic, it was argued in their favour, seldom attempts to rise to a higher condition than that in which he is placed, while the Negro often makes the attempt with success. Had not the old Puritan Oliver Cromwell, while the traffic in black slaves was on, sold all the Irish not killed in the Drogheda Massacre, into Barbados? Free and fugitive Negroes in New York and Pennsylvania were in constant conflict with this group and the bitter hostility showed itself most violently in the draft riots of the New York. These Hibernians controlled the hod carrying and the common labour jobs, opposing every approach of the Negro as a menace to their slight hold upon America and upon a means of livelihood."

Such was the *de facto* condition of the Roman slave and the American Negro slave. Is there anything in the condition of the Untouchables of India which is comparable with the condition of the Roman slave and the American Negro slave? It would not be unfair to take the same period of time for comparing the condition of the Untouchables with that of the slaves under the Roman Empire. But I am prepared to allow the comparison of the condition of the slaves in the Roman Empire to be made with the condition of the

Untouchables of the present day. It is a comparison between the worst of one side and the best of the other, for the present times are supposed to be the golden age for the Untouchables. How does the *de facto* condition of the Untouchables compare with the *de facto* condition of the slaves? How many Untouchables are engaged as the slaves in Rome were, in professions such as those of Librarians, Amanuenses, Shorthand writers? How many Untouchables are engaged, as the slaves in Rome were, in such intellectual occupations as those of rhetoricians, grammarians, philosophers, tutors, doctors and artists? How many Untouchables are engaged, as the slaves in Rome? Can any Hindu dare to give an affirmative answer to anyone of these queries? The Untouchables are completely shut out from any of these avenues in which the slaves found so large a place. This proves how futile is the line of defence adopted by the Hindus to justify untouchability. The pity of the matter is that most people condemn slavery simply because they hold that for one man or class to have by law the power of life and death over another is wrong. They forget that there can be cruel oppression, tyranny, and persecution, with the train of misery, disappointment and desperation even when there is no slavery. Those who will take note of the facts stated above relating to the *de facto* condition of the slaves will admit that it is idle to condemn slavery lightly or hurriedly on the mere *de jure* conception of it. What the law permits is not always evidence of the practices prevalent in society. Many a slave would readily have admitted that they owed everything to slavery, and many did so whether they would have admitted it or not.

Slavery, it must be admitted, is not a free social order. But can untouchability be described as a free social order? The Hindus who came forward to defend untouchability no doubt claim that it is. They, however, forget that there are differences between untouchability and slavery, which makes untouchability a worse type of an unfree social order. Slavery was never obligatory. But untouchability is obligatory. A person is *permitted* to hold another as his slave. There is no compulsion on him if he does not want to. But an Untouchable has no option. Once he is born an Untouchable, he is subject to all the disabilities of an Untouchable. The law of slavery permitted emancipation. Once a slave always a slave was not the fate of the slave. In untouchability there is no escape. Once an Untouchable always an Untouchable.

The other difference is that untouchability is an indirect and therefore the worst form of slavery. A deprivation of a man's freedom by an open and direct way is a preferable form of enslavement. It makes the slave conscious of his enslavement and to become conscious of slavery is the first and most important step in the battle for freedom. But if a man is deprived of his liberty indirectly he has no consciousness of his enslavement. Untouchability is an indirect form of slavery. To tell an Untouchable 'you are free, you are a citizen, you have all the rights of a citizen', and to tighten the rope in such a way as to leave him no opportunity to realise the ideal is a cruel deception. It is enslavement without making the Untouchables conscious of their enslavement. It is slavery though it is untouchability. It is real though it is indirect. It is enduring because it is unconscious. Of the two orders, untouchability is beyond doubt the worse.

Neither slavery nor untouchability is a free social order. But if a distinction is to be made—and there is no doubt that there is distinction between the two—the test is whether education, virtue, happiness, culture, and wealth is possible within slavery or within untouchability. Judged by this test it is beyond controversy that slavery is hundred times better than untouchability. In slavery there is room for education, virtue, happiness, culture, or wealth. In untouchability there is none. Untouchability has none of the advantages of an unfree social order such as slavery. It has all the disadvantages of a free social order. In an unfree social order such as slavery there is the advantage of apprenticeship in a business, craft or art or what Prof. Mures calls 'an initiation into a higher culture'. Neither the crushing of untouchability nor the refusal of personal growth was necessary inherent in slavery, especially slavery as it existed in Roman Empire. It is therefore over hasty to say that slavery is better than untouchability.

This training, this initiation of culture was undoubtedly a great benefit to the slave. Equally it involved considerable cost to the master to train his slave, to initiate him into culture. 'There can have been little supply of slaves educated or trained before enslavement. The alternative was to train them when young slaves in domestic work or in skilled craft, as was indeed done to some extent before the Empire, by Cato, the Elder, for example. The training was done by his owner and his existing staff.... indeed the household of the rich contained special pedagogue for this purpose. Such training took many forms, industry, trade, arts and letters'.

The reason why the master took so much trouble to train the slave and to initiate him in the higher forms of labour and culture was undoubtedly the motive of gain. A skilled slave as an item was more valuable than an unskilled slave. If sold, he would fetch better price, if hired out he would bring in more wages. It was therefore an investment to the owner to train his slave.

In an unfree social order, such as slavery, the duty to maintain the slave in life and the body falls upon the master. The slave was relieved of all responsibility in respect of his food, his clothes and his shelter. All this, the master was bound to provide. This was, of course, no burden because the slave earned more than his keep. But a security for boarding and lodging is not always possible for every freeman, as all wage earners now know to their cost. Work is not always available even to those who are ready to toil and a workman cannot escape the rule according to which he gets no bread if he finds no work. This rule—no work no bread—has no applicability to the slave. It is the duty of the master to find bread and also to find work. If the master fails to find work, the slave does not forfeit his right to bread. The ebbs and tides of business, the booms and depressions are vicissitudes through which all free wage earners have to go. But they do not affect the slave. They may affect his master. But the slave is free from them. He gets his bread, perhaps the same bread, but bread whether it is boom or whether it is depression.

In an unfree social order, such as slavery, the master is bound to take great care of the health and well being of the slave: The slave was property of the master. But this very disadvantage gave the slave an advantage over a freeman. Being property and therefore valuable, the master for sheer self-interest took great care of the health and well-being of the slave In Rome, the slaves were never employed on marshy and malarial land. On such a land only freemen were employed. Cato advises Roman farmers never to employ slaves on marshy and malarial land. This seems strange. But a little examination will show that this was quite natural. Slave was valuable property and as such a prudent man who knows his interest will not expose his valuable possession to the ravages of malaria. The same care need not be taken in the case of freeman because he is not valuable property. This consideration resulted into the great advantage of the slave. He was cared for as no one was.

THE PERSISTENCE OF UNTOUCHABILITY AND ATROCITIES

Abetment Of Exploitative Bondage

Closely related to the persistence of untouchability and atrocities is the existence of SCs as bonded labourers. As the second report of the Commission for SCs and STs noted, "bonded labourers represent the extreme situation of abject prostration of landless agricultural labourers in the rural economy".

The 21st report of the commissioner for SCs and STs described the bonded labour system as follows: The prominent feature of the system is that a man pledges his person or sometimes a member of his family against a loan. The pledger or his nominee is released only on its discharge. Until then the man himself or the member of the family is required to work for his creditor against his daily meals. Since he gets no money, he has to depend upon someone in the family to procure the sum required for his release and this, of course, is rarely available. The relationship lasts for months and sometimes years, occasionally for an entire life time and not infrequently follows the male heir.

The Bonded Labour System Act of 1976 is intended to abolish this evil practice, and identify, free, and rehabilitate its victims of whom at least 80 per cent are reported to be SCs and STs. But its implementation has not served this purpose so far.

For one thing, under this act the term bonded labour itself is defined in a limited sense. Of this the fifth report of the Commission for SCs and STs wrote: The very definition of the term 'bonded labour' restricts its meaning so much that its connotation excludes many who are virtually compelled but may not be forced to work as bonded labourers.

It is particularly difficult to establish the element of force applied by the creditors with the result that many labourers are excluded from the meaning of the term though their condition is by no means better than that of others. Because of the apparent loophole in the law, in states like Bihar systems like "attached labour" cannot be brought under the purview of the Bonded Labour System Act, 1976.

Terms like "attached labour" are nothing but a euphemism for bonded labour. For another, the implementation of the act has been far from effective even to release and rehabilitate those bonded labourers who come under its purview. Consequently, in practice the system still persists in some form or another in many parts of the country. Data available in the eighth report of the Commission for SCs and STs reveal that as on March 31, 1986 only about 2 lakh bonded labourers were identified and freed, and of them only about 1.6 lakh were rehabilitated. But, if the estimate of bonded labourers in the country at about 22.4 lakh as made by a survey conducted in 1978 by the Gandhi Peace Foundation in collaboration with the National Labour Institute is any indication, by its implementation the act has so far only scratched the surface.

Even going by the conservative estimate of 3.4 lakh as made by the 32nd round of the NSS, the implementation of the act has to cover a lot more ground. What is more, due to inadequacies in the rehabilitation scheme and lack of follow up action, even the freed bonded labourers are either back in or on the verge of further bondage.

Of this, the fifth report of the Commission for SCs and STs wrote: Rehabilitation measures in many cases do not appear to be sufficient or are adopted unimaginatively. One of the reasons for unimaginative rehabilitation is that, due to poverty, illiteracy and economic backwardness, freed bonded labourers are not in a position to exercise option and preference for a particular scheme of rehabilitation. In such a situation the field functionaries have to decide for themselves the role of freed bonded labourers, taking a decision about what would be the form of rehabilitation.

As examples the report pointed out that in certain land-based schemes the agricultural land allotted was too inadequate for the maintenance of a family, and that sometimes such land itself was fallow and unfit for cultivation.

UNTOUCHABLE COMMUNITY

The '*Times of India*' in its issue of 4th January 1928 reports the tyranny and oppression practised upon the Balais who form an Untouchable community in Central India for their daringness to wear clean clothes and golden ornaments. Says the 'Times': In May (1927) high caste Hindus *viz.*, Kalotas Rajputs and Brahmins including the Patils and Patwaris of villages Kanana, Bicholee Hafsi, Bicholi Mardana and of about 15 other villages in the Indore district informed the Balais of their respective villages that if they wished to live among them, they must conform to the following rules:

1. Balais must not wear gold lace bordered pugrees;
2. They must not wear dhoties with coloured or fancy borders;
3. They must convey intimation of the death of any Hindu to relatives of the deceased—no matter how far away these relatives may be living;
4. In all Hindu marriages, the Balais must play music before the processions, and during the marriages;
5. The Balai women must not wear fancy gowns for jackets;
6. Balai women must attend all cases of confinement of Hindu women;
7. The Balais must render services without demanding remuneration, and must accept whatever a Hindu is pleased to give;
8. If the Balais do not agree to abide by these terms, they must clear out of the villages.

The Balais refused to comply; and the Hindu element proceeded against them. Balais were not allowed to get water from the village wells; they were not allowed to let their cattle to graze. Balais were prohibited from passing through land owned by a Hindu; so that if the field of a Balai was surrounded by fields owned by Hindus, the Balai could have no access to his own field. The Hindus also let their cattle graze down the fields of Balais. The Balais submitted petitions to the Darbar of Indore against these persecutions, but as they could get no timely relief, and the oppression continued, hundreds of Balais with their wives and children, were obliged to abandon their homes in which their ancestors lived for generations, and to migrate to adjoining states, *viz.* to villages in Dhar, Dewas, Bangali, Bhopal, Gwalior and other states.

Only a few days ago the Hindus of Reoti village barely 8 miles to the North of Indore city ordered the Balais to sign a stamped agreement in accordance with the rules framed against the Balais by the Hindus of other villages. The Balais refused to comply, It, is alleged that some of them were beaten by the Hindus; and one Balai was fastened to a post, and was told that he would be let go, on agreeing to sign the agreement. He signed the agreement, and was released ". The next is from the *'Arya Gazette'* dated 21st January, 1928: "Up till now the tales of woe that were usually related of the persecution of the Harijans were mostly from the Madras province, but now thanks to the treatment of the Maharana of the Simla Hills, one has not to go so far to search for these stories. In the Simla district, their dwells a caste called 'Collie' whose members are very handsome and hard working. The Hindus of that area consider them to be Untouchables although they do not engage in any such work which should render them objectionable in the eyes of the Hindu religion. The members of this caste are not only powerful and well built but intelligent also. Almost all the songs that the dwellers of the Simla Hills sing are composed by the 'Collies'. These people labour all day long and venerate the Brahmins excessively but still they cannot so much as pass near the house of a Brahmin. Their children cannot read in schools and 'Pathashalas' (religious monastic schools). Their women folk cannot wear gold ornaments. It has even been reported that some Collies have gone to the Punjab and earned some money with which they have bought gold rings and earrings. When however they have brought these back to their homes, they have been cast into the jail and not freed until the ornaments had passed into the pockets of the State Officers."

The following letter appeared in the *'Pratap'* of 23rd June 1926: "Swami Ramanandji Sanyasi writes: On the 23rd of March 1926, in the evening a Chamar came to me who had recently managed to escape from the clutches of the Jats. He related to me a moving tale of the sufferings that his caste had to put up with in the village of Kheri near Faridabad in the District of Gurgaon. On the morning of 24th March I reached Faridabad in the District of Gurgaon, so as to investigate the state of affairs myself. The result of my enquiries is briefly as follows: "On the 5th of March the marriage took place of the daughter of a Chamar called Gorkhi. The financial condition of the Chamar was comparatively good and he entertained his guests in the same way as people of the high castes do. Moreover, before handing away his daughter, he gave her three gold ornaments. This news spread amongst the Jats and was widely discussed. It was decided finally that the high castes had been insulted by the fact that the lower castes have started viewing with them. Till the 20th of March nothing untoward happened but on the morning of the 21st the Jats called a meeting of the Panchayat (village council) to consider the matter. Just at that moment a party of the Chamars of which the greater portion was composed of boys, girls and women was setting out for Faridabad on its daily duty. The party had just gone out of the village as far as the

Dharmashala when the Jats attacked it. All the men of the party were belaboured and the women were thrashed with shoes. The backs of some were broken and of some the arms. Not only this, even their implements were robbed. A Muslim happened to pass along that way and the Jats took hold of him also and robbed him of his big gold earrings as well as of twenty-eight rupees. On the 22nd of March some groups of the Jats went into the fields of the Chamar and played havoc with them. The crop thus destroyed was estimated at about a thousand rupees. At that time, Nanwa, the son of Kori, was working in the fields. The Jats gave him also a thorough beating. On the 22nd of March again a party of the Jats sallied forth armed with flaming torches dipped in Kerosene oil, with the intention of setting fire to the houses of the Chamars but later came away. On the 23rd of March at midnight a house was set on fire belonging to the grandfather of that married girl who has been mentioned above. The house is now a heap of ashes. It contained sixteen skins ready to be made into shoes and worth 90 rupees. They also got burnt up together with the other household goods. The general situation now is that the Jats have surrounded the town and no Chamar is allowed to go out. The Baniyas also, out of fear of the Jats, have refused to sell anything to the Chamars. For three days the Chamars as well as their cattle have been starving."

The following is a more recent occurrence. It has happened in Malabar. The facts of the case are revealed by the following resolution passed at the first Chirakal Taluka Harijan Conference held at Cherukunn in Malabar on 5th June 1945 with Shri K. Kannan, M.L.A., presiding: "This Conference invites the urgent attention of the Government and the public to the increasing cases of inhuman oppressions of the Scheduled Castes of Malabar by Hindus, Muslims and Christians, particularly to the severest type of oppression now going on, almost with impunity, in the Nattika Firka, Ponnani Taluk, where something like a regular Harijan hunting is taking place every day as a result of the Harijans trying to wear gold ornaments and use clean clothes and umbrellas. In addition to numerous cases of assaults a Harijan marriage party was waylaid and assaulted and the shirts of men and the sarees of women removed by force and a Harijan student mercilessly beaten in Vadanpilly on 27th May 1945.

This Conference while congratulating the progressive Thiya youths of the place under the enlightened leadership of Messrs. C. S. Gopalan, M. S. Sankaranarayan and P. C. Ramakrishna Vydier for their magnificient efforts to help the Harijans, most emphatically protests against the callous indifference of the local authorities, particularly/of the Police Department in that the ill-treated Harijans did not get any timely protection from them. This conference desires to state that almost in all cases of the above-said oppressions, the aggrieved Harijans have received neither protection nor justice from the police. There are instances where poor Harijans were even beaten by the Police for their coming forward to give evidence in such cases. In so far as these events have reduced the Harijans of Malabar to a very miserable plight and the situation, if left alone, is likely to develop into a crisis endangering the lives of all progressive Harijans who are trying to break the shackles of caste and economic exploitation of the vested interests in Malbar. This Conference most earnestly appeals to the Government of India, the Hon'ble Dr. B. R. Ambedkar and all the enlightened people in the country to see that the Harijans are allowed to live in this land as free citizens of a democratic country unmolested by any people and promptly protected by the administration whenever they are oppressed by others."

The Untouchables must not eat rich food even if they can afford it. It is an offence for the Untouchables to live above their station in life. The *'Pratap'* of 26th February 1928 relates the following occurrence: "In the State of Jodhpur at a place Chandayal, you will still see men who do not think that the Harijans have even the right to eat Halva. One of the Untouchable castes is that of Sargaroes. Sometime back on the occasion of the Marriage ceremony of two or three girls, Halva was prepared for the members of the marriage party. For this purpose, maida (white flour) was brought from the Thakur Sahib. At mealtime, the marriage party came for meals but just at that time the Kanwar Sahib of Chandawala sent orders to the Saragaroes that they could not eat Halva. Some cringing sycophants negotiated a compromise in this way that the Kanwar Sahib be presented with Rs. 200 and then permission will be given to eat Halva. At this the Sargaroes got infuriated and refused to pay the money."

To lead a marriage procession through the main streets of the village is the right of every caste Hindu. It is also in evidence that the community, which enjoys this right, is accepted as a respectable community. The Untouchables have no such right. But they have been seeking to establish such a right by taking their marriage procession through the main streets of the village with the object of establishing their social status.

The following incidents show how the Hindus have dealt with this claim. From the *'Adi-Hindu'* dated July 1927: "Bangalore, 27th May 1927: Seven Brahmins were sentenced to pay a fine of hundred rupees each, by the First Class Magistrate. These men had wantonly attacked a procession of the well-known Pariah Untouchable caste when it was passing along the Mallkot Road where only Brahmins live."

From the *'Pratap'* dated 25th October 1931: "In the village of Hargaon, district Garhwal when the high caste Hindus heard that a marriage party of the Untouchables was coming and the bridegroom was sitting in a palanquin they sallied forth in great numbers and surrounded the party and gave it a severe beating. In intense cold they held up the marriage party and kept it without food for 24 hours. The members of the party were inhumanly treated and were only rescued from this difficult situation by the coming of the Police."

From the *'Satya Samwad'* Lahore dated 3rd November 1931: "A marriage party was passing near Delhi, carrying the bridegroom in a palanquin. The high caste Hindus took offence at this for they thought it to be an insult to them. They held up the party for two days and gave it nothing either to eat or drink. At last the police came and chased away these tyrants and rescued the marriage party."

The *'Jivan'* a Hindu journal for June 1938 reports,

1. "In village Sevra, the Golas (Purva Thakurs) who boast of being Congressites, have so mercilessly beaten with spears and lathis the unarmed Jatavs of that village that five of them were lying wounded in the hospital with arms and ribs broken. Bansi has sustained fracture of the skull bone and is still unconscious in the hospital. All this happened because when a marriage party came to the village the bridegroom was wearing a glittering crown (Pukka Mohar) which offended the Thakurs, who wanted to attack the marriage party; but desisted because of the party's superior strength and were therefore content with only insulting the marriage party within the Zamindari at that time."
2. "In village Dorra, Tehsil Fatechand, District Agra, a marriage party came to the house of Moti Ram Jatav from village Rampur. The bridegroom was wearing a glittering crown and the party also brought band music and fireworks. The Caste Hindus objected to the party proceeding with the music band playing and displaying fireworks. Moti Ram protested against this and said that they were also as good human beings as any others. On this, the caste Hindus caught hold of Moti Ram and gave him a severe beating and also attacked the marriage party. A sum of Rs. 15-1-0 tied in Moti Ram's turban was also removed."
3. "While a marriage party was on its way to the house of Prem Singh and Girvar Singh, Jatavs of village Khurva, Police post Sakini, District Aligarh, it was prevented by the caste Hindus from proceeding further unless the music band stopped playing, and the procession was threatened to be killed and looted if the music was not stopped. Caste Hindus were also enraged for refusal by the Jatavs to do 'Begar" and

for the audacity to have music band playing with a marriage party. On the marriage party's refusal to stop music, the caste Hindus were so much enraged that they threw brickbats and stones at the party."

The *'Hindustan Times'* of the 24th of March 1945 reports the following incident relating to the same subject: "A Shilpakar marriage party of the village of Dhanuri in Lands down sub-division carrying the bridegroom in a 'palki' was proceeding to the bride's house in the village of Mall Dhangu. A man introducing himself as an agent of the Patwari of Mall Dhangu advised the party to go through an out of the way route to avoid disturbance by caste Hindus. The party, accordingly, took a forest path and when they were at a lonely spot a whistle brought out about 200 caste Hindus who, it is alleged, attacked the party and carried away the 'palki". The Shilpakar party reached the bride's house two days later and the marriage was, it is reported, performed in the presence of the Sub-divisional Magistrate and a police party brought by him. The Patwari has been suspended in this connection."

The *Civil and Military Gazette of Lahore* in its issue of 24th June 1945 reports: "A party of Rajputs, armed with axes, lathis and daggers, attacked yesterday Harijans of a village in Gwalior State, killing one and inflicting serious injuries on four. The Rajputs and the Harijans of the village were on hostile terms for some time past ever since the Harijans took out a procession to celebrate the birth of an heir apparent to the Gwalior Darbar. The Rajputs strongly protested against it, as according to them, Harijans were not entitled to the privileges of such celebrations. Last month, a proclamation was issued by the Maharaja giving equal rights to the Harijans."

Here are a few cases to show how the Hindus treat with violence any attempt on the part of the Untouchables to imitate the ways and manners of the Hindus and to have a little pride in themselves. The following is from the *"Bombay Samachar"* of 4th November 1936: "At Uttapalam (in Malabar) an Ezhava by caste named Sivaraman, aged 17, went to the shop of a caste Hindu to buy salt and asked in the Malayalam language for 'uppu'. In Malabar, according to custom, caste Hindus alone can use the word 'uppu' for salt; being only a Harijan he ought to have used the word 'pulichatan'. Consequently, the high caste grocer was very angry and is alleged to have thrashed Sivaraman so severely that the latter died."

The following instances are collected from the *'Samata':*

(1) "At Kathi (District Poona) the people have begun to persecute the Untouchables because the latter have begun saying 'Ram, Ram and Namaskar'. Be it known to the un-intimated that these are salutations which only the higher castes have the right to employ; the Mahars, etc. must say 'Johar' or 'Paya Lagu' (I touch your feet) to the people.

(2) The Untouchables of Tanoo (District Poona) tried to behave 'like Touchable Hindu people'; the result of this impudent encroachment is that many of them have had to leave the village and some have migrated to Bavda.

(3) At Valapur (District of Sholapur) the Mahars are persecuted because they have dared to refuse to address Touchables as 'Saheb' and to say 'Paya Lagu' ('I touch your feet') in salutation.

(4) At Jambad (District Sholapur) the Untouchables refused to make 'Nautch' and 'Tamasha' for the diversion of their Touchable lords. Therefore these Untouchables were thrashed, their huts were burnt down or pulled down, and they were driven out of the village limits.

(5) At Bavda (District Poona) some Untouchables exhorted their fellow-outcastes to give up eating the leavings of higher caste people, dead animals, etc., and to refuse to do the dirty work of the people. The elders of the village have told these Mahars with new fanglad notions that it is their 'Dharma' to eat what they have always been eating and do what they have been doing. Those Mahars who do not follow their ancient and eternal 'Dharma' have been thrashed by the people and threatened with expulsion from the village."

The Hindu treats the Untouchables as being born to serve the Hindu community. It being his duty to serve, the Untouchables cannot refuse to serve the Hindu whenever the latter call upon to do so. The Hindus of the village hold the belief that they can commandeer the labour of the Untouchables. The system is known as '*Begar*', or forced labour. A few instances will show that dire consequences follow from the refusal of the Untouchables to submit to the system. The '*Jivan*' of December 1938 report the following incidents: "On 29th November 1938, the Jatavs of village Kohana, district Muttra were seriously tortured by the Jats and Brahmins for refusing Begar.

The Thakkurs and the Brahmins of this village used to extract Begar from the Jatavs and to harass them. The latter decided not to do Begar and do only that work for which wages were paid. Recently, a bullock died in the village and the Thakkurs and other caste Hindus tried to force the Jatavs to lift it, but they said that they could do that only if they were paid. This enraged the caste Hindus so much that they asked a sweeper to fill the Jatavs' well with excreta and make them not to go to their fields for ablutions and decided to tease them in every way. When the Jatavs prevented the Sweeper from putting excreta in their well, he called the Jats, Thakkurs and Brahmins who were all ready for an attack.

They attacked the Jatavs with lathis and seriously belaboured them and also set fire to their houses as a result of which six houses were burnt to ashes and 18 Jatavs were wounded seriously and a lot of their household property was taken away by the rowdies." The same *Journal* in its issue of February 1939 reports: "The Jats of village Abhaipura, tehsil Kirvali, district Agra, are used to extract Begar (Forced labour) from the poor Scheduled Caste people and beat them on demanding wages. Some three months back Sukhi Jat forced Sukh Ram, Ghanshyam and Humka, Jatavs to do work for them and did not pay any wages. These persons are so much fed up with such high-handedness that they have left the villages and lived with their relatives in other villages, while their utensils and other household goods have been taken away by the Jats and concealed in some barn."

The '*Savadhan*' in its issue of 3rd June 1945 reports the following incident: "Mehraji Kori, a Scheduled Caste woman has filed a complaint in the court of Mr. Mahboob Alam, City Magistrate under Sections 376, 341 and 354-A against Brahma Singh, Sulaiman and Aftab, constables of Jubi Police post. It is alleged that at about 10-30 p.m. on 2nd May 1945 these three constables, Sumar, Kahar, Kallu Bibis son and some others came and searched her house and then took her to the police station and kept her there for the whole night. In the early hours of the morning these constables took her to a small room bolted it and then all three of them violated her modesty one by one. Then she was removed to another small room where charcoal and pieces of paper were filled in her private part and they put their private organs in her mouth. Her clothes were torn and saturated with blood. The following day her mother was forced to do begar work for the whole day and then both of them were left off at 10 p.m. Murala, wife of Maharaji's husband's younger brother has also filed a similar complaint. She has alleged that the same constables took her to the police post the same night and returned her to her house. On the way she was caught by Madari Teli, near Kumar Tola, to the ruins of a house and her modesty violated. Messrs. Munna Lal, Bhushan and Ram Bharose, advocates are appearing for the complainant."

In the '*Hindustan Times*' of 15th April 1945 occurs the following news item: "For refusal to do forced labour, it is alleged, a large number of Harijans in the village of Dukheri in Ambala District were recently assaulted by a party of Rajputs. A man and a woman, both Harijans, were killed. It is also alleged that a large number of houses belonging to Harijans were set on fire. Telegrams have been sent to the Commissioner and the Deputy Inspector General of Police to inquire into the matter."

From these instances, it will be clear to anyone that the Hindus do not hesitate to use violence to hold down the Untouchables and maintain the established order and even to commit, murder. Mr. Lajpat Rai in his book'.Unhappy India' in which he tried to reply to and refute the charges levelled by Miss Mayo in her 'Mother India' gives a lengthy and lucid description of the lynching of the Negroes in the United States and the atrocities committed upon them by the members of the Ku Klux Klan and asks: "What however is very relevant to her to ask is: is the unjustifiable and cruel attitude of the Brahmins towards the *Pariah* more unjustifiable and more cruel than that of the Klansmen of America towards the Negroes?" "What are the caste cruelties of India put by the side of what the whiteman has done to the non-white people?"

Lala Lajpatrai, if he had cared to investigate could have found that the cruelties and atrocities practised by the Hindus against the Untouchables were no less than those practised by the Americans upon the Negroes. If these atrocities are not so well known to the world as are those practised upon the Negro, it is not because they do not exist. They are not known because there is no Hindu, who will not do his best to conceal truth in order to hide his shame, Some might think that this description of the Established Order and the rules made thereunder are matters of ancient past. This is a complete mistake. The Established Order subsists even today and the rules are as operative today as they were when they were made. This will be evident from the two following statements on the condition of the Untouchables which have appeared in the *'Hindustan Times'*. The first appeared in the issue of 8th March 1945. The first one is written by one Kesarilaiji Bordia, Headmaster of a school called Vidya Bhuwan in Udaipur. It reads as follows: Many are the disabilities under which the Harijans in Mewar live. They cannot enter temples, nor can they draw water from public wells. They cannot join the caste Hindus in festivals and processions.

They have to take out their Rath Yatra or Doll procession through a different route and on a different day. And they cannot ride through the village. Even silver ornaments, let alone gold ones on their person are resented by the caste Hindus. The result is, they have to content themselves with tin and brass articles. Age-old usage prevents them from using butter or gur in wedding feasts. In Schools and other public places, Harijan boys cannot sit with the children of caste Hindus. They are asked to absent themselves on the inspection day in order to save the Inspector from embarrassment.

A memorandum has been submitted to the State Government. If the Government chooses to declare in unequivocal terms the disapproval of these disabilities, the hands of non-official bodies which are fighting untouchability will be strengthened." The second is in the form of a statement issued by the President of the *Harijan Sevak Sangh* and refers to the condition of the Untouchables in the State of Mewar. It reads as under: The Mewar Harijan Sevak Sangh has sent a Memorandum to the Mewar Government drawing their attention to the various disabilities of Harijans in the State and their consequent hardships. The Memorandum brings out how civil liberties of Harijans are curtailed in several ways by the orthodoxy and prejudices of caste Hindus.I enumerate below some of the unjust practices, which still persist in the State and for the rectification of which the State has taken no effective measures. They are as follows:

1. Harijans have no liberty in the selection of clothes to wear. The form of dress must follow the age-long pattern; personal tastes and desires have no place in the choice of the dress.
2. At wedding feasts they have no choice in the selection of food materials. Even on payment they cannot use costly articles.
3. They cannot ride the village on a horse.
4. They are not allowed accommodation in public vehicles.
5. On religious festivals they cannot take out procession of their idols except through specified routes.
6. They have no access to wells and temples."

"Three years ago in company with Thakkur Bapa, I travelled all over the State and placed before the Government and public my impressions of the conditions obtaining there and pleaded for reform. On perusal of the above mentioned memorandum and other reports sent to me, I find that the past few years have hardly brought any change and conditions are more or less static. It is heart breaking to find that passage of time cuts no ice with us. The result is that there is hardly any change in our age-long practices and prejudices. This perversity which blinds us to the tyranny and injustices of our ways also makes us impervious to the incalculable harm we have already suffered as a result of it. Even if the ignorant prejudice of the common man is unshaken the enlightened Governments of the twentieth century ought to be more alive to their responsibilities."

The dates of these communications are important. They are of the year 1945. None can say that this Hindu Established Order is a thing of the ancient past. The fact that these latest accounts refer to the Indian States should not be understood to mean that the established Order has vanished from British India. The chapters to follow will present enough evidence to show that the same Established Order is very much alive in British India.

In the *"Times of India"* of 31st August 1950 occurs the following news item: The following facts of a case revealed in the hearing of an appeal in the Allahabad High Court, are illustrative of the socio-economic conditions of lower castes in the rural areas: Chiranji, a dhobi of the village of Sarras in the District of Etah, went out as a military employee in the last war and remained out of his village for four or five years. When he was discharged, he returned to his home. He stopped washing clothes and used to go about in the village in his military uniform. This coupled with the fact that he refused to wash clothes even for the men of the Raja of Sarras the sole zamindar in the village, was resented by the villagers.

On December 31, 1947, when the dhobi was washing his clothes, four villagers, including the Raja's servants, approached him and asked him to wash their clothes which he refused. The villagers took Chiranji to the Raja's house and gave him a beating. His mother and mother's sister went there to intercede on his behalf but they too were assaulted. The attackers then went away leaving Chiranji in the custody of one Ram Singh; finding him alone, Chiranji was alleged to have slapped him and run away. Ram Singh and other servants of the Raja chased him to his house where he had taken shelter. The villagers insisted upon his opening the door but when there was no response, his house was set on fire. A number of other huts were also reduced to ashes.

The dhobi lodged a complaint with the Police who disbelieved his story and wanted to prosecute him for a false report. He then filed a complaint in a Magistrate's Court. The accused were convicted and sentenced to three years' imprisonment, each. The High Court upheld the sentences imposed by the Magistrate. The following news item has appeared in the '*Indian News Chronicle*' dated 31st August 1950. Inhuman Treatment towards Harijans in Pepsu: Depressed Classes League's Memorandum to Government.

Patiala, August 1950: "The unprovoked thrashing of the Backward Class people, inhuman insults heaped upon their women folk, indiscriminate detachment of the Harijans from the lands, the virtual confinement of the Harijans and their cattle in their mud houses for days together without any fault is a long tale of suffering whose echoes are rising in proportion to the diminishing echoes of crime in general," says a memorandum presented by the PEPSU Provincial Depressed Classes League to the State Government. "While crime in PEPSU is on the decrease due to the vigorous efforts of the police," the memorandum adds, "it is a pity that the sector of the Backward Class should be deprived of the protection from the unsociable elements". The Backward Classes economically handicapped as they are, find it very difficult to ventilate their day-to-day grievances to the authorities concerned who could immediately come to their rescue, and are perforce, compelled to submit to their lot, to the encouragement of the aggressor, and thus the wail of disgust against the present state of affairs grows still louder which in its turn is made stock of by the interested parties."

The Provincial Depressed Classes League further quoted an instance to show how much inhuman treatment was being meted out to Harijans in PEPSU. Chand Singh a Harijan of village Katu, district Bernala, was made to go round the village on the back of donkey with face blackened for the fault of having drunk water at the well of a high caste zamindar. "In the changed atmosphere of free India, the members of the Scheduled Castes in the PEPSU are daily finding themselves put in a tight corner as a result of the unprecedented repression let loose upon them by the members of high castes."[1]

The Provincial Depressed Classes League has further suggested formation of district and central special commissions in the State with wide powers to deal with the complaints on Harijans on the spot and afford them other facilities. Concluding, the League has urged upon the State Government that pending an all-India enactment in this connection, it may, temporarily be provided that the Harijans have equal rights in the village common, to ease the situation from further deterioration.

UNTOUCHABILITY AND LAWLESSNESS

There are many people who must be wondering as to how such an established order so full of inequalities could have survived. What are the forces, which go to support it? The forces which sustain the system the most important is the determination of the Hindus to maintain it at all cost. The Hindus are prepared to use every means to suppress the Untouchables whenever the Untouchables try to upset it even in the slightest degree. The ordinary non-violent Hindu will not hesitate to use the utmost violence against the Untouchables. There is no cruelty, which he will not practice against them to sustain the established order. Not many will readily believe this. But this is a fact. For those who have any doubt on the point, I reproduce below some cases of tyrannies and oppressions practised by the Hindus against the Untouchables as have been reported from time to time in the newspapers:

The following news item appeared in the "*Tej*" of Delhi in its issue of 4th September 1927:

> *"The Shiva Temple of Vykom has been desecrated by the Harijans by their coming too near to the temple. Now the Hindus of that area have decided that the ceremony of purifying the temple should be elaborately performed at great expense before the place is fit for worship again."*

The correspondent of '*Pratap*' reports the following incident which appears in its issue of 2nd September 1932:

> *"Meerut August 1932. On the day of Janmashtami some Harijans tried to gain admittance into Caste Hindu Temple but nothing came except widespread troubles and unrest. This year the local Dalit Association has decided that if the doors of the temples are not opened to them, they will undertake*

Satyagraha. When the Hindus came to know of this, they started making plans to defeat the moves of the Harijans. At last on the night of Janmashtami, the members of the Harijan community came in the form of a procession and tried to gain access to the temple Gods. The priests, however, refused them permission to enter and said, "You can have audience of the Gods standing outside on the street." Upon this a great crowd gathered at the place. The priests tried to enter the temple and thus a clash took place between the two parties and blows were freely exchanged."

The Hindus do not allow the Untouchables to enter the Hindu temples. It would be thought that they would allow the Untouchables to have their own temples and install therein the image of God. That is a mistake. The Hindus will not allow even that. It is enough to quote two instances. One is from the *"Pratap"* of 12th February 1923:

"In the District of Agra, a Chamar who had seen a Brahmin worshipping the image of Vishnu in his house, began to do the same himself. When the Brahmin came to know of this he was most indignant and with the help of a number of villagers caught hold of the ill-fated Harijan, gave him a sound beating saying, 'How dare you try to win over the God Vishnu'. Finally, they stuffed his mouth with filth and left him. In sheer desperation the Chamar abandoned the Hindu faith and embraced Islam."

The other is from the *'Hindu'* of 4th July 1939:

"A meeting of the Bellary District Harijan Advisory Board was held on 29th June 1939 at the Collector's Bunglow. Mr. A. D. Crombie, CIE., ICS., President of the Committee and Collector presided. With regard to the grievances of the Harijans of Narayanadevarakeri including allegations of extraction of forced labour from them and harassment by moneylenders, the Committee decided to call for official report, with a view to taking action, if necessary. The religious disabilities of the Harijans residing in Kudathini village were brought to the notice of the Committee. It was alleged that though the Harijans constructed a temple in their colony as long as twelve years ago, they could not install the image of God which was also ready in the temple, owing to the objections raised by a section of the Caste Hindus in the place to the Harijans taking out the image in procession in the village before the installation."

How any attempt to take water from the Hindu well is dealt with by the Hindus can be seen from the following instances. The first one appeared in the *'Pratap'* of 12th February 1923:

"Mahashaya Chhedi Lalji has reported that a Chamar was going for idol worship, when on the way he felt thirsty. He cast his own iron pail into a well and drew out some water. Upon this he was rebuked by a high caste

Hindu and then soundly beaten and locked up in a room. As it happened, I was passing by and when I enquired why this man was being kept under lock and key, the Diwan Saheb replied that this man cast his own pail into our well and wants to profane religion."

That even the Hindu women will not hesitate to take part in the assaults committed by the Hindus against the Untouchables who dare to take water from the Hindu well is a fact. Compare the following report which appeared in the '*Pratap*' of 26th February 1932:

"On 19th February 1932, a very tragic incident took place in the village of Pul Bajwan. This happened when Mahashaya Ramlal went to fetch some water from a well, the same well at which on 13th January 1932 some Rajputs had belaboured Mahashaya Ramlal and his companion. Pandit Bansilal. At that time, a crowd of Rajput women came up armed with all sorts of bats and sticks and gave such a sound beating to the Mahashaya that it is difficult to describe. All his body was covered with blood by the time the Rajput women had done with him. At this time, he is admitted in the hospital of Phuklian."

That even the support of an officer of Government in the exercise of their right to take water from the well will not save the Untouchables from assault is clear from the following incident which appeared in the '*Milap*' of 7th June 1924:

"Some days ago, an officer of the Canal Department came to the village of Rahian in Tehsil Sabha and he ordered some Megha Untouchables to help in drawing out water from a well. At first they refused but the officer rebuked them sternly and forced them to draw water. The next day the Hindus gathered at the well and sent for the Megha through a Chowkidar and asked them why they dared to climb up to the well. One Megha replied that they were obliged to do so and it was no fault of theirs. For this cheek he was attacked by the Hindus with sticks and hands and until the time of writing this, he is lying unconscious. Although the doctor has declared that the injuries are minor ones, a report of attempted murder and unlawful assembly has been filed with the Police. This however has been ignored and the indifference of the police has created a feeling of great insecurity among the Megha people. The villagers are persecuting the Meghas very much, even their cattle are not allowed to drink water and all wells and ponds have been closed to them."

The Untouchables cannot take water from the Hindu well is not all. They must not build a pucca brick well for themselves even though they may have the money to do so. For having a pucca well for them selves means an attempt to raise themselves to the status of the Hindus which is contrary to the Established Order. The '*Milap*' of 6th June 1934 reports the following incidents:

"Lala Ram Prashadji, Secretary of the Achhut Udharak Committee, Punjab, has written to the following effects:

> *"During this hot season, complaints are being received from everywhere that the supply of water is becoming a great problem. The Depressed Class people, who have no wells of their own sit near the well with their vessels in their hands. If someone is kind enough to pour out some water, well and good, otherwise they sit helpless. In some places, however, no one is allowed to pour out water to these people even for money and if anyone does so, mortal fights ensue. Not only is the use of the village wells forbidden to them, but they are not even allowed to make wells of their own with their own money."*

To the same effect is the incident reported in the "*Tej*" of 21st April 1924:

> *"The Chamars of the village, Opad, numbered about 250. About a month and half ago, they gave up drinking water out of the leather bags of the Muslim water carriers (on the suggestions of the Arya Samaj Pandits?) and now they are in great difficulties about their water supply. The Jats of the village not only refuse to let them draw water out of the village wells but do not even let them make wells of their own. The poor Chamars are living on water from ponds and ditches. Yesterday, Dr. Sukhdevji, Secretary of Dalit Sudhar (Harijan Uplift) Committee came to make investigations in Upad and saw everything with his own eyes. He found the condition of the Chamars abject beyond words and their persecution by the Jats a real fact."*

The following is from the '*Times of India*' dated 9th May 1931:

> *"In the Baroda State the Untouchables are supposed to be better treated than in the adjoining British territory, because the State has made laws recognising the equality of the Antyaja with caste people. And yet in Padras Taluka the other day the standing crop of a poor Antyaja woman was fired and she herself brutally assaulted, because she dared to send her little son to the local primary school. Now comes a tale of woe from Chanasma in Kadi Prant where an artisian well has been sunk and built with the labour of the Antayajas who were promised the use of the well. But when the well was ready for use they were first flatly told it was not for them, and when they complained to the Punch the latter generously allowed them to lay a pipe 500 feet long at the end of which they could have a tap all for themselves. Now an unexpected owner of the land at the tap had cropped up, so the pipeline was taken somewhere near to the local tank, but this meant pollution of the tank and therefore of the dirty linen washed there. So the tap was accommodated elsewhere. But did this mean the end of the trouble? No, the enraged caste people have cut the pipeline several times and the Antyajas are without water to drink. How very 'adequate' to use Mr. Gandhi's term, must the Untouchables feel the treatment given to them by their coreligionists."*

Mr. Sanjana in a letter to the *'Times of India'* of the 7th November 1928 reports what Mr. Thakkar saw in the year 1927 regarding the awful plight of the Untouchables in the matter of water.

"In Balsad Taluk, Mr. Thakkar saw a Bhangi woman waiting near a well for some merciful 'people' to give her some water. She had waited from morning till noon, and none had given her any. But the most exquisite touch of spirituality is revealed in the manner of giving water to the Bhangis; it cannot be poured direct into their pots—any 'people' doing so would get polluted. Says, Mr. Thakkar, once our teacher Chunibhai had shown the temerity of pouring water direct from his bucket into a Bhangi's pot and he had received a stern warning in consequence 'Master this sort of thing won't be (tolerated) here'. A small cistern is built below the slope of the well. Anyone who is moved by pity may pour some water in the cistern. A bamboo pipe just out of the cistern, and the Bhangi women must put her pot under the pipe, and it may get filled in an hour or so. For, adds Mr. Thakkar, it is only the unwanted water remaining over in the bucket of the woman drawing it that is as a rule thrown into the cistern, and that too if she takes pity on the waiting Bhangi woman."

Under the established order, the Untouchables have no right to education and certainly have no right to be admitted to the village school. Those Untouchables who have dared to make a breach in these rules of the Established Order have been severely punished by the Hindus.

The following are only a few of the numerous cases that have happened: From the *"Arya Gazette"* of Lahore dated 30th June 1921:

"A Mahashaya wrote an article in the paper 'Young India", *in which he reported that in district surat there is a village called Sisodri. In a very short span of time it has made such progress on the path of nationalism that it could be held up as a model of noncooperation. With all this, however, the old contempt for the Harijan remains. The writer says that in the nationalist school of that place, I saw a Dhed caste child sitting all apart in one corner of I the classroom and proclaiming by his very looks that he was an untouchable. I asked the students why they did not let this boy sit with them and they replied that this could not be until the Harijan left drinking wine and eating meat. The Harijan boy at once said that he had already given these up. The high caste students could say nothing now."*

From the *'Pratap'* of 12th February 1923: "Mahashaya Santramji has reported: It happened recently that a Brahmin teacher was appointed by the Government to go and teach in a village school for Chamar boys. When he came there, the Brahmins, Kshatrias and others boycotted the teacher saying,

'You have come here to teach the Chamars and raise them to our level. Have You?" From the *'Tej'* of 11th April 1924:

> *"Swami Shradhanandji has written: There was a nationalist school in Khatsayas which I visited towards the end of November 1921. When I enquired how many Harijan children read there, I was told only three and they too, sit outside the classroom in the verandah. In my lecture I objected to this procedure and said that in a nationalist institution, it was only proper that these boys should be allowed to sit inside the classroom. The manager of the school acted on my advice. The next day the benches of the school were all deserted and till this day the Grand building of that nationalist school stands locked out and dreary."*

From *"Milap"* dated 18th April 1924:

> *"Here is an incident from Hoshungabad. The district Council sent a circular letter to the schools that the Harijan children should be educated in the schools. The headmasters began to act on the orders. When one of the schools admitted some Harijan children the Honorary Magistrate took great offence at it and withdrew his children from that school; other guardians also followed suit and all together got a meeting of the school committee convened and resolutions passed in it, that the education of Harijans in the school is against the Public wishes. They said that after coming into contact with Harijans, the Brahmin children change their Janayu (a religious thread) therefore this school committee could not undertake the education of Harijan children."*

From *"Pratap"* dated 3rd April 1932:

> *"Ahmedabad, 1st April 1932: A report has been received from the village of Nawagaon, Baroda State, that ever since the Harijan schools were closed down and permission given to the Harijans to enter the ordinary village schools, the villagers have been subjecting the Harijans to endless persecution. It is reported that the thousand stacks of hay belonging to Harijan farmers, were burnt down, Kerosine oil has been sprinkled into the Harijan wells and attempts made to set fire to their houses. A Harijan boy was assaulted on his way to school and a general boycott of the Harijans has been declared."*

The *"Hindustan Times"* in its issue of 26th May 1939 says:

> *"Several persons are reported to have raided a night school in village Catipore in the district where Kisans and others used to be taught. The teacher was caught hold of by them, and asked to close the school on the ground that the boys of the Untouchables, after acquiring education will begin to assert themselves to treat them on a footing of equality. When the teacher refused to do so he was belaboured and the students were asked to disperse."*

The last instance I would like to refer occurred in the year 1935 in *the* village of Kavitha in Dholka Taluka of the Ahmedabad District of the Bombay

Presidency. The incident occurred on 8th August 1935. As the Bombay Government had issued orders requiring the admission of the children of the Untouchables in public schools, the Untouchables of village Kavitha thought of taking advantage of the order. What happened to them is reported below:

> *"On 8-8-1935, the Untouchables of the village Kavitha took four of their children to be admitted in the village school. Much caste Hindus from the village had gathered near the school to witness this. This occasion for admission passed off quietly and nothing untoward happened. From the next day however the caste Hindus of the village withdrew their children from the school as they did not like their children sitting with those of the Untouchables and getting themselves polluted."*

"Some time thereafter an Untouchable from the village was assaulted by a Brahmin on 13th August 1935. The male members of the Untouchables of the village had come to Dholka to file a criminal complaint against the Brahmin in the court of the Magistrate. Coming to know that the adult members of the Untouchables were absent the Hindus of the village invaded the quarters of the Untouchables. They were armed with sticks, spears and swords.

Among the invaders was caste Hindu women. They started attacking the old men and women of the Untouchables. Some of the victims fled into the jungle some shut themselves up. These invaders directed their vehemence against those Untouchables who were suspected to have taken a lead in the matter of the admission of their children in the village school. They broke open their doors and not finding them in, they broke the tiles and the rafters of the roofs over their houses.

"Terror-stricken these Untouchables men and women who were assaulted and beaten were anxious about the safety of those of their elders who had gone to Dholka and who were expected back that night. The caste Hindus knowing that the leaders of Untouchables who had gone to Dholka would be returning had concealed themselves behind the bushes and shrubs on the way to the village. Having come to know of this, an old Untouchable woman sneaked out of the village in the dark, met the leaders who were returning and informed them that armed gangs of caste Hindus were hiding themselves to waylay them and that therefore they should not come into the village. They refused to listen fearing that the caste Hindus might do greater mischief in their absence.

At the same time, they were afraid that if they did enter they might be assaulted. They therefore decided to wait outside the village in the field till after midnight. In the meantime, the gang of caste Hindus who were in ambush waited and waited and finally gave up the game and retired. The leaders of the Untouchables entered the village after about 3 a.m. in the night. If they had come earlier and met the murderous gang they would probably have been done to death. On seeing the harm done to person and property they left the village for Ahmedabad before day break, and informed the Secretary of the Harijan Sevak Sangh, a body organised by Mr. Gandhi to look after the welfare of the Untouchables.

But the Secretary was helpless. Not only did the caste Hindus use physical violence, but they conspired to make the life of the Untouchables intolerable. They refused to engage them as labourers; they refused to sell them foodstuffs. They refused to give them facilities for grazing their cattle and they used to commit stray assaults on Untouchable men and women. Not only this, but the caste Hindus in their frenzy poured kerosine oil in the well from which the Untouchables used to get their supply of drinking water. This, they did for days together. The result was that the Untouchables of the village had no water. When things reached this stage the Untouchables thought of filing criminal complaint before a Magistrate which they did on 17th October, making some of the caste Hindus as the accused." The strange part of the case is the part played by Mr. Gandhi and his henchman, Sardar Vallabhbhai Patel. With all the knowledge of tyranny and oppression practised by the caste Hindus of Kavitha against the Untouchables all that Mr. Gandhi felt like doing was to advise the Untouchables to leave the village. He did not even suggest that the miscreants should be hauled up before a court of law. His henchman Mr. Vallabhbhai Patel, played a part which was still more strange. He had gone to Kavitha to persuade the caste Hindus not to molest the Untouchables.

But they did not even give him a hearing. Yet this very man was opposed to the Untouchables hauling them up in a court of Law and getting them punished. The Untouchables filed the complaint notwithstanding his opposition. But he ultimately forced them to withdraw the complaint on the caste Hindus making some kind of a show of an understanding not to molest, an undertaking, which the Untouchables can never enforce. The result was that the Untouchables suffered and their tyrants escaped with the aid of Mr. Gandhi's friend, Mr. Vallabhbhai Patel.

The Untouchables are claimed by the Hindus as Hindus. But the dead body of an Untouchable cannot be cremated in the Hindu cremation ground. The *"Free Press"* of 7th June, 1946 reports the following:

> *"Citing a recent criminal case in which two Madura Harijans were sentenced to four months rigorous imprisonment for doing an act which was likely to wound the feelings of others, Mr. A. S. Vaidyanatha lyer in a communication to the press draws the attention of the public to the 'cruel suffering which the Harijans have to bear by reason of Untouchability."*

Mr. Vaidyanatha lyer says: 'A Madura Harijan who had lost his eldest child cremated the body in the Madura municipal burning ghat in a shed which is said to be set apart for caste Hindus instead of in the one reserved for Harijans. The Harijan's plea was, he did not know of any such reservation, that it was drizzling and that the former place was better. No caste Hindu raised any objection nor was there any proof that anyone's feelings were wounded. The incident came to the notice of the Madura police who prosecuted the father of the child and another near relation on the ground that such act was likely to wound the feelings of others because the Harijans were Untouchables. Mr. lyer adds, "he brought this case to the notice of the Madras Ministry." The *'Savadhan'* of 22nd April, 1945 says:

> *"On 18th March, 1945, a sweeper died in the village Floda, District Muzaffarnagar. The Sweepers of the village took the dead body to the cremation grounds. This enraged the Tyagi Brahmins of the village who abused the sweepers for their audacity in bringing their dead to the caste Hindu grounds. The sweepers protested that they were Hindus and would cremate the dead. But the Brahmins were not at all amenable to reason and told the sweepers that irrespective of their being Hindus and Muslims they must bury their dead and if they failed to do it they (Brahmins) would themselves bury the dead body. When the poor sweepers were thus threatened and were also afraid of being beaten they buried the dead body."*

This is not all. There is a further point to benoted. The Touchable Hindus dispose of the dead body by cremating it. Just because it is a presumption on the part of the Untouchables to initiate the ways of the Hindus, which are marks of their superior status, the Untouchables must necessarily bury their dead even if they do not wish to do so. An instance of this compulsory burial was reported in the *'Milap'* of 6th June 1924:

> *"The chief cause of the awakening among the Untouchables is the tyranny of the Hindus. I was not aware of this but the reports that I have received from various workers has caused me much pain. From one place I am informed that the Untouchables of that place are not allowed to even burn their dead. This, however it seems has created a new spirit among the sweepers of the place. They have started burying their dead with the head downwards probably to distinguish themselves from others who bury the corpse in a lying position. The Sweepers think that if they also act in imitation of others, it is derogatory."*

The wearing of the sacred thread is evidence of noble birth. The Untouchables with the idea of ennobling themselves thought of wearing the sacred thread. The atrocities committed by the caste Hindus on the Untouchables of the village Ringwari in Garhwal District in U. P. are reported in the *'National Herald'* of 6th June "After leading a fugitive life for well nigh two months as a result of persecution at the hands of the caste Hindus, ten families consisting of 33 Harijans have now been able to return to their-homes in village Ringwari of Chandkot with the help of the district authorities of Garhwal. These Harijans, it may be recalled, had taken full advantage of the social movement started for their uplift by Mahatma Gandhi and the late Swami Shradhanand.

PERPETRATION OF UNTOUCHABILITY

Closely related to the persistence of untouchability is the perpetration of atrocities against the SCs. The atrocity cases registered have continued to be relatively more in Bihar, Gujarat, Kerala, Madhya Pradesh, Maharashtra, Rajasthan, Tamil Nadu, and Uttar Pradesh. Of late, there has also been a considerable increase in the number of atrocity cases in some states, especially in Gujarat, Madhya Pradesh, Rajasthan, and Tamil Nadu. Of the different types of atrocity cases registered in the whole country at least one-fourth have involved grievous hurt, followed by arson, rape, and murder.

The nature of disposal of these cases has not been any better: Data available for some of the states indicate that of the total atrocity cases for disposal by the police during 1985 only about 53 per cent were 'challenged', that of the total cases for disposal by the courts only about 5 per cent were disposed of, and that of these only about 34 per cent ended up in conviction. Stated differently, of the total cases for disposal by the police not even 10 per cent ended up in confusion. The performance was especially poor if, Karnataka, Madhya Pradesh, Orissa, Punjab, and Tamil Nadu. These cases again do not reflect the magnitude of atrocities; more so when contrasted against the recurrent press reports from different parts of the country about the crimes on the SCs. The reasons for the PCR cases also apply to this and to the large number of cases pending with the courts and ending up in acquittal. As atrocities against the SCs are closely related to untouchability, their perpetration has to be partly explained by the persistence of untouchability and by the increasing resentment of the SCs against the social indignities emanating from its practice in different forms.

These include denial of entry into public places of worship, discrimination and differential treatment in hotels and teastalls, refusal of service by washermen and barbers, and restriction on movement in certain localities, on wearing sandals, riding horses, and leading marriage processions through certain caste-Hindu localities. The other major factors listed in the various reports of the Commission/er for SCs and STs include envy of the caste-Hindus for the various welfare measures adopted by the government to ameliorate the socioeconomic conditions of the SCs, the wide economic disparities arising out of landlessness, wage labour, bondage, non-payment of fair share of agricultural produce to the SC sharecroppers, forced harvesting of crops, forced eviction of the SC ` from their land and house-sites, dispute over non-payment of minimum wages prescribed by the state, and land disputes, especially as a result of land reforms and the redistribution of surplus lands.

The reports also reveal that of late many of the atrocities committed have been by some of the affluent parts of the middle caste peasantry—the so-called backward classes—,who have been the major beneficiaries of agrarian reforms and other rural development programmes and of the resultant changes in the economic and political structure in the villages. It is important to note that, as observed in the seventh report of the Commission for SCs and STs, the incidence of atrocities is relatively lower in states where literacy rates and economic development of the SCs are relatively higher.

GANDHI & THE BLACK UNTOUCHABLES

As opposed to the popular perceptions, here you will see Gandhi's image from the eyes of a very famous untouchable leader, named, Dr. B.R. Ambedkar (1893-1956). Born and raised as an untouchable, Dr. Ambedkar received his masters and Ph.D. from Columbia University, which later on also conferred upon him the Doctor of Law. Dr. Ambedkar also received a D.Sc. degree from London School of Economics, and the Bar-at-Law from the Grays Inn, London. Suffice to say, Dr. Ambedkar's sharp intellect has provided us an insight into Gandhi, some of which we will like to share with you all. We recommend the following:1. Nichols, Beverley. Verdict on India. New York: Harcourt, Brace and Company, 1944.

A book we highly recommend. Beverley Nichols, a famous novelist, musician, playwright, essayist, reporter, and a journalist visited British India. During this visit, he met Dr. Ambedkar, who told him:

"Gandhi is the greatest enemy the untouchables have ever had in India."

So what did Ambedkar mean? Mr. Nichols explained it as follows:

[We can best explain it by a parallel. Take Ambedkar's remark, and for the word "untouchable" substitute the word "peace." Now imagine that a great champion of peace, like Lord Cecil, said, "Gandhi is the greatest enemy of peace the world has ever had." What would he mean, using these words of the most spectacular pacifist of modern times? He would mean that passive resistance—which is Gandhi's form of pacifism—could only lead to chaos and the eventual triumph of brute force; that to lie down and let people trample on you (which was Gandhi's recipe for dealing with the Japanese) is a temptation to the aggressor rather than an example to the aggressed; and that in order to have peace you must organize, you must be strong, and that you must be prepared to use force. Mutatis mutandis, that is precisely what Ambedkar meant about the untouchables. He wanted them to be recognized and he wanted them to be strong. He rightly considered that the best way of gaining his object was by granting them separate electorates; a solid block of 60 million would be in a position to dictate terms to its oppressors. Gandhi fiercely opposed this scheme. "Give the untouchables separate electorates," he cried, "and you only perpetuate their status for all time." It was a queer argument, and those who were not bemused by the Mahatma's charm considered it a phoney one. They suspected that Gandhi was a little afraid that 60 million untouchables might join up with the 100 million Muslims—(as they nearly did)—and challenge the dictatorship of the 180 million orthodox Hindus. With such irreverent criticisms were made to him, Gandhi resorted to his usual tactics: he began to fast unto death. (As if that altered the situation by a comma or proved anything but his own obstinacy!) There was a frenzy of excitement, ending in a compromise on the seventh day of the fast. The untouchables still vote in the same constituencies as the caste Hindus, but a substantial number of seats are now reserved for them in the provincial legislatures. It is better than nothing, but it is not nearly so good as it would have been if Gandhi had not interfered. That is what Doctor Ambedkar meant. And I think that he was right.]

2. Ambedkar, B.R. What Congress and Gandhi Have Done to the Untouchables? Bombay: Thacker & Co., Ltd, 2nd edition, 1946. Excerpts from this book were published in: Gandhi: Maker of Modern India? Edited by Martin Deming Lewis. Boston: D.C. Heath and Co., 1965. Here is the report which you must read in its entirety:

Mr. Gandhi's views on the caste system–which constitutes the main social problem in India–were fully elaborated by him in 1921-22 in a Gujrati journal called Nava-Jivan. The article is written in Gujrati. I give below an English translation of his views as near as possible in his own words. Says Mr. Gandhi:

(1) I believe that if Hindu Society has been able to stand it is because it is founded on the caste system.

(2) The seeds of swaraj are to be found in the caste system. Different castes are like different sections of military division. Each division is working for the good of the whole....

(3) A community which can create the caste system must be said to possess unique power of organization.

(4) Caste has a ready made means for spreading primary education. Each caste can take the responsibility for the education of the children of the caste. Caste has a political basis. It can work as an electorate for a representative

body. Caste can perform judicial functions by electing persons to act as judges to decide disputes among members of the same caste. With castes it is easy to raise a defense force by requiring each caste to raise a brigade.

(5) I believe that interdining or intermarriage are not necessary for promoting national unity. That dining together creates friendship is contrary to experience. If this was true there would have been no war in Europe.... Taking food is as dirty an act as answering the call of nature. The only difference is that after answering call of nature we get peace while after eating food we get discomfort. Just as we perform the act of answering the call of nature in seclusion so also the act of taking food must also be done in seclusion.

(6) In India children of brothers do not intermarry. Do they cease to love because they do not intermarry? Among the Vaishnavas many women are so orthodox that they will not eat with members of the family nor will they drink water from a common water pot. Have they no love? The caste system cannot be said to be bad because it does not allow interdining or intermarriage between different castes.

(7) Caste is another name for control. Caste puts a limit on enjoyment. Caste does not allow a person to transgress caste limits in pursuit of his enjoyment. That is the meaning of such caste restrictions as interdining and intermarriage.

(8) To destroy caste system and adopt Western European social system means that Hindus must give up the principle of hereditary occupation which is the soul of the caste system. Hereditary principle is an eternal principle. To change it is to create disorder. I have no use for a Brahmin if I cannot call him a Brahmin for my life. It will be a chaos if every day a Brahmin is to be changed into a Shudra and a Shudra is to be changed into a Brahmin.

(9) The caste system is a natural order of society. In India it has been given a religious coating. Other countries not having understood the utility of the caste system, it existed only in a loose condition and consequently those countries have not derived from caste system the same degree of advantage which India has derived. These being my views I am opposed to all those who are out to destroy the caste system.

In 1922, Mr. Gandhi was a defender of the caste system. Pursuing the inquiry, one comes across a somewhat critical view of the caste system by Mr. Gandhi in the year 1925. This is what Mr. Gandhi said on 3rd February 1925:

I gave support to caste because it stands for restraint. But at present caste does not mean restraint, it means limitations. Restraint is glorious and helps to achieve freedom. But limitation is like chain. It binds. There is nothing commendable in castes as they exist to-day. They are contrary to the tenets of the Shastras. The number of castes is infinite and there is a bar against intermarriage. This is not a condition of elevation. It is a state of fall.

In reply to the question: What is the way out? Mr. Gandhi said:

The best remedy is that small castes should fuse themselves into one big caste. There should be four big castes so that we may reproduce the old system of four Varnas.

In short, in 1925 Mr. Gandhi became an upholder of the Varna system.

The old Varna system prevalent in ancient India had the society divided into four orders: (1) Brahmins,whose occupation was learning; (2) Kshatriyas, whose occupation was warfare; (3) Vaishyas, whose occupation was trade and (4) Shudras,whose occupation was service of the other classes. Is Mr. Gandhi's Varna system the same as this old Varna system of the orthodox Hindus? Mr. Gandhi explained his Varna system in the following terms:

(1) I believe that the divisions into Varna is based on birth.

(2) There is nothing in the Varna system which stands in the way of the Shudra acquiring learning or studying military art of offense or defense. Contra it is open to a Kshatriya to serve. The Varna system is no bar to him. What the Varna system enjoins is that a Shudra will not make learning a way of earning a living. Nor will a Kshatriya adopt service as a way of learning a living. [Similarly a Brahmin may learn the art of war or trade. But he must not make them a way of earning his living. Contra a Vaishya may acquire learning or may cultivate the art of war. But he must not make them a way of learning his living.]

(3) The Varna system is connected with the way of earning a living. There is no harm if a person belonging to one Varna acquires the knowledge or science and art specialized in by persons belonging to other Varnas. But as far as the way of earning his living is concerned he must follow the occupation of the Varna to which he belongs which means he must follow the hereditary profession of his forefathers.

(4) The object of the Varna is to prevent competition and class struggle and class war. I believe in the Varna system because it fixes the duties and occupations of persons.

(5) Varna means the determination of a man's occupation before he is born.

(6) In the Varna system no man has any liberty to choose his occupation. His occupation is determined for him by heredity.

The social life of Gandhism is either caste or Varna.Though it may be difficult to say which, there can be no doubt that the social ideal of Gandhism is not democracy. For, whether one takes for comparison caste or Varnaboth are fundamentally opposed to democracy....

That Mr. Gandhi changed over from the caste system to the Varna system does not make the slightest difference to the charge that Gandhism is opposed to democracy. In the first place, the idea of Varna is the parent of the idea of caste. If the idea of caste is a pernicious idea it is entirely because of the viciousness of the idea of Varna. Both are evil ideas and it matters very little whether one believes in Varna or in caste.

Turning to the field of economic life, Mr. Gandhi stands for two ideals. One of these is the opposition to machinery... evidenced by his idolization of charkha (the spinning wheel) and by insistence upon hand-spinning and hand-weaving. His opposition to machinery and his love for charkha are not matter of accident. They are a matter of his philosophy of life....

The second ideal of Mr. Gandhi is the elimination of class war and even class struggle in the relationship between employers and employees and between landlords and tenants....Mr. Gandhi does not wish to hurt the propertied class. He is even opposed to a campaign against them. He has no passion for economic equality. Referring to the propertied class Mr. Gandhi said quite recently that he does not wish to destroy the hen that lays the golden egg. His solution for the economic conflict between the owners and the workers, between the rich and the poor, between the landlords and the tenants and between the employers and the employees is very simple. The owners need not deprive themselves of their property. All they need do is to declare themselves trustees for the poor. Of course, the trust is to be a voluntary one carrying only a spiritual obligation.

Is there anything new in the Gandhian analysis of economic ills? Are the economics of Gandhism sound? What hope does Gandhism hold out to the common man, to the down and out? Does it promise him a better life, a life of joy and culture, a life of freedom, not merely freedom from want but freedom to rise, to grow to the full stature which his capacities can reach?

There is nothing new in the Gandhian analysis of economic ills, insofar as it attributes them to machinery and the civilization that is built upon it. That machinery and modern civilization help to concentrate management and control into relatively few hands, and with the aid of banking and credit facilitate the transfer into still fewer hands of all materials and factories and mills in which millions are bled white in order to support huge industries thousands of miles away from their cottages, maimings and cripplings far in excess of the corresponding injuries by war, and are responsible for disease and physical deterioration due directly and indirectly to the development of large cities with their smoke, dirt, noise, foul air, lack of sunshine and outdoor life, slums, prostitution and unnatural living which they bring about, are all old and worn-out arguments. There is nothing new in them. Gandhism is merely repeating the views of Rousseau, Ruskin, Tolstoy and their school.

The ideas which go to make up Gandhism are just primitive. It is a return to nature, to animal life. The only merit is their simplicity. As there is always a large corps of simple people who are attracted by them, such simple ideas do not die, and there is always some simpleton to preach them. There is, however, no doubt that the practical instincts of men–which seldom go wrong–have found them unfruitful and which society in search of progress has thought it best to reject.

The economics of Gandhism are hopelessly fallacious. The fact that machinery and modern civilization have produced many evils may be admitted. But these evils are no argument against them. For the evils are not due to machinery and modern civilization. They are due to wrong social organization, which has made private property and pursuit of personal gain, matters of absolute sanctity. If machinery and civilization have not benefited everybody, the remedy is not to condemn machinery and civilization but to alter the organization of society so that the benefits will not be usurped by the few but will accrue to all.

In Gandhism, the common man has no hope. It treats man as an animal and no more. It is true that man shares the constitution and functions of animals, nutritive, reproductive, etc. But these are not distinctively human functions. The distinctively human function is reason, the purpose of which is to enable man to observe, meditate, cogitate, study and discover the beauties of the Universe and enrich his life and control the animal elements in his life. Man thus occupies the highest place in the scheme of animate existence. If this is true what is the conclusion that follows: The conclusion that follows is that while the ultimate goal of a brute's life is reached once his physical appetites are satisfied, the ultimate goal of man's existence is not reached unless and until he has fully cultivated his mind. In short, what divides the brute from man is culture. Culture is not possible for the brute, but it is essential for man. That being so, the aim of human society must be to enable every person to lead a life of culture, which means the cultivation of mind as distinguished from the satisfaction of mere physical wants. How can this happen?

Both for society as well as for individual[s] there is always a gulf between merely living and living worthily. In order that one may live worthily one must first live. The time and energy spent upon mere life, upon gaining of subsistence detracts from that available for activities of a distinctively human nature and which go to make up a life of culture. How then can a life of culture be made possible? It is not possible unless there is sufficient leisure. For, it is only when there is leisure that a person is free to devote himself to a life of culture.

The problem of all problems, which human society has to face, is how to provide leisure to every individual. What does leisure mean? Leisure means the lessening of the toil and effort necessary for satisfying the physical wants of life. How can leisure be made possible? Leisure is quite impossible unless some means are found whereby the toil required for producing goods necessary to satisfy human needs is lessened. What can lessen such toil? Only when machine takes the place of man. There is no other means of producing leisure. Machinery and modern civilization are thus indispensable for emancipating man from leading the life of a brute, and for providing him with leisure and for making a life of culture possible. The man who condemns machinery and modern civilization simply does not understand their purpose and the ultimate aim which human society must strive to achieve.

Gandhism may well be well suited to a society which does not accept democracy as its ideal. A society which does not believe in democracy may be indifferent to machinery and the civilization based upon it. But a democratic society cannot. The former may well content itself with a life of leisure and culture for the few and a life of toil and drudgery for the many. But a democratic society must assure a life of leisure and culture to each one of its citizens. If the above analysis is correct then the slogan of a democratic society must be machinery, and more machinery, civilization and more civilization. Under Gandhism the common man must keep on toiling ceaselessly for a pittance and remain a brute. In short, Gandhism with its call of back to nature, means back to nakedness, back to squalor, back to poverty and back to ignorance for the vast mass of the people....

Gandhism insists upon class structure. It regards the class structure of society and also the income structure as sacrosanct with the consequent distinctions of rich and poor, high and low, owners and workers, as permanent parts of social organization. From the point of view of social consequences, nothing can be more pernicious.... It is not enough to say that Gandhism believes in a class structure. Gandhism stands for more than that. A class structure which is a faded, jejune, effete thing–a mere sentimentality, a mere skeleton is not what Gandhism wants. It wants class structure to function as a living faith. In this there is nothing to be surprised at. For, class structure in Gandhism is not a mere accident. It is its official doctrine.

The idea of trusteeship, which Gandhism proposes as a panacea and by which the moneyed classes will hold their properties in trust for the poor, is the most ridiculous part of it. All that one can say about it is that if anybody else had propounded it the author would have been laughed at as a silly fool, who had not known the hard realities of life and was deceiving the servile classes by telling them that a little dose of moral rearmament to the propertied classes–those who by their insatiable cupidity and indomitable arrogance have made and will always make this world a vale of tears for the toiling millions–will recondition them to such an extent that they will be able to withstand the temptation to misuse the tremendous powers which the class structure gives them over servile classes....

Mr. Gandhi sometimes speaks on social and economic subjects as though he was a blushing Red. Those who will study Gandhism will not be deceived by the occasional aberrations of Mr. Gandhi in favor of democracy and against capitalism. For, Gandhism is in no sense a revolutionary creed. It is conservatism in excelsis. So far as India is concerned, it is a reactionary creed blazoning on its banner the call of Return to Antiquity. Gandhism aims at the resuscitation and reanimating of India's dread, dying past.

Gandhism is a paradox. It stands for freedom from foreign domination, which means the destruction of the existing political structure of the country. At the same time, it seeks to maintain intact a social structure which permits the domination of one class by another on a hereditary basis which means a perpetual domination of one class by another....

The first special feature of Gandhism is that its philosophy helps those who want to keep what they have and to prevent those who have not from getting what they have a right to get. No one who examines the Gandhian attitude to strikes, the Gandhian reverence for caste and the Gandhian doctrine of Trusteeship by the rich for the benefit of the poor can deny that this is an upshot of Gandhism. Whether this is the calculated result of a deliberate design or whether it is a matter of accident may be open to argument. But the fact remains that Gandhism is the philosophy of the well-to-do and the leisure class.

The second special feature of Gandhism is to delude people into accepting their misfortunes by presenting them as best of good fortunes. One or two illustrations will suffice to bring out the truth of this statement.

The Hindu sacred law penalized the Shudras (Hindus of the fourth class) from acquiring wealth. It is a law of enforced poverty unknown in any other part of the world. What does Gandhism do? It does not lift the ban. It blesses the Shudra for his moral courage to give up property. It is well worth quoting Mr. Gandhi's own words. Here they are:

The Shudra who only serves (the higher caste) as a matter of religious duty, and who will never own any property, who indeed has not even the ambition to own anything, is deserving of thousand obeisance...The very

Gods will shower flowers on him. Another illustration in support is the attitude of Gandhism towards the scavenger. The sacred law of the Hindus lays down that a scavenger's progeny shall live by scavenging. Under Hinduism scavenging was not a matter of choice, it was a matter of force. What does Gandhism do? It seeks to perpetuate this system by praising scavenging as the noblest service to society! Let me quote Mr. Gandhi: As a President of a Conference of the Untouchables, Mr. Gandhi said:

I do not want to attain Moksha. I do not want to be reborn. But if I have to be reborn, I should be born an untouchable, so that I may share their sorrows, sufferings and the affronts levelled at them, in order that I endeavor to free myself and them from that miserable condition. I, therefore prayed that if I should be born again, I should do so not as a Brahmin, Kshatriya, Vaishya, or Shudra, but as an AtiShudra....

I love scavenging. In my ashram, an eighteen-years-old Brahmin lad is doing the scavenger's work in order to teach the ashram scavenger cleanliness. The lad is no reformer. He was born and bred in orthodoxy.... But he felt that his accomplishments were incomplete until he had become also a perfect sweeper, and that, if he wanted the ashram sweeper to do his work well, he must do it himself and set an example. You should realize that you are cleaning Hindu Society.

Can there be a worse example of false propaganda than this attempt of Gandhism to perpetuate evils which have been deliberately imposed by one class over another? If Gandhism preached the rule of poverty for all and not merely for the Shudra the worst that could be said about it is that it is mistaken idea. But why preach it as good for one class only?... In India a man is not a scavenger because of his work.

He is a scavenger because of his birth irrespective of the question whether he does scavenging or not. If Gandhism preached that scavenging is a noble profession with the object of inducing those who refuse to engage in it, one could understand it. But why appeal to the scavenger's pride and vanity in order to induce him and him only to keep on to scavenging by telling him that scavenging is a noble profession and that he need not be ashamed of it?

To preach that poverty is good for the Shudra and for none else, to preach that scavenging is good for the Untouchables and for none else and to make them accept these onerous impositions as voluntary purposes of life, by appeal to their failings is an outrage and a cruel joke on the helpless classes which none but Mr. Gandhi can perpetrate with equanimity and impunity....

Criticism apart, this is the technique of Gandhism to make wrongs done appear to the very victim as though they were his privileges. If there is an "ism" which has made full use of religion as an opium to lull the people into false beliefs and false security, it is Gandhism. Following Shakespeare, one can well say: Plausibility! Ingenuity! Thy name is Gandhism.

Such is Gandhism. Having known what is Gandhism the answer to the question, "Should Gandhism become the law of the land what would be the lot of the Untouchables under it?" cannot require much scratching of the brain.... In India even the lowest man among the caste Hindus–why even the aboriginal and the Hill Tribe man–though educationally and economically not very much above the Untouchables. The Hindu society accepts him claim to superiority over the Untouchables. The Untouchable will therefore continue to suffer the worst fate as he does now namely, in prosperity he will be the last to be employed and in depression the first to be fired.

What does Gandhism do to relieve the Untouchables from this fate? Gandhism professes to abolish Untouchability. That is hailed as the greatest virtue of Gandhism. But what does this virtue amount to in actual life? To assess the value of this anti-Untouchability which is regarded as a very big element in Gandhism, it is necessary to understand fully the scope of Mr. Gandhi's programme for the removal of Untouchability. Does it mean anything more than that the Hindus will not mind touching the Untouchables? Does it mean the removal of the ban on the right of the Untouchables to education? It would be better to take the two questions separately.

To start wit the first question. Mr. Gandhi does not say that a Hindu should not take a bath after touching the Untouchables. If Mr. Gandhi does not object to it as a purification of pollution then it is difficult to see how Untouchability can be said to vanish by touching the Untouchables. Untouchability centers round the idea of pollution by contact and purification by bath to remove the pollution. Does it mean social assimilation of the Untouchables with the Hindus? Mr. Gandhi has most categorically stated that removal of Untouchability does not mean interdining or intermarriage between the Hindus and the Untouchables.

Mr. Gandhi's anti-Untouchability means that the Untouchables will be classes as Shudras instead of being classed as AtiShudras [i.e., "beyond Shudras"]. There is nothing more in it. Mr. Gandhi has not considered whether the old Shudras will accept the new Shudras into their fold. If they don't then the removal of Untouchability is a senseless proposition for it will still keep the Untouchables as a separate social category. Mr. Gandhi probably knows that the abolition of Untouchability will not bring about the assimilation of the Untouchables by the Shudras.That seems to be the reason why Mr. Gandhi himself has given a new and a different name to the Untouchables. The new name registers by anticipation what is likely to be the fact. By calling the Untouchables Harijans, Mr. Gandhi has killed two birds with one stone. He has shown that assimilation of the Untouchables by the Shudras is not possible. He has also by his new name counteracted assimilation and made it impossible.

Regarding the second question, it is true that Gandhism is prepared to remove the old ban placed by the Hindu Shastras on the right of the Untouchables to education and permit them to acquire knowledge and learning. Under Gandhism the Untouchables may study law, they may study medicine, they may study engineering or anything else they may fancy.

So far so good. But will the Untouchables be free to make use of their knowledge and learning? Will they have the right to choose their profession? Can they adopt the career of lawyer, doctor or engineer? To these questions the answer which Gandhism gives is an emphatic "no."

The untouchables must follow their hereditary professions. That those occupations are unclean is no excuse. That before the occupation became hereditary it was the result of force and not volition does not matter. The argument of Gandhism is that what is once settled is settled forever even it was wrongly settled. Under Gandhism the Untouchables are to be eternal scavengers. There is no doubt that the Untouchables would much prefer the orthodox system of Untouchability.

A compulsory state of ignorance imposed upon the Untouchables by the Hindu Shastras made scavenging bearable. But Gandhism which compels an educated Untouchable to do scavenging is nothing short of cruelty. The grace in Gandhism is a curse in its worst form. The virtue of the anti-Untouchability plant in Gandhism is quite illusory. There is no substance in it.

What else is there in Gandhism which the Untouchables can accept as opening a way for their ultimate salvation? Barring this illusory campaign against Untouchability, Gandhism is simply another form of Sanatanism which is the ancient name for militant orthodox Hinduism. What is there in Gandhism which is not to be found in orthodox Hinduism? There is caste in Hinduism, there is caste in Gandhism. Hinduism believes in the law of hereditary profession, so does Gandhism. Hinduism enjoins cow-worship. So does Gandhism. Hinduism upholds the law of karma, predestination of man's condition in this world, so does Gandhism. Hinduism accepts the authority of the Shastras. So does Gandhism. Hinduism believes in idols. So does Gandhism. All that Gandhism has done is to find a philosophic justification for Hinduism and its dogmas. Hinduism is bald in the sense that it is just a set of rules which bear on their face the appearance of a crude and cruel system. Gandhism supplies the philosophy which smoothens its surface and gives it the appearance of decency and respectability and so alters it and embellishes it as to make it even more attractive....

What hope can Gandhism offer to the Untouchables? To the Untouchables, Hinduism is a veritable chamber of horrors. The sanctity and infallibility of the Vedas, Smritis and Shastras, the iron law of caste, the heartless law of karma and the senseless law of status by birth are to the Untouchables veritable instruments of torture which Hinduism has forged against the Untouchables. These very instruments which have mutilated, blasted and blighted the life of the Untouchables are to be found intact and untarnished in the bosom of Gandhism. How can the Untouchables say that Gandhism is a heaven and not a chamber of horrors as Hinduism has been? The only reaction and a very natural reaction of the Untouchables would be to run away from Gandhism.

Gandhists may say that what I have stated applies to the old type of Gandhism. There is a new Gandhism, Gandhism without caste. This has reference to the recent statement of Mr. Gandhi that caste is an anachronism. Reformers were naturally gladdened by this declaration of Mr. Gandhi. And who would not be glad to see that a man like Mr. Gandhi having such terrible influence over the Hindus, after having played the most mischievous part of a social reactionary, after having stood out as the protagonist of the caste system, after having beguiled and befooled the unthinking Hindus with arguments which made no distinction between what is fair and foul should have come out with this recantation? But is this really a matter for jubilation?

Does it change the nature of Gandhism? Does it make Gandhism a new and a better "ism" than it was before? Those who are carried away by this recantation of Mr. Gandhi, forget two things. In the first place, all that Mr. Gandhi has said is that caste is an anachronism. He does not say it is an evil. He does not say it is anathema. Mr. Gandhi may be taken to be not in favor of caste. but Mr. Gandhi does not say that he is against the Varna system. And what is Mr. Gandhi's Varna system? It is simply a new name for the caste system and retains all the worst features of the caste system.

The declaration of Mr. Gandhi cannot be taken to mean any fundamental change in Gandhism. It cannot make Gandhism acceptable to the Untouchables. The untouchables will still have ground to say: "Good God! Is this man Gandhi our Savior?"

3

Ambedkar: Father of Indian Constitution

Dr. Bhim Rao Ambedkar was the most important leader of the oppressed untouchable minority in the history of India. He acquired the honorific name Babasaheb. Fighting for his people, he angered Mohandas K. Gandhi, the revered leader of the Indian nationalist movement, as well as many Hindu traditionalists.

When India became an independent country, he served in its cabinet and drafted its constitution. Near the end of his life, he became a Buddhist and encouraged other untouchables to do likewise; he had lost hope of justice for his people within Hinduism.

In Hinduism most people belonged to four hierarchical castes, but a large minority were excluded from the caste system and were regarded as beneath it. They did jobs that other Hindus rejected as ritually unclean and were not allowed to pray in temples or to draw water from communal wells.

Nearly all of them were desperately poor. In English these people often are called untouchables, or pariahs. Gandhi, wishing to improve their status, called them harijans, or children of God. To underscore their miserable condition, untouchables preferred to be called dalits, a name that means oppressed.

B. R. Ambedkar was born to an untouchable family as its 14th child. At the time of his birth his father was a soldier. Untouchables were divided into numerous hereditary subgroups, or jatis. Ambedkar belonged to the Mahar jati. Despite the disadvantages of poverty, family responsibilities, and untouchable status, he acquired an advanced education. In 1912 he earned a B.A. degree from Elphinstone College at Bombay University. The ruler of a princely state then financed his education in the United States and Britain. In 1916 Columbia University awarded him a Ph.D. in economics. He continued his studies at the London School of Economics. In 1921 it awarded him a second doctorate. He studied law at Gray's Inn and in 1923 was called to the bar in Britain. He also studied briefly at a German university.

In India he practiced law, taught, edited newspapers, and entered politics. Although he was elected to the Bombay legislature, his real political career was as the leader of the formerly passive untouchable community. Ambedkar's nonviolent protests mobilized tens of thousands of dalits for the right to draw water from wells and public tanks and to pray in temples. Although Gandhi saw himself as a friend of the untouchables, he got along poorly with Ambedkar. They quarreled at the Round Table Conferences on India's future held in London.

When Britain decided to grant India extensive political autonomy, its government grappled with the problem of the diversity within the Indian population. In 1932 Britain offered separate electorates to the untouchables, so that this oppressed minority would control the selection of its representatives. The Indian National Congress strongly opposed any separate electorates. Gandhi began a fast to put pressure on Ambedkar to reject the special electorates for his people. Reluctantly, he did so. The Indian National Congress offered Ambedkar concessions in what was known as the Poona Pact. The number of seats reserved for untouchable candidates was increased, but the entire electorate, not just untouchables, would vote on the candidates for these seats.

In 1936 Ambedkar organized the Independent Labour Party. In contrast with Gandhi and the Indian National Congress, Ambedkar and his party supported the British government in India during World War II. In 1942 he became a member of the viceroy's executive council. In the same year he organized a new political party, the Scheduled Castes' Federation. When India became independent, Ambedkar joined the new government that the Indian National Congress dominated. From 1947 to 1951, he was a member of the cabinet. More important, he chaired the committee that drafted the national constitution and was its principal author. In the final years of his life, Ambedkar turned to Buddhism, a religion with Indian roots that rejected the Hindu caste system and the concept of untouchability. He formally converted to Buddhism in October 1956. Hundreds of thousands of untouchables joined him in leaving Hinduism for Buddhism. A few weeks after his conversion ceremony, Ambedkar died.

FATHER OF INDIA'S CONSTITUTION

Upon India's independence on August 15, 1947, the new Congress-led government invited Ambedkar to serve as the nation's first law minister, which he accepted. On August 29, Ambedkar was appointed Chairman of the Constitution Drafting Committee, charged by the Assembly to write free

India's new Constitution. Ambedkar won great praise from his colleagues and contemporary observers for his drafting work. In this task Ambedkar's study of sangha practice among early Buddhists and his extensive reading in Buddhist scriptures were to come to his aid. Sangha practice incorporated voting by ballot, rules of debate and precedence and the use of agendas, committees and proposals to conduct business. Sangha practice itself was modelled on the oligarchic system of governance followed by tribal republics of ancient India such as the Shakyas and the Lichchavis. Thus, although Ambedkar used Western models to give his Constitution shape, its spirit was Indian and, indeed, tribal. Granville Austin has described the Indian Constitution drafted by Dr. Ambedkar as 'first and foremost a social document.' ... 'The majority of India's constitutional provisions are either directly arrived at furthering the aim of social revolution or attempt to foster this revolution by establishing conditions necessary for its achievement.'

The text prepared by Ambedkar provided constitutional guarantees and protections for a wide range of civil liberties for individual citizens, including freedom of religion, the abolition of untouchability and the outlawing of all forms of discrimination Ambedkar argued for extensive economic and social rights for women, and also won the Assembly's support for introducing a system of reservations of jobs in the civil services, schools and colleges for members of scheduled castes and scheduled tribes, a system akin to affirmative action. India's lawmakers hoped to eradicate the socio-economic inequalities and lack of opportunities for India's depressed classes through this measure, which had been originally envisioned as temporary on a need basis. The Constitution was adopted on November 26, 1949 by the Constituent Assembly.

Ambedkar resigned from the cabinet in 1951 following the stalling in parliament of his draft of the Hindu Code Bill, which sought to expound gender equality in the laws of inheritance, marriage and the economy. Although supported by Prime Minister Nehru, the cabinet and many other Congress leaders, it received criticism from a large number of members of parliament. Ambedkar independently contested an election in 1952 to the lower house of parliament, the Lok Sabha, but was defeated. He was appointed to the upper house, of parliament, the Rajya Sabha in March 1952 and would remain a member until his death.

EVOLUTION OF THE CONSTITUTION

Acts of British Parliament before 1935

After the Indian Rebellion of 1857, the British Parliament took over the reign of India from the British East India Company, and British India came under the direct rule of the Crown. The British Parliament passed the Government of India Act of 1858 to this effect, setting up the structure of government in India. It established in England the office of the Secretary of State for India through whom Parliament would exercise its rule, along with a Council of India to aid him.

It also established the office of the Governor-General of India along with an Executive Council in India, consisting of high officials of the British Government. The Indian Councils Act of 1861 provided for a Legislative Council consisting of the members of the Executive council and non-official members.

The Indian Councils Act of 1892 established provincial legislatures and increased the powers of the Legislative Council. These acts increased the representation of Indians in the government, however their power remained limited. The Government of India Acts of 1909 and 1919 further expanded participation of Indians in the government.

Government of India Act 1935

The provisions of the Government of India Act of 1935, though never implemented fully, had a great impact on the constitution of India. Many key features of the constitution are directly taken from this Act. The federal structure of government, provincial autonomy, bicameral legislature consisting of a federal assembly and a Council of States, separation of legislative powers between the center and provinces are some of the provisions of the Act which are present in the Indian constitution.

The Cabinet Mission Plan

In 1946, British Prime Minister Clement Attlee formulated a cabinet mission to India to discuss and finalize plans for the transfer of power from the British Raj to Indian leadership as well as provide India with independence under Dominion status in the Commonwealth of Nations.

The Mission discussed the framework of the constitution and laid down in some detail the procedure to be followed by the constitution drafting body. Elections for the 296 seats assigned to the British Indian provinces were completed by August 1946. The Constituent Assembly first met and began work on 9 December 1946.

Indian Independence Act 1947

The Indian Independence Act, which came into force on 18 July 1947, divided British Indian territory into two new states: India and Pakistan, which were to be dominions under the Commonwealth of Nations until their constitutions were in effect. The Constituent Assembly was divided into two for the separate states. The Act relieved the British Parliament of any further rights or obligations towards India or Pakistan, and granted sovereignty over the lands to the respective Constituent Assemblies.

When the Constitution of India came into force on 26 January 1950, it repealed the Indian Independence Act. India ceased to be a dominion of the British Crown and became a sovereign democratic republic. 26 November 1949 is also known as National Law Day.

CONSTITUENT ASSEMBLY OF INDIA

The Constituent Assembly of India was elected to write the Constitution of India, and served as its first Parliament as an independent nation.

Election

The Constituent Assembly of India was set up as a result of negotiations between the Indian leaders and members of the British Cabinet Mission. The constituent assembly was elected indirectly by the members of the Provincial legislative assembly. The Congress secured an overwhelming majority in the general seats while the Muslim League managed to sweep almost all the seats reserved for Muslims. The Congress had a majority of 69%. There were also members from smaller parties like the Scheduled Caste Federation, the Communist Party of India and the Unionist Party. It first met on December 9, 1946 in Delhi, while India was still under British rule. It originally included the provinces that now compose Pakistan and Bangladesh, and the representation of the princely states of India. In June 1947, the delegations from the provinces of Sindh, East Bengal, Baluchistan, West Punjab and the North West Frontier Province formed the Constituent Assembly of Pakistan in Karachi.

The final Constituent Assembly had two hundred and seven representatives, including fifteen women. Only 28 members of the Muslim League finally joined the Indian Assembly. Later, 93 members were nominated from the princely states. The Congress thus secured a majority of 82%. On August 15, 1947, India became an independent nation, and the Constituent Assembly became India's Parliament.

Organization

Dr. Sachchidananda Sinha was the first president (temporary Chairman of the Assembly)of the Constituent Assembly when it met on December 9, 1946. Dr. Rajendra Prasad then became the President of the Constituent Assembly, and would later become the first President of India. The Vice

President of the Constituent Assembly was Professor Harendra Coomar Mookerjee, former Vice-Chancellor of Calcutta University and a prominent Christian from Bengal who also served as the Chairman of the Minorities Committee of the Constituent Assembly. He was appointed Governor of West Bengal after India became a republic.

The Assembly approved the Constitution on November 26, 1949, making it official. On January 26, 1950, the Constitution took effect — a day now commemorated as Republic Day nationwide.

At this point, the Constituent Assembly became the Provisional Parliament of India, until the first elections under the new Constitution took place in 1952.

CONSTITUTION AND DR. AMBEDKAR

"Without going into the merit of constitution, however good and faultless a constitution may be, but if those who implement it are incompetent and useless, that constitution results in an evil. Similarly however defective a constitution may be, but if its executors are good the same constitution results in the good of the people", such was the view expressed by Dr. Baba Saheb Ambedkar while replying to the discussion on the Constitution on November 26, 1949. How prophetic were his statement! The, Congress rulers during the last 40 years have made a travesty of the Constitution. They needlessly amended the original charter several times to perpetuate their single-party rule. Actually the Congress rulers have no moral right to speak on the sanctity of the Constitution.

Hindutva Challenge and Congress: In recent years the Congress has been facing a formidable challenge from the protagonists of Hindutva. It must be noted that the Hindutva challenge is to the Congress, and not to the Constitution, the judiciary or the democratic system. But a systematic Goebellsian propaganda blitzkrieg is conducted by the Congress and those whose vested interests lie in perpetuating the Congress rule and the Congress culture to present Hindutva as the worst challenge to the Constitution. The vilification campaign is joined by all those who have an eye on the main chance, and the Congress party is the highest bidder.

The Congress hangers-on have formed a Constitution Preservation committee as a part of this anti-Hindu propaganda campaign. Anything is grist for their propaganda mill. No falsehood or abuse is too base or too mean for them. They have no compunction to use shady methods. They argue: (1) The Sangh Parivar is out to scrap the Indian Constitution. (2) Its aim is to establish the system propounded by Manu. (3) If elected to power, Bharatiya Janata Party will rescind all legal provisions giving certain social rights to the dalits. (4) The dalits will again be dumped in the traditional ditch of untouchability and all the disabilities associated with it. The source of this offensive of falsehoods is far from any love for the Constitution. The whole business springs from the single-point programme of perpetuation of the Congress rule, the sole host of these parasites. Political propaganda should be matched on a political plane. Yet there is enough occasion to have a hard look at the issue in dispute, "Dr. Baba Saheb Ambedkar, Constitution and Hindutva". Let us first consider Hindutva.

Hindutva is, these days, being discussed from various angles. The dominant being the accusation that Hindutva is none else than the abuse of Hindutva for political mileage by Sangh Parivar. Even the courts of law have taken the stand that Hindutva is a religious concept. And following this, elections of several Members of Parliament and State Legislative Assemblies have been declared void. But Hindutva is not a mere religious concept. At least the Sangh Parivar does not subscribe to this view. Hindutva is a concept that is related to nationhood. The part "Hindu" in the word "Hindutva" is not used to denote a group of people following any particular way of worship. The late V.D. Savarkar has defined the word "Hindu" as "the one whose country, India, spreads between the two seas and who regards it as his fatherland and sacred land".

RSS has not defined Hindu, and Hindutva. But what the Sangh understands by these words has been amply clarified. Sangh believes Hindu to be a way of life. Guruji has stated regarding this way of life: "We have perceived the entire society as a body. It is the great social person (virat samajapuruṣh). All men are indeed limbs and organs of the great social corpus spiritualis. Society as a mammoth humanoid body and the eternal undying spirit that dwells in that body and this realization is the specific and unique aspect of the Indian spiritual thinking. All existent objects, including all human beings are parts of that eternal existence. And that is the fount of the basic unity. Since the eternal spirit inform everyone in equal measure, the social system should be so organised as to make everyone happy. A social order where all will have equal self-interest."

Shri Guruji calls these "the principles of Hindu way of life". He further says: "The ever present principle of Hindu life, that one truth pervades in all, is the ultimate truth. That alone is the link that joins all. The selfsame truth appears in diverse forms. Therefore it is our natural duty to create all manner of scope for all to lead their life according their diverse tastes".

It should be, noted that Shri Guruji does not define Hindu-Hindutva in religious terms. He does not link Hindutva with any specific method of worship. It should be appreciated that he sheds light on the fact that the substance of Hindutva relates to the wellbeing of mankind. The Sarsanghchalak Shri Balasaheb Deoras while addressing the Maharashtra State-level camp at Tuljai declared: "The Sangh goal is to create an egalitarian society free from exploitation."

The concept of Hindutva does not imply total trust in a single scripture, neither does it strictly adhere to a single religious regimen. It does not reserve all its faith for one Prophet, nor does it profess to tailor society to the measurements given by a religious tone. Deoras has elaborated the thoughts on social system intended in Hindutva in his book Hindu Organisation and Social Equality where he says: "Untouchability should be eradicated from our society permanently, It must go lock, stock and barrel. The Hindutva of the Sangh does not accept the sense of high and low based on caste. So there is no question of Sangh justifying the present caste inequality."

The Hindutva of the RSS-is not based on any religious sect, so it has no room for religious hatred against any sect. Guruji says: "There is a deliberate attempt to create confusion around the word Hindu. Some are driven by their selfish motives to describe Hindus as opposed to Muslims, Christians, Sikhs, Jains and dalits."

They do not do this after any serious study of the issue. The Hindu thinking and the Hindu way of life have been in the world even before Islam and Christianity were yet to emerge. How could Hindus be against a religion that was not in existence, either Islam or Christianity, Sikhs, Jains, etc. are indeed under the general conceptual umbrella of Hinduism. To oppose them is a indulge in suicidal attempt to cut one's limbs. The term Hindu is never used to oppose or discriminate against any sect. The term is a positive one and could never be construed to mean anything negative.

Constitutional Idealism: While discussing the Constitution, one has to bear in mind this wider meaning of the term Hindutva. Our Constitution has three types of idealism. The political idealism, social idealism and economic idealism. The blend of these three ideals becomes the national idealism. The Constitution explains to us the objectives to be kept always before our eyes in the context of individual-society relationship.

The freedom struggle was not at all limited to political freedom only. India aimed at three kinds of freedom. The political freedom was to be followed by social and economic freedoms. The great leaders at the helm of the freedom struggle had mainly the Hindu society before, their vision. The Muslim community did not fully participate in the freedom struggle. Muslim leaders were without any big following. There was hardly any Muslim League representative in the Constituent Assembly.

The kind of political freedom the leaders in the freedom struggle had envisaged is reflected in the Constitution in the form of the fundamental rights. This freedom was not demanded by the Muslims. Because their overwhelming majority had demanded a separate land for Muslims. And the factor of social freedom in the struggle for the freedom of the country was a hundred-per-cent Hindu social reform movement. Untouchability, social inequality, traditional superstition, injustice to women, child-marriage, widow remarriage an so on and so forth were all issues of social reforms in Hindu society.

The incursion of social justice in the Constitution is the outcome of these agitations for social reforms. The demand for the country's liberation from the foreign economic yoke and all-out efforts for gaining that were the activities of Hindus. Though the Parsis like Jamshedji Tata and Dadabhoy Naoroji were at the forefront of the country's economic liberation they were different only in their manner of worship. They were in fact a factor in the all-round movement for economic emancipation carried out by Lokmanya Tilak, Mahatma Gandhi, Lalchand Hirachand in their own way. The economic ideal enshrined in the Constitution is the fruit of their efforts.

Because the ideals of political, social and economic liberaties are enshrined in the Constitution the responsibility for their fulfilment devolves on the government machinery and the citizens are granted some of these liberties in the form of the fundamental rights. All these are intended to achieve the goal of highest interests and welfare of the people, and therefore Hindutva cannot have any quarrel with these.

The noble ideals included in the Constitution, if viewed uninhibited by political considerations and those of Hindutva, would appear to have no contradictions. Hindutva does not deny individual liberty, equality and fraternity. It also does not deprive anyone of his freedom of worship. The founding fathers of our Constitution felt that such ideals must be enshrined in our Constitution, because they were deeply impressed by Indian traditions in social thought.

In this context Dr. Ambedkar's interpretation is very significant. He says: "I have not borrowed liberty, equality and fraternity from the French Revolution. I have learnt them from the teachings of Lord Buddha. To allow every person to adopt a way of worship dictated by his conscience is in the best of Hindu tradition. It is not in the Hindu tradition to oppress anyone only because he happens to worship his lord in a different manner. This has been beautifully expressed in the Mahimnastotra which says: "O Lord, you are the destination of all people reaching you by various ways, straight or crooked according to their taste as waters of various rivers flowing whichever way reach the sea." The Constitution also merely paraphrases the contents of this stotra (praise to Lord).

Social Justice : The social ideals of our Constitution are as important as the political ones. There was dual slavery in our country. One political and the other social. Under the social slavery it was mainly the scheduled castes which were trampled under the injustices by higher castes. They had no political or social rights. Their lowest state in society was determined by their birth. Great savants raised a relentless revolt against this social slavery prevalent in the Hindu society. Sages like Maharshi Dayanand, social reformers like Mahatma Phule, political leaders like Mahatma Gandhi and Swatantrya Veer Savarkar ceaselessly agitated against this social slavery. Ambedkar fought the final battle against the Hindu society. The strugglers reflected in our Constitution.

"I entered the Constituent Assembly to safeguard the interests of the dalits", said Dr. Ambedkar while explaining his purpose in joining the Constituent Assembly. He further stated: "I did not go there to draft the Constitution. But that responsibility crane upon me for certain reasons. It is a matter of pride for me to have been associated with the architects of the Constitution." Dr. Ambedkar's is the lion's share in clearly defining the social and economic ideals in our Constitution. Article 17 of the Constitution eradicates untouchability. Article 15 guarantees that no discrimination would be allowed on the basis of religion race, caste, gender or domicile. Article 16 guarantees that the State will grant equal opportunities to all citizens. And the same Article 16 makes provision for reservations for the backward people.

Political Democracy: This is a special feature of our Constitution. All adults enjoy the right to vote. All votes are of equal weightage. This right of the citizens is very important and this has invested the common man with full control on the State power. With the ballot-power the Constitution itself grants to the majority of the citizens the power to rule. To extend the right to select their rulers to the common people is politically a revolutionary measure. Politicians playing caste-card organise their parties on various caste-lines and try to acquire majority. The Ahirs, the Jats, the Rajputs, the Yadavs, the dalits and the Muslims are yoked together to present what is named as Bahujan Samaj. But this is an election strategy. Some others try to garner castes other than the Brahmins, the Kshatriyas and the Kayasthas, and try to present them as Bahujan Samaj.

But Hindutva is opposed to such fissiporous business of strengthening divisive caste sentiments through politician means because a very narrow sentiment is detrimental to national unity. The political organisation of the Indian society should be undertaken on the basis of the wide and comprehensive content of Hindutva. If caste is conceived as the basis of political activity the hallowed social ideals in the Constitution would be gathering dust in the statute. The protagonists of Hindutva in the widest ken of the term-aspire to bring a Hindu-again in the wide connotation-rule in the country.

The adult franchise granted in the Constitution is bound to result in the majority rule, *i.e.*, Hindu rule. No one can change this foregone conclusion. The limited demand of the Hindutva protagonists is that those politicians who play caste politics, who foster communal division for their politician ends and who deny the just share of the national life to the dalits and the backward sections of society should not be allowed to usurp power by formenting fissiparous, communal and caste passions.

Hindutvists are not opposed to the principle of political democracy consecrated in the Constitution. Their objection and opposition is to the policies of implementing the democracy promoted by political parties with their eye on the main chance without any compunction regarding national interests.

Economic Justice: Our Constitution has vowed to render economic justice to all citizens. The directive principles laid down in the Constitution have recorded the economic goals to be achieved by the States. Article 36 to 51 comprise such directive principles, Two of them are relevant here. Article 38 enjoins on the State to establish a social system which will ensure social, political and economic justice to its citizens. Article 39 directs the State to formulate policies of distribution of physical means which will result in the greatest good of all and will provide adequate means of livelihood to all its citizens, men and women. The principle of equal remuneration for equal work should be implemented. The States should not allow centralisation of wealth and the means of-production which harm the society.

A part from these, there are other directives which have extensively discussed the responsibilities of the States regarding adult education, unemployment, children, women, etc., and how the States should execute these responsibilities. The administrators and the government are guided by these directive principles to achieve, the goals included in the preamble of the Constitution.

Dr. Ambedkar in commenting on this says: "These directive principles are not mere decorative pieces showing noble sentiments. The executive and the judiciary should keep those principles in their minds while taking any decisions in future." The economic ideals in the Constitution guide the States in their actions in the relevant field. In the present age the government field of action is not limited to maintaining peace and order. It will be seen that these ideals are but the concrete form of the Hindu directive principle:

Sarve Santu Sukhinah, Sarve Santu Niramayah,

Sarve Bhadrani Pashyantu ma Kashchit Duhkhabhag Bhavet.

(Let all be happy and healthy. Let all see the vision of universal wellbeing. Let no one suffer miseries.)

If liberty and equality are to materialise in the practical life of the people then economic justice should be granted to all without exception. All the rights enumerated in the Constitution are swallowed by the enormous dragon of poverty and destitution. Dr. Ambedkar says: "On 26 January 1950, India will awake in political freedom, but in the social and economic field the darkness of inequality will persist. We must strive to remove this contradiction between political freedom and economic and social bondage, as soon as possible. If we do not succeed in removing this contradiction, then those masses who are the victims of this contradiction will certainly raze to ground the lofty edifice of political democracy, the Constituent Assembly has so painstakingly and assiduously erected."

Hindutvists have never suggested that the State may deny economic equality-economic justice. On the contrary they have for so long been opposing those very policies that have impaired economic justice. Because the political policies so far carried out have denied this very economic justice to the masses, the rich have snowballed into affluent giants, the poor have been lowered into utter destitution. The directive principles have evaporated in their implementation. The State apparatus has installed and operated an economic machinery that diligently preserves the vested interests of a particular tiny but powerful group. The country is groaning under the unbearable load of foreign debt. Indigenous industries are facing insurmountable difficulties created by multinationals riding on the backs of the ruling coterie. The economic policies that help these multinationals to ascend the ruling backs are wrong. And so these policies should be opposed. Opposition to these policies cannot be construed to mean opposition to economic ideals enshrined in the Constitution.

Framework of Constitution: The Hindutva ideology is not in conflict with the framework of the Constitution that lays down the political, economic and social ideals and the ideals regarding freedom of worship. The foregoing discussion would have brought to light two reasons for this. One, the framework of Constitution upholds certain guiding principles and these principles are but a reflection of the noblest ideals held dear for centuries by Indian thinkers. And two, the Hindutva philosophy has already assimilated the ideals our Constitution so explicitly proclaims. Therefore the Hindutva protagonists have no warrant to wage a war against the lofty values they have cherished all their life.

Congress and Constitution: The malicious, mendacious and mean campaign to malign the Hindutva camp springs from causes that are far from the high plane of the directive principles. These are: One for the last several decades the Congress has been operating the Constitution for its narrow political ends.

There is nowhere any proof of Congress efforts to bring into practice the noble values enshrined in our Constitution. Whenever their was imminent threat to the Congress hold on political power, the Congress has never flinched from abusing and wrongfully amending the Sections of the Constitution to save its rule from being overthrown.

In 1969 the threat to Indira Gandhi's premiership was staring in the face. So she abused the economic ideal of the Constitution to nationalize the banks and abolish the privy purses of the native princes and shouted from the housetops the slogan of "Garibi Hatao".

In 1975 she was again threatened with loss of her seat in the Lok Sabha; she took recourse to the Emergency, abrogated fundamental rights granted by the Constitution, amended the very preamble by interpolating the words "secular" and "socialist". The Constitution cannot slap any specific restricting ideology on the society. The State cannot be bound by such partisan ideology. Dr. Ambedkar astutely skirted these two words but equally sagely incorporated the ideas of freedom of worship and economic justice. He intended to ensconce the soul of these ideas, whereas the late prime minister, Indira Gandhi wanted to use these words as catchwords to attract and abuse popular sentiments without granting anything of substance.

For, the Congress programme for the last four decades had nothing really secular or really socialistic. This travesty of the directive principles is a breach of the sanctity of the Constitution. The Hindutvists' present struggle is against the Congress. But how can the fight against the Congress be considered as a fight against Constitution? The, propaganda that the Hindutvists are opposed to the Constitution is politically motivated to save the Congress rule.

For some years now all the political parties have been celebrating 14 April,Dr. Ambedkar's birthday in a big way; for most of them it is a ritual.

Some of the major parties indulge in unalloyed hypocrisy in that they do two things simultaneously. One, their think tanks attack Dr. Ambedkar mercilessly; they are very angry that there are more statues of Dr. Ambedkar than that of Gandhiji, and that, too, of a larger size; angry because Dr. Ambedkar is called the father/architect of the Indian Constitution. They are dismissive of the perpetual suffering and unequal status of the depressed section of our population and Dr. Ambedkar's fight for their right to be human. Two, on 14 April the leaders garland Dr. Ambedkar's "oversized" statues, hail him as the architect of the Constitution and as one who sowed the seeds of social democracy and social equality.

The think tank—the 'ideologues' of 'patriotic' political formations—shed crocodile tears over Ambedkar's disagreement with Gandhiji on a number of issues. They, however, conveniently forget what Gandhiji thought of Ambedkar: "If Ambedkar does not break our heads, it is an act of self-restraint on his part. Dr. Ambedkar has had to suffer humiliations and insults which should make any one of us bitter and resentful. Had I been in his place, I would have been as angry. We shall be unfit to gain Swaraj so long as we keep in bondage a fifth of the population. In the history of world religions there is perhaps nothing like our treatment of the suppressed classes. Caste Hindu well-wishers of untouchables have no right to speak for them."

Dr. Ambedkar was a revolutionary, rationalist-humanist, human rights intellectual-activist, a man who looked ahead of his time. He wondered "why the Hindus having traditions of charity and humanity—their regard for animal life-should behave so heartlessly towards their fellow human beings and in such unreasonable ways. The Hindu community is set in the steel frame of the caste system, in which one caste is lower than another in social gradation involving particular privileges, rights, inhibition and disabilities with regard to each caste. This system has created vested interests which depend upon maintaining the inequalities resulting from the system".

He, therefore, "unfurled the banner of equality". He was not satisfied with the abolition of untouchability only, leaving the caste system along with "the inequalities inherent in the system". Dr. Ambedkar embraced Buddhism because the Buddhist dharma is based on scientific reasoning, it seeks to achieve human freedom, equality, liberty and fraternity. According to him Buddhism is the only religion which does not sanctify poverty and inequality: nirvana is the way "to remove injustice and inhumanity that man does to man." Buddha taught "social freedom, intellectual freedom, and political freedom. He taught equality, equality not between man and man only but between man and woman. His concern was to give salvation to man in his life on earth, and not to promise it to him in heaven after he is dead".

Many progressives whisper that Dr. Ambedkar accepted a cabinet post in Pandit Nehru's government because he wanted, political, power. Like all political leaders he too wanted power, but unlike most of them he accepted a cabinet post to empower those who have remained depressed and deprived for centuries. But for him the progressive provisions in the Constitution might not have been incorporated. He devoted his whole life to the cause of human rights of the depressed; his mission in life was to restore human dignity to those who have been victims of an ugly and unjust hierarchical social order which gave rise to injustice and, inequality. "My hear breaks", he said, "to see the pitiable sight of your faces and hear your sad voices".

To the Hindus he said. "If you say that Hindu religion is our religion, then your right and ours must be equal. But is this the case?" Dr. Ambedkar fought a relentless battle against this social order and was one of the very few Indian leaders who was forthright, and called a spade a spade: "I hate all injustice, tyranny, pompousness and humbug". Dr. Ambedkar believed that if he succeeded in his struggle—struggle for a just social order—it will prove a blessing for all Indians, not merely any group or community. He wanted the dominating section of our people to adopt a strong position against the hierarchical social order.

Dr. Ambedkar will be remembered for all time to come as the architect of the Indian Constitution, specially for the Fundamental Rights and Directive Principles Chapters which, aim at eradicating "all injustice and tyranny" and ushering in social democracy and social equality. He was however, disappointed that the dominating section of our society did not rise to the occasion and did not water the plants that he had planted. Our political rulers have failed Ambedkar and his vision. It is now for human rights groups and grassroots activists to make social democracy and equality a way of life in the absence of which political democracy will always stand on a shaky foundation.

CONSTITUENT ASSEMBLY

The Constitution was drafted by the Constituent Assembly, which was elected by the elected members of the provincial assemblies. Jawaharlal Nehru, C. Rajagopalachari, Rajendra Prasad, Sardar Vallabhbhai Patel, Maulana Abul Kalam Azad, Shyama Prasad Mukherjee and Nalini Ranjan Ghosh were some important figures in the Assembly. There were more than 30 members of scheduled classes.

Frank Anthony represented the Anglo-Indian community, and the Parsis were represented by H. P. Modi. The Chairman of the Minorities Committee was Harendra Coomar Mookerjee, a distinguished Christian who represented all Christians other than Anglo-Indians. Ari Bahadur Gururng represented the Gorkha Community.

Prominent jurists like Alladi Krishnaswamy Iyer, B. R. Ambedkar, Benegal Narsing Rau and K. M. Munshi were also members of the Assembly. Sarojini Naidu and Rajkumari Amrit Kaur were important women members. The first president of the Constituent Assembly was Sachidanand Sinha later, Rajendra Prasad was elected president of the Constituent Assembly. The members of the Constituent Assembly met for the first time in 1946 on 9 December.

Drafting

In the 14 August 1947 meeting of the Assembly, a proposal for forming various committees was presented. Such committees included a Committee on Fundamental Rights, the Union Powers Committee and Union Constitution Committee. On 29 August 1947, the Drafting Committee was appointed, with Dr Ambedkar as the Chairman along with six other members. A Draft Constitution was prepared by the committee and submitted to the Assembly on 4 November 1947.

The Assembly met, in sessions open to the public, for 166 days, spread over a period of 2 years, 11 months and 18 days before adopting the Constitution. After many deliberations and some modifications, the 308 members of the Assembly signed two hand-written copies of the document on 24 January 1950. Two days later, the Constitution of India became the law of all the Indian lands. Constitution of India has undergone 94 amendments in less than 60 years since its enactment.

STRUCTURE

The debate on the 'basic structure' of the Constitution, lying somnolent in the archives of India's constitutional history during the last decade of the 20th century, has reappeared in the public realm. While setting up the National Commission to Review the Working of the Constitution, the National Democratic Alliance government (formed by a coalition of 24 national and regional level parties) stated that the basic structure of the Constitution would not be tampered with.

Justice M.N. Venkatachalaiah, Chairman of the Commission, has emphasised on several occasions that an enquiry into the basic structure of the Constitution lay beyond the scope of the Commission's work. Several political parties—notably the Congress (I) and the two Communist parties which are in the opposition—have made it clear that the review exercise was the government's ploy to seek legitimacy for its design to adopt radical constitutional reforms thus destroying the basic structure of the document.

Much of the public debate has been a victim of partial amnesia as even literate circles of urban India are unsure of the ramifications of this concept, which was hotly debated during the 1970s and 1980s. The following discussion is an attempt to chart the waters of that period rendered turbulent by the power struggle between the legislative and the judicial arms of the State.

According to the Constitution, Parliament and the state legislatures in India have the power to make laws within their respective jurisdictions. This power is not absolute in nature. The Constitution vests in the judiciary, the power to adjudicate upon the constitutional validity of all laws. If a law made by Parliament or the state legislatures violates any provision of the Constitution, the Supreme Court has the power to declare such a law invalid or ultra vires.

This check notwithstanding, the founding fathers wanted the Constitution to be an adaptable document rather than a rigid framework for governance. Hence Parliament was invested with the power to amend the Constitution.

Article 368 of the Constitution gives the impression that Parliament's amending powers are absolute and encompass all parts of the document. But the Supreme Court has acted as a brake to the legislative enthusiasm of Parliament ever since independence.

With the intention of preserving the original ideals envisioned by the constitution-makers, the apex court pronounced that Parliament could not distort, damage or alter the basic features of the Constitution under the pretext of amending it. The phrase 'basic structure' itself cannot be found in the Constitution.

The Supreme Court recognised this concept for the first time in the historic Kesavananda Bharati case in 1973. Ever since the Supreme Court has been the interpreter of the Constitution and the arbiter of all amendments made by Parliament.

The pre-Kesavanada position

Parliament's authority to amend the Constitution, particularly the chapter on the fundamental rights of citizens, was challenged as early as in 1951. After independence, several laws were enacted in the states with the aim of reforming land ownership and tenancy structures.

This was in keeping with the ruling Congress party's electoral promise of implementing the socialistic goals of the Constitution [contained in Article 39 (b) and (c) of the Directive Principles of State Policy] that required equitable distribution of resources of production among all citizens and prevention of concentration of wealth in the hands of a few. Property owners—adversely affected by these laws—petitioned the courts.

The courts struck down the land reforms laws saying that they transgressed the fundamental right to property guaranteed by the Constitution. Piqued by the unfavourable judgements, Parliament placed these laws in the Ninth Schedule of the Constitution through the First and Fourth amendments (1951 and 1952 respectively), thereby effectively removing them from the scope of judicial review. [Parliament added the Ninth Schedule to the Constitution through the very first amendment in 1951 as a means of immunising certain laws against judicial review.

Under the provisions of Article 31, which themselves were amended several times later, laws placed in the Ninth Schedule—pertaining to acquisition of private property and compensation payable for such acquisition—cannot be challenged in a court of law on the ground that they violated the fundamental rights of citizens. This protective umbrella covers more than 250 laws passed by state legislatures with the aim of regulating the size of land holdings and abolishing various tenancy systems.

The Ninth Schedule was created with the primary objective of preventing the judiciary-which upheld the citizens' right to property on several occasions-from derailing the Congress party led government's agenda for a social revolution.] Property owners again challenged the constitutional amendments which placed land reforms laws in the Ninth Schedule before the Supreme Court, saying that they violated Article 13 (2) of the Constitution. Article 13 (2) provides for the protection of the fundamental rights of the citizen.

Parliament and the state legislatures are clearly prohibited from making laws that may take away or abridge the fundamental rights guaranteed to the citizen. They argued that any amendment to the Constitution had the status of a law as understood by Article 13 (2).

In 1952 (Sankari Prasad Singh Deo v. Union of India) and 1955 (Sajjan Singh v. Rajasthan), the Supreme Court rejected both arguments and upheld the power of Parliament to amend any part of the Constitution including that which affects the fundamental rights of citizens. Significantly though, two dissenting judges in Sajjan Singh v. Rajasthan case raised doubts whether the fundamental rights of citizens could become a plaything of the majority party in Parliament.

The Golaknath verdict

In 1967 an eleven-judge bench of the Supreme Court reversed its position. Delivering its 6:5 majority judgement in the Golaknath v. State of Punjab case, Chief Justice Subba Rao put forth the curious position that Article 368, that contained provisions related to the amendment of the Constitution, merely laid down the amending procedure. Article 368 did not confer upon Parliament the power to amend the Constitution. The amending power (constituent power) of Parliament arose from other provisions contained in the Constitution (Articles 245, 246, 248) which gave it the power to make laws (plenary legislative power). Thus, the apex court held that the amending power and legislative powers of Parliament were essentially the same.

Therefore, any amendment of the Constitution must be deemed law as understood in Article 13 (2). The majority judgement invoked the concept of implied limitations on Parliament's power to amend the Constitution. This view held that the Constitution gives a place of permanence to the fundamental freedoms of the citizen. In giving the Constitution to themselves, the people had reserved the fundamental rights for themselves.

Article 13, according to the majority view, expressed this limitation on the powers of Parliament. Parliament could not modify, restrict or impair fundamental freedoms due to this very scheme of the Constitution and the nature of the freedoms granted under it. The judges stated that the fundamental rights were so sacrosanct and transcendental in importance that they could not be restricted even if such a move were to receive unanimous approval of both houses of Parliament.

They observed that a Constituent Assembly might be summoned by Parliament for the purpose of amending the fundamental rights if necessary. In other words, the apex court held that some features of the Constitution lay at its core and required much more than the usual procedures to change them. The phrase 'basic structure' was introduced for the first time by M.K. Nambiar and other counsels while arguing for the petitioners in the Golaknath case, but it was only in 1973 that the concept surfaced in the text of the apex court's verdict.

Nationalisation of Banks and Abolition of Privy Purses

Within a few weeks of the Golaknath verdict the Congress party suffered heavy losses in the parliamentary elections and lost power in several states. Though a private member's bill-tabled by Barrister Nath Pai-seeking to restore the supremacy of Parliament's power to amend the Constitution was introduced and debated both on the floor of the house and in the Select Committee, it could not be passed due to political compulsions of the time.

But the opportunity to test parliamentary supremacy presented itself once again when Parliament introduced laws to provide greater access to bank credit for the agricultural sector and ensure equitable distribution of wealth and resources of production and by:

- Nationalising banks and
- Derecognising erstwhile princes in a bid to take away their Privy purses, which were promised in perpetuity-as a sop to accede to the Union-at the time of India's independence.

Parliament reasoned that it was implementing the Directive Principles of State Policy but the Supreme Court struck down both moves. By now, it was clear that the Supreme Court and Parliament were at loggerheads over the relative position of the fundamental rights vis-à-vis the Directive Principles of State Policy. At one level, the battle was about the supremacy of Parliament vis-à-vis the power of the courts to interpret and uphold the Constitution.

At another level the contention was over the sanctity of property as a fundamental right jealously guarded by an affluent class much smaller than that of the large impoverished masses for whose benefit the Congress government claimed to implement its socialist development programme. Less than two weeks after the Supreme Court struck down the President's order derecognising the princes, in a quick move to secure the mandate of the people and to bolster her own stature Prime Minister Indira Gandhi dissolved the Lok Sabha and called a snap poll.

For the first time, the Constitution itself became the electoral issue in India. Eight of the ten manifestos in the 1971 elections called for changes in the Constitution in order to restore the supremacy of Parliament. A.K. Gopalan of the Communist Party of India (Marxist) went to the extent of saying that the Constitution be done away with lock stock and barrel and be replaced with one that enshrined the real sovereignty of the people.

The Congress party returned to power with a two-thirds majority. The electorate had endorsed the Congress party's socialist agenda, which among other things spoke of making basic changes to the Constitution in order to restore Parliament's supremacy. Through a spate of amendments made between July 1971 and June 1972 Parliament sought to regain lost ground. It restored for itself the absolute power to amend any part of the Constitution including Part III, dealing with fundamental rights.

Even the President was made duty bound to give his assent to any amendment bill passed by both houses of Parliament. Several curbs on the right property were passed into law. The right to equality before the law and equal protection of the laws (Article 14) and the fundamental freedoms guaranteed under Article 19 were made subordinate to Article 39 (b) and (c) in the Directive Principles of State Policy. Privy purses of erstwhile princes were abolished and an entire category of legislation dealing with land reforms was placed in the Ninth Schedule beyond the scope of judicial review.

Emergence of the Basic Structure Concept: the Kesavanada milestone

Inevitably, the constitutional validity of these amendments was challenged before a full bench of the Supreme Court (thirteen judges). Their verdict can be found in eleven separate judgements. Nine judges signed a summary statement which records the most important conclusions reached by them in this case.

Granville Austin notes that there are several discrepancies between the points contained in the summary signed by the judges and the opinions expressed by them in their separate judgements. Nevertheless, the seminal concept of 'basic structure' of the Constitution gained recognition in the majority verdict. All judges upheld the validity of the Twenty-fourth amendment saying that Parliament had the power to amend any or all provisions of the Constitution.

All signatories to the summary held that the Golaknath case had been decided wrongly and that Article 368 contained both the power and the procedure for amending the Constitution. However they were clear that an amendment to the Constitution was not the same as a law as understood by Article 13 (2).

It is necessary to point out the subtle difference that exists between two kinds of functions performed by the Indian Parliament:

1. It can make laws for the country by exercising its legislative power and
2. It can amend the Constitution by exercising its constituent power.

Constituent Power is Superior to Ordinary Legislative Power

Unlike the British Parliament which is a sovereign body (in the absence of a written constitution), the powers and functions of the Indian Parliament and State legislatures are subject to limitations laid down in the Constitution. The Constitution does not contain all the laws that govern the country. Parliament and the state legislatures make laws from time to time on various subjects, within their respective jurisdictions.

The general framework for making these laws is provided by the Constitution. Parliament alone is given the power to make changes to this framework under Article 368. Unlike ordinary laws, amendments to constitutional provisions require a special majority vote in Parliament.

Another illustration is useful to demonstrate the difference between Parliament's constituent power and law making powers. According to Article 21 of the Constitution, no person in the country may be deprived of his life or personal liberty except according to procedure established by law. The Constitution does not lay down the details of the procedure as that responsibility is vested with the legislatures and the executive.

Parliament and the state legislatures make the necessary laws identifying offensive activities for which a person may be imprisoned or sentenced to death.

The executive lays down the procedure of implementing these laws and the accused person is tried in a court of law. Changes to these laws may be incorporated by a simple majority vote in the concerned state legislature. There is no need to amend the Constitution in order to incorporate changes to these laws. However, if there is a demand to convert Article 21 into the fundamental right to life by abolishing death penalty, the Constitution may have to be suitably amended by Parliament using its constituent power.

Most importantly seven of the thirteen judges in the Kesavananda Bharati case, including Chief Justice Sikri who signed the summary statement, declared that Parliament's constituent power was subject to inherent limitations. Parliament could not use its amending powers under Article 368 to 'damage', 'emasculate', 'destroy', 'abrogate', 'change' or 'alter' the 'basic structure' or framework of the Constitution.

Basic Features of the Constitution according to the Kesavanada verdict

Each judge laid out separately, what he thought were the basic or essential features of the Constitution. There was no unanimity of opinion within the majority view either.

Sikri, C.J. explained that the concept of basic structure included:

- Supremacy of the Constitution
- Republican and democratic form of government
- Secular character of the Constitution
- Separation of powers between the legislature, executive and the judiciary
- Federal character of the Constitution

Shelat, J. and Grover, J. added two more basic features to this list:

1. The mandate to build a welfare state contained in the Directive Principles of State Policy
2. Unity and integrity of the nation

Hegde, J. and Mukherjea, J. identified a separate and shorter list of basic features:

- Sovereignty of India
- Democratic character of the polity
- Unity of the country
- Essential features of the individual freedoms secured to the citizens
- Mandate to build a welfare state

Jaganmohan Reddy, J. stated that elements of the basic features were to be found in the Preamble of the Constitution and the provisions into which they translated such as:

- Sovereign democratic republic parliamentary democracy
- Three organs of the State

He said that the Constitution would not be itself without the fundamental freedoms and the directive principles. Only six judges on the bench (therefore a minority view) agreed that the fundamental rights of the citizen belonged to the basic structure and Parliament could not amend it.

The minority view

The minority view delivered by Justice A.N. Ray (whose appointment to the position of Chief Justice over and above the heads of three senior judges, soon after the pronunciation of the Kesavananda verdict, was widely considered to be politically motivated), Justice M.H. Beg, Justice K.K. Mathew and Justice S.N. Dwivedi also agreed that Golaknath had been decided wrongly. They upheld the validity of all three amendments challenged before the court.

Ray, J. held that all parts of the Constitution were essential and no distinction could be made between its essential and non-essential parts. All of them agreed that Parliament could make fundamental changes in the Constitution by exercising its power under Article 368.

In summary the majority verdict in Kesavananda Bharati recognised the power of Parliament to amend any or all provisions of the Constitution provided such an act did not destroy its basic structure. But there was no unanimity of opinion about what appoints to that basic structure. Though the Supreme Court very nearly returned to the position of Sankari Prasad (1952) by restoring the supremacy of Parliament's amending power, in effect it strengthened the power of judicial review much more.

Basic Structure concept reaffirmed: the Indira Gandhi Election case

In 1975, The Supreme Court again had the opportunity to pronounce on the basic structure of the Constitution. A challenge to Prime Minister Indira Gandhi's election victory was upheld by the Allahabad High Court on grounds of electoral malpractice in 1975. Pending appeal, the vacation judge-Justice Krishna Iyer, granted a stay that allowed Smt. Indira Gandhi to function as Prime Minister on the condition that she should not draw a salary and speak or vote in Parliament until the case was decided.

Meanwhile, Parliament passed the Thirty-ninth amendment to the Constitution which removed the authority of the Supreme Court to adjudicate petitions regarding elections of the President, Vice President, Prime Minister and Speaker of the Lok Sabha. Instead, a body constituted by Parliament would be vested with the power to resolve such election disputes. Section 4 of the Amendment Bill effectively thwarted any attempt to challenge the election of an incumbent, occupying any of the above offices in a court of law.

This was clearly a pre-emptive action designed to benefit Smt. Indira Gandhi whose election was the object of the ongoing dispute. Amendments were also made to the Representation of Peoples Acts of 1951 and 1974 and placed in the Ninth Schedule along with the Election Laws Amendment Act,

1975 in order to save the Prime Minister from embarassment if the apex court delivered an unfavourable verdict.

The mala fide intention of the government was proved by the haste in which the Thirty-ninth amendment was passed. The bill was introduced on August 7, 1975 and passed by the Lok Sabha the same day. The Rajya Sabha (Upper House or House of Elders) passed it the next day and the President gave his assent two days later. The amendment was ratified by the state legislatures in special Saturday sessions. It was gazetted on August 10.

When the Supreme Court opened the case for hearing the next day, the Attorney General asked the Court to throw out the case in the light of the new amendment. Counsel for Raj Narain who was the political opponent challenging Mrs. Gandhi's election argued that the amendment was against the basic structure of the Constitution as it affected the conduct of free and fair elections and the power of judicial review.

Counsel also argued that Parliament was not competent to use its constituent power for validating an election that was declared void by the High Court. Four out of five judges on the bench upheld the Thirty-ninth amendment, but only after striking down that part which sought to curb the power of the judiciary to adjudicate in the current election dispute. One judge, Beg, J. upheld the amendment in its entirety. Mrs. Gandhi's election was declared valid on the basis of the amended election laws. The judges grudgingly accepted Parliament's power to pass laws that have a retrospective effect.

Basic Features of the Constitution according to the Election case verdict

Again, each judge expressed views about what amounts to the basic structure of the Constitution: According to Justice H.R. Khanna, democracy is a basic feature of the Constitution and includes free and fair elections. Justice K.K. Thomas held that the power of judicial review is an essential feature.

Justice Y.V. Chandrachud listed four basic features which he considered unamendable:

1. Sovereign democratic republic status
2. Equality of status and opportunity of an individual
3. Secularism and freedom of conscience and religion
4. 'Government of laws and not of men' *i.e.* the rule of law

According to Chief Justice A.N. Ray, the constituent power of Parliament was above the Constitution itself and therefore not bound by the principle of separation of powers. Parliament could therefore exclude laws relating election disputes from judicial review. He opined, strangely, that democracy was a basic feature but not free and fair elections. Ray, C.J. held that ordinary legislation was not within the scope of basic features. Justice K.K. Mathew agreed with Rày, C.J. that ordinary laws did not fall within the purview of basic structure.

But he held that democracy was an essential feature and that election disputes must be decided on the basis of law and facts by the judiciary. Justice M.H. Beg disagreed with Ray, C.J. on the grounds that it would be unnecessary to have a Constitution if Parliament's constituent power were said to be above it. Judicial powers were vested in the Supreme Court and the High Courts and Parliament could not perform them.

He contended that supremacy of the Constitution and separation of powers were basic features as understood by the majority in the Kesavananda Bharati case. Beg, J. emphasised that the doctrine of basic structure included within its scope ordinary legislation also. Despite the disagreement between the judges on what constituted the basic structure of the Constitution, the idea that the Constitution had a core content which was sacrosanct was upheld by the majority view.

The Kesavananda Review Bench

Within three days of the decision on the Election case Ray, C.J. convened a thirteen judge bench to review the Kesavanada verdict on the pretext of hearing a number of petitions relating to land ceiling laws which had been languishing in high courts. The petitions contended that the application of land ceiling laws violated the basic structure of the Constitution.

In effect the Review bench was to decide whether or not the basic structure doctrine restricted Parliament's power to amend the Constitution. The decision in the Bank Nationa-lisation case was also up for review. Meanwhile Prime Minister Indira Gandhi, in a speech in Parliament, refused to accept the dogma of basic structure.

It must be remembered that no specific petition seeking a review of the Kesavananda verdict filed before the apex court-a fact noted with much chagrin by several members of the bench. N.N. Palkhivala appearing for on behalf of a coal mining company eloquently argued against the move to review the Kesavananda decision. Ultimately, Ray, C.J. dissolved the bench after two days of hearings. Many people have suspected the government's indirect involvement in this episode seeking to undo an unfavourable judicial precedent set by the Kesavananda decision.

However no concerted efforts were made to pursue the case. The declaration of a National Emergency in June 1975 and the consequent suspension of fundamental freedoms, including the right to move courts against preventive detention, diverted the attention of the country from this issue.

Sardar Swaran Singh Committee and the Forty: second amendment

Soon after the declaration of National Emergency, the Congress party constituted a committee under the Chairmanship of Sardar Swaran Singh to study the question of amending the Constitution in the light of past experiences.

Based on its recommendations, the government incorporated several changes to the Constitution including the Preamble, through the Forty-second amendment (passed in 1976 and came into effect on January 3, 1977).

Among other things the amendment:

- Gave the Directive Principles of State Policy precedence over the Fundamental Rights contained in Article 14 (right to equality before the law and equal protection of the laws), Article 19 (various freedoms like freedom of speech and expression, right to assemble peacefully, right to form associations and unions, right to move about and reside freely in any part of the country and the right to pursue any trade or profession) and Article 21 (right to life and personal liberty). Article 31C was amended to prohibit any challenge to laws made under any of the Directive Principles of State Policy;
- Laid down that amendments to the Constitution made in the past or those likely to be made in future could not be questioned in any court on any ground;
- Removed all amendments to fundamental rights from the scope of judicial review and
- Removed all limits on Parliament's power to amend the Constitution under Article 368.

Basic structure doctrine reaffirmed: the Minerva Mills and Waman Rao cases

Within less than two years of the restoration of Parliament's amending powers to near absolute terms, the Forty-second amendment was challenged before the Supreme Court by the owners of Minerva Mills (Bangalore) a sick industrial firm which was nationalised by the government in 1974. Mr. N.A. Palkhivala, renowned constitutional lawyer and counsel for the petitioners, chose not to challenge the government's action merely in terms of an infringement of the fundamental right to property.

Instead, he framed the challenge in terms of Parliament's power to amend the Constitution.

Mr. Palkhivala argued that Section 55 of the amendment had placed unlimited amending power in the hands of Parliament. The attempt to immunise constitutional amendments against judicial review violated the doctrine of basic structure which had been recognised by the Supreme Court in the Kesavananda Bharati and Indira Gandhi Election Cases.

He further contended that the amended Article 31C was constitutionally bad as it violated the Preamble of the Constitution and the fundamental rights of citizens.

It also took away the power of judicial review. Chief Justice Y.V. Chandrachud, delivering the majority judgement (4:1), upheld both contentions. The majority view upheld the power of judicial review of constitutional amendments.

They maintained that clauses (4) and (5) of Article 368 conferred unlimited power on Parliament to amend the Constitution. They said that this deprived courts of the ability to question the amendment even if it damaged or destroyed the Constitution's basic structure.

The judges, who concurred with Chandrachud, C.J. ruled that a limited amending power itself is a basic feature of the Constitution. Bhagwati, J. the dissenting judge also agreed with this view stating that no authority howsoever lofty, could claim to be the sole judge of its power and actions under the Constitution.

The majority held the amendment to Article 31C unconstitutional as it destroyed the harmony and balance between fundamental rights and directive principles which is an essential or basic feature of the Constitution. The amendment to Article 31C remains a dead letter as it has not been repealed or deleted by Parliament.

Nevertheless cases under it are decided as it existed prior to the Forty-second amendment. In another case relating to a similar dispute involving agricultural property the apex court, held that all constitutional amendments made after the date of the Kesavananda Bharati judgement were open to judicial review.

All laws placed in the Ninth Schedule after the date of the Kesavananda Bharati judgement were also open to review in the courts. They can be challenged on the ground that they are beyond Parliament's constituent power or that they have damaged the basic structure of the Constitution. In essence, the Supreme Court struck a balance between its authority to interpret the Constitution and Parliament's power to amend it.

SYSTEM OF GOVERNMENT

The basic form of the Union Government envisaged in the Constitution is as follows, A democratic executive must satisfy three conditions:

1. It must be a stable executive, and
2. It must be a responsible executive.
3. It must be impartial to all religion, caste and community.

Unfortunately, it has not been possible so far to devise a system which can ensure both conditions in equal degree...... The daily assessment of responsibility, which is not available in the American system is, it is felt, far more effective than the periodic assessment and far more necessary in a country like India. The Draft Constitution in recommending the parliamentary system of Executive has preferred more responsibility to stability.

Federal Structure

The constitution provides for distribution of powers between the Union and the States. It enumerates the powers of the Parliament and State Legislatures in three lists, namely Union list, State list and Concurrent list. Subjects like national defence, foreign policy, issuance of currency are reserved to the Union list. Public order, local governments, certain taxes are examples of subjects of the State List, on which the Parliament has no power to enact laws in those regards, barring exceptional conditions.

Education, transportation, criminal law are a few subjects of the Concurrent list, where both the State Legislature as well as the Parliament have powers to enact laws. The residuary powers are vested with the Union. The upper house of the Parliament, the Rajya Sabha, which consists of representatives of States, is also an example of the federal nature of the government.

Parliamentary Democracy

The President of India is elected by the Parliament and State Legislative Assemblies, and not directly by the people. The President is the Head of the State, and all the business of the Executive and Laws enacted by the Parliament are in his/her name. However, these powers are only nominal, and the President must act only according to the advise of the Prime Minister and the Council of Ministers.

The Prime Minister and the Council of Ministers enjoy their offices only as long as they enjoy a majority support in the Lok Sabha, the lower house of the Parliament, which consists of members directly elected by the people. The ministers are answerable to both the houses of the Parliament. Also, the Ministers must themselves be elected members of either house of the Parliament.

Thus, the Parliament exercises control over the Executive. A similar structure is present in States, where the directly elected Legislative Assembly enjoys control over the Chief Minister and the State Council of Ministers.

Independent Judiciary

The Judiciary of India is free of control from either the executive or the Parliament. The judiciary acts as an interpreter of the constitution, and an intermediary in case of disputes between two States, or between a State and the Union. An act passed by the Parliament or a Legislative Assembly is subject to judicial review, and can be declared unconstitutional by the judiciary if it feels that the act violates some provision of the Constitution. Constitutional remedy against any action of the government is available in a High Court or the Supreme Court, if the action violates any of the fundamental rights of an individual as enumerated in the Constitution.

CHANGING THE CONSTITUTION

Amendments to the constitution are made by the Parliament, the procedure for which is laid out in Article 368. An amendment bill must be passed by both the Houses of the Parliament by a super-majority consisting of 2/3rd of the members present and voting, and half of the total membership of the House. In addition to this, certain amendments which pertain to the federal nature of the Constitution must be ratified by a majority of state legislatures.

As of September 2010, there have been 108 amendment bills presented in the Parliament, out of which 94 have been passed to become Amentment Acts. The Supreme Court has ruled, controversially, that not every constitutional amendment is permissible. An amendment must respect the "basic structure" of the constitution, which is immutable. In 2000 the National Commission to Review the Working of the Constitution (NCRWC) was setup to look into updating the constitution of India.

JUDICIAL REVIEW OF LAWS

Judicial review is adopted in the Indian constitution from the constitution of the United States of America. In the Indian constitution, Judicial Review is dealt with under Article 13. Judicial Review refers that the Constitution is the supreme power of the nation and all laws are under its supremacy.

Article 13 states that:

- All pre-constitutional laws, after the coming into force of constitution, if in conflict with it in all or some of its provisions then the provisions of constitution will prevail and the provisions of that pre-constitutional law will not be in force until an amendment of the constitution relating to the same matter. In such situation the provision of that law will again come into force, if it is compatible with the constitution as amended. This is called the Theory of Eclipse.

- In a similar manner, laws made after adoption of the Constitution by the Constituent Assembly must be compatible with the constitution, otherwise the laws and amendments will be deemed to be void-ab-initio.

In such situations, the Supreme Court or High Court interprets the laws as if they are in conformity with the constitution. If such an interpretation is not possible because of inconsistency, and where a separation is possible, the provision that is inconsistent with constitution is considered to be void. In addition to article 13, articles 32, 124, 131, 219, 226 and 246 provide a constitutional basis to the Judicial review in India.

COMMITTEES UNDER THE CONSTITUENT ASSEMBLY

- Committee on the Rules of procedure - Rajendra Prasad
- Steering Committee *Rajendra Prasad*
- Finance and Staff Committee *Anugrah Narayan Sinha*
- Credential Committee *Alladi Krishnaswamy Iyer*
- House Committee *B. Pattabhi Sitaramayya*
- Order of Business Committee *K.M. Munshi*
- Ad hoc Committee on the National Flag *Rajendra Prasad*
- Committee on the Functions of the Constituent Assembly *G.V. Mavalankar*
- States Committee *Jawaharlal Nehru*
- Advisory Committee on Fundamental Rights, Minorities
- Tribal and Excluded Areas Vallabhbhai Patel
- Minorities Sub-Committee *H.C. Mookherjee*
- Fundamental Rights Sub-Committee *J.B. Kripalani*
- North-East Frontier Tribal Areas and Assam. Excluded & Partially Excluded Areas Sub-Committee *Gopinath Bardoloi*
- Excluded and Partially Excluded Areas (Other than those in Assam) Sub-Committee *A.V. Thakkar*
- Union Powers Committee *Jawaharlal Nehru*
- Union Constitution Committee *Jawaharlal Nehru*
- Drafting Committee *B.R. Ambedkar.*

MEMBERS OF THE INDIAN CONSTITUENT ASSEMBLY

Indian National Congress

- Pandit Jawaharlal Nehru, 1st Prime Minister
- Sardar Vallabhbhai Patel, Deputy Prime Minister cum Home Minister
- Maulana Azad, Minister for Education,
- Dr. Rajendra Prasad, Chairman of the Assembly
- C. Rajagopalachari, Governor General
- Sarat Chandra Bose
- Sri Krishna Sinha, Chief Minister, Bihar
- Shyam Nandan Prasad Mishra
- Anugrah Narayan Sinha, Deputy Chief Minister cum Finance Minister,Bihar
- Rafi Ahmed Kidwai
- Asaf Ali
- Syama Prasad Mookerjee, President, Hindu Mahasabha
- Rajkumari Amrit Kaur, Minister for Health
- Hansa Mehta, President, All India Women's Conference
- Prof. N.G. Ranga
- Deep Narayan Singh
- P. Subbarayan
- Kailashnath Katju
- N.G Ayyangar
- T.T. Krishnamachari
- Rameshwar Prasad Sinha
- Durgabai Deshmukh
- K.M. Munshi
- Krishana Vallabh Sahay
- Frank Anthony, Anglo Indian representative
- Sarvepalli Radhakrishnan
- Dr. John Mathai
- Pratap Singh Kairon
- Prof. Shibbanlal Saxena
- R. K. Shanmukham Chetty
- Alladi Krishnaswamy Iyer

- Jagjivan Ram, President, All India Depressed Classes League
- Pandit Govind Ballabh Pant, Premier, United Provinces
- Minoo Masani
- Renuka Ray
- Purushottam Das Tandon
- Mahavir Tyagi
- Thakur Das Bhargava
- Bhagwan Das
- Feroze Gandhi
- B. Shiva Rao
- Jairamdas Daulatram
- Pattom A. Thanu Pillai
- R. Sankar
- P. S. Nataraja Pillai
- K. A. Mohamed
- P. T. Chacko, Pullolil
- Panampilly Govinda Menon
- Annie Mascarene
- Bhograju Pattabhi Sitaramayya
- Kamraj
- Ammu Swaminathan
- Purnima Banerjee
- Vijayalakshmi Pandit
- Ramnath Goenka, Editor of the Indian Express
- Sarojini Naidu
- Jaipal Singh Munda, President, Adibasi Mahasabha
- Jagjivan Ram
- Dakshayani Velayudan
- Reverend Jerome D'Souza
- Reverend JJM Nichols-Roy
- Gopinath Bordoloi
- Dharanidhar Basumatari
- Malati Choudhury
- Homi Mody
- Leela Roy

- Biswanath Das, Premier of Orissa
- Acharya Kriplani
- Sucheta Kriplani
- Harendra Coomar Mookerjee
- Gopi Krishna Vijayvargiya
- Pandit Raghunath Vinayak Dhulekar
- D.H. Chandrasekharaiya
- Nibaran Chandra Laskar
- Ari Bahadur Gururng, Gorkha Community (Darjeeling)
- Ch. Ranbir Singh Hooda.

Muslim League

- Begum Aizaz Rasul, Vice President (later President) Muslim League (India)
- Maulana Hasrat Mohani
- Nawab Mohammad Ismail Khan
- Kazi Syed Karimuddin
- Chaudhry Khaliquzzaman, President, Muslim League (India)
- Naziruddin Ahmad
- Z.H. Lari
- Mohammad Saadullah, Premier of Assam
- Aziz Ahmed Khan
- Maulana Daud Ghazhnavi
- Tajamul Hussain
- Hussain Imam
- Mahboob Ali Baig Sahib Bahadur
- Pocker Sahib Bahadur.

Others

Scheduled Caste Federation:

- Dr. Ambedkar.

Akalis:

- Sardar Hukam Singh.

Communist:

- Somnath Lahiri.

4

Ambedkar and Dalit

The first question which arises is: Why did Ambedkar not endorse the nationalist discourse of this period? There are several answers to this. One explanation for this is given by Omvedt when she writes: "It is impossible to conceptualise the Dalit movement in India in the absence of Ambedkar, it is equally difficult to imagine, sociologically, Ambedkar coming of any other region than the Marathi-speaking areas of British presidency". Let us explore this a little bit more.

Omvedt refers to the existence of an important tradition of anti-caste movement in Maharashtra that needs to be seen as part of the response to industrialisation and urbanisation. This was the site of the radical movement of Jotiba Phule's Satyashodhak Samaj, and from the time of Tilak, it had also provided a strong base for Hindu revivalism in the form of a Hindu Mahasabha. In fact, the Indian National Congress held its first session in 1885 in Bombay.

There was another reason for Ambedkar's critical position on nationalist politics. He was a Mahar, the largest untouchable caste in Maharashtra. His actions, then, according to Zelliot, "were moulded not only by his own personal background, and achievements, and the Maharashtrian thinking of his day, but also by his status as an untouchable". This group he came from had begun social and political movements before he assumed a position of leadership. Behind this identification with a non-Brahmin group lay the logic of a movement that was essentially anti-caste and not simply a movement for 'untouchability removal' or 'self-reform'. This is not to say that the Mahar movement in the later 19th century was an isolated movement but only to suggest that all these influences constantly streaming in are employed by Ambedkar in a new sense and directed towards a new solution.

To what extent does his work, in this political scenario, represent more than a resuscitation of known and traditional ideas and to what extent does it deviate from the traditional mode and contain new and original thought? There is no doubt that Ambedkar's writings chiefly captured the political tradition of their time: the philosophical views of that time must be at least in part responsible for his dissatisfaction with the nationalist discourse – the new political mood after the Montague-Chelmsford Reforms; an awakening among the minorities for safeguarding their interests in relation to the Hindu majority which pointed towards wider political participation in the national movement.

Yet, his thesis does not fit in with the dominant discourse on nationalism. One of the reasons behind Ambedkar's verdict on the national movement and its leaders, was their general indifference to caste issues. The intelligentsia, as part of the Congress leadership, organised first as social reformers against the British, and also organised as nationalists to challenge many aspects of Indian tradition. But they remained very ambiguous towards removal of the caste system. Linked to the debate on social and political reform was the issue of class. Many communist leaders analysed caste in a mechanical class framework and sought to override traditional identities rather than reinterpret them.

Therefore, a plausible explanation could be found in his own solution for liberating the dalits. Ambedkar realised that the identification of Indian culture with Hinduism is incorrect.

Because he believed that absorption into Hinduism meant the acceptance of Hindu leadership in the national movement, he felt it would be wiser to take chances with a religion which has many safeguards. At first, he tried to assert the path of radical autonomy, encouraged the dalits to form their own organisations and to deal independently with some basic issues. It means that the dalits themselves, "would have to redefine and reconstitute their relations with the whole of Hindu society". But if the dalits were not Hindus, what were they? In fact, a non-Hindu choice seems to have led him finally, to identify with Buddhism.

At the theoretical level, Ambedkar's language turned out to be singularly open to misconstruals. It was not easy for many to accept the Indian National Congress, social reform organisations and the Hindu Mahasabha as irreconcilable opponents of the dalits; neither was it easy to accept the praise accorded by Ambedkar to the British state for raising the status of untouchables.

Even more open to misunderstanding was Ambedkar's critique of nationalism: whereas Ambedkar attacked the Congress for their failure to recognise caste issues, he was erroneously taken to reject nationalism altogether. He was supposed to be not only anti-national but to advocate a separatist policy which was anti-sectarian as well. Opposed by both traditionalists and Congress leaders, Ambedkar reserved his most bitter attack for Gandhi's reformism.

AMBEDKAR: IN PURSUIT OF HISTORICAL TRUTH

One may derive Ambedkar's 'historical method' in all his major writings on Indian history, culture and philosophy. The writings on this kind of issues not only provoked the scholars, political leaders of nationalist movement and orthodox Hindus of his times but helped deconstruct the dominant construction of ideas of Indian society.

He made a systematic attempt to construct the histories and genealogies of the submerged social groups of Indian society by questioning the elite and dominant established Brahminical positions. He seems confident of his position by declaring it as 'fresh insights and new visions' in looking at Indian history and philosophy.

In the year 1946, Ambedkar identified five streams of thoughts among the Hindus of Indian society in his writing on 'who are Shudras'- Orthodox, Aryasamajists, respecters of law (Hindu social system is all wrong, but who holds that there is no necessity to attack it. Since law does not recognize it, it is dying, if not dead system) Political minded (Swaraj is important than social reform) and Rationalists (regard social reform as primary and even more important than Swaraj). Among these five classes of Hindus, Ambedkar would like to identify his position with rationalist Hindus who were arguing for social reform as immediate agenda rather than any other. In the words of Ambedkar; "I claim that in my research I have been guided by the best tradition of the historian who treats all literature as vulgar- I am using the word in its original sense of belonging to the people –to be examined and tested by accepted rules of evidence without recognizing any distinction between the sacred and profane and with the sole object of finding the truth."

As has been well said, an historian ought to be exact, sincere, and impartial; free from passion, unbiased by interest, fear, resentment or affection; and faithful to the truth, which is the mother of history, the preserver of great actions, the enemy of oblivion, the witness of the past, the director of the future. In short he must have an open mind, though it may not be an empty mind, and readiness to examine all evidence even though it be spurious. The non-brahmin scholar may find it difficult to remain true to this spirit of historian. He is likely to import the spirit of non-brahmin politics in the examination of the truth or falsity of ancient literature which is not justifiable. I feel certain that in my research I have kept myself free from such prejudice. In writing about sudras I have had present in my mind no other consideration except that of pure history. Respect and reverence for the sacred literature cannot be made to order.

They are results of social factors which make such sentiments natural in one case and quite unnatural in another. Respect and reverence for sacred literature of the Hindus is natural to a Brahmin scholar. But it is quite unnatural in a non-Brahmin scholar. In the historical method of Ambedkar; man is the maker of history: Ambedkar evaluates the three different views on the causes of historical changes, Augustine, Buckle and Marx.

Augustinian, history is only an unfolding of divine plan in which mankind is to continue through war and suffering until that divine plan is completed at the day of judgment. Ambedkar pointed out that this is not acceptable to many except theologians. For Buckle, history was made by geography and physics.

As per Marx, history was the result of economic forces. Ambedkar finds the limitations of these three arguments by holding the opinion that none of these would admit that history is the biography of great men. Indeed they deny man any place in making of history. He considers there is a truth in Buckle and Marx, but their views do not represent the whole truth. They are quite wrong in holding that impersonal forces are everything and that man is no factor in the making of history. That these impersonal forces are a determining factor can not be denied, however, the effect of impersonal forces depends on man must also be admitted.' The methods employed by Ambedkar in reconstructing the history are unique and convincing.

In developing an historical method he followed Goethe, as he said 'the historian's duty is to separate the truth from false, the certain from the uncertain...' Ambedkar agrees with Goethe in bringing out the relevant and necessary facts to forefront. Ambedkar proceeds further and points out into what the duty of historian in reconstructing the authentic history in situations, where he confronts with many missing links, *i.e.* when no direct evidence of connected relations between important events is available.

He himself faced this kind of situation in explaining the origin of sudras and untouchables as in both cases no documentary evidences were available or its antiquity. "In case of reconstructing history where there are no texts, and if there are, they have no direct bearing on the question. In such circumstances what one has to do is to strive to divine what the texts conceal or suggest without being even quite certain of having found the truth.

The task is one of gathering survivals of the past, placing hem together and making them tell the story of their birth. The task is analogous to that of the archaeologist who constructs a city from broken stones or of the paleontologist who conceives an extinct animal from scattered bones and teeth or of a painter who reads the lines of the horizon and the smallest vestiges on the slopes of the hill to make up a scene."

Ambedkar appears very much aware of the role of historian's social affinity in dealing the material in relation to the problems of social history.

In an introduction to 'who are the Shudras', he made this point more clear. He finds the difference between the non-Brahmin scholar and Brahmin scholar in treating the same source material of sacred literature of Hindus. The Brahmin scholar's attitude is identified as uncritical commendation, and where as the Non-Brahmins attitude in dealing this is unsparing condemnation. Ambedkar finds both the attitudes are harmful to historical research. It is often argued by many Brahmins that sacred literature has to be treated with reverence and respect.

Ambedkar staunchly believes that in pursuit of historical truth, there is nothing wrong in exposure of these very sacred texts which are responsible for the decline and fall of nation and society. It is the duty of a scholar to treat the literature without having any distinction of sacred or profane in pursuing truth. It is quite natural for Brahmin scholar to treat it as sacred with lot of respect and reverence. More over its object is to sustain the superiority and privileges of Brahmins as against the non-brahmins.

Since he finds the comfort and privilege, it is not possible for the Brahmin scholar to be critical about sacred literature. In fact, it is his whole production and finds livelihood on it. 'Knowing that what is called the sacred literature contains an abominable social philosophy which is responsible for their social degradation, the non-brahmin reacts to it in a manner quite opposite to that of the brahmin..... I am a non-brahmin, not even a non-brahmin, but an untouchable.'

Ambedkar had more focus on philosophy of religion in understanding the socio-historical phenomenon and the moral basis of Indian society, than exclusively depending on either religion or philosophy. He developed it as a method. It seems in evolving this method, he got influenced by John Dewey. Dewey is one of those pragmatic philosophers who wrote extensively on philosophy of religion from this perspective. In the west, religion is identified with faith, and philosophy is with reason/science/rationality, in the age of enlightenment. It is also understood as tradition and modernity dichotomy. Religion and science started considering adverse to each other. In this backdrop pragmatism of Dewey got importance by considering religion on practical utility. Religion is an institution or an influence and like all social influences and institutions, it may help or harm a society which is in its grip. Religion not only crossed everywhere the wrap of Indian history it forms the wrap and woof of Hindu mind. The life of the Hindu is regulated by religion at every moment of his life. Besides religion acts as a social force, and it stands for a scheme of divine governance. The scheme becomes an ideal for society to follow. 'The power of religious ideal depends upon its power to confer material benefit'. Ambedkar favours for religion that stand for reason rather negating religion. He felt that Hindu religion need to undergo a reform. Caste is a natural outcome of certain religious beliefs which have the sanction of shastras. To abolish the sanctity and sacredness of caste, one has to destroy the authority of the shastras and Vedas. One has to destroy the religion of sruti and smriti. Ambedkar not only proposed the religion that should stand for reason, but also tries to link it up with the governing principle of politics. In simple terms, he thought reason and critical analysis as a method used for the study of religion.

ORIGINS OF INDIAN DALIT

The origin of the Dalit community, and of the caste system itself, is unclear. Adherents of the Aryan migration hypothesis theorize that the caste system was a product of the invasion, with the Aryans reserving the higher castes for themselves and relegating the darker-skinned, native inhabitants that they conquered to lower castes and untouchable status. An alternative theory accepts this general outline, but holds that Dalit existed before the Aryan migration as an oppressed class among the native Dravidian peoples of South Asia. In this latter theory, the Dalit status was simply preserved and expanded by the Aryans as part of the integration of Aryan and Dravidian societies.

In the context of traditional Hindu beliefs, Dalit status has often been historically associated with occupations regarded as ritually impure: any occupation involving killing or handling dead bodies, or anything involving disposing of refuse or human waste. Engaging in these activities was considered to be polluting to the individual who performed them, and this pollution was considered to be 'contagious'.

As a result, Dalits were commonly banned from fully participating in Hindu religious life (they could not enter the premises of a temple), and elaborate precautions were sometimes observed to prevent incidental contact between Dalits and higher-caste Hindus.

Historically, there may not have been clear demarcation between Dalit castes and the lowest Shudra castes. Before the freezing of lands and territories during the British colonial period, it may have been possible for Dalits to move up the ladder as Shudras or higher castes. In the same way, some people from the lowest Shudra communities may have been reduced in status to that of the Dalits. Culturally there appears to be continuity across the caste spectrum.

In modern India the word 'Dalit' has been applied to all people who do not belong to any of the four castes of Hinduism. Defined in this way, 'Dalit' includes not only low-caste or outcaste Hindus, but also aboriginal followers of animist religions, and possibly may have included immigrant communities that subscribed to beliefs that were seen as incompatible with orthodox brahman ist and Hindu traditions.

Dalits are not a single identifiable race or caste. Instead, they are divided into various subcastes known as or ' jati s', the lowest ranking of which is generally considered to be the Bhangi s.

Most genetic studies have found no significant evidence that members of 'untouchable' groups are substantially different from other groups in similar locations. Castes within a region are probably less genetically different than people of the same caste across different regions. While at least one studyfound a correlation between caste status and genetic markers seeming to indicate a more European lineage, no clear biological basis for caste distinctions has been conclusively revealed.

The absence of strong genetic differentiation between Dalits and non-Dalits is often regarded as evidence that the caste barrier was historically more permeable than commonly perceived. Intermarriage (which is again growing in popularity in Indian society), or sexual infidelity (the prevalence of which is difficult to assess) across caste lines may be more common than was previously thought. Additionally, Dalit diversity may be due to newly outcaste individuals or communities over the years. It is noteworthy that certain regional tribes that are considered Dalits are sometimes seen by Indians as racially distinct- they are often regarded as more closely related to Burmese, Thais , and other Southeast and East Asians.

Many Dalits who have converted to other religions in the past few centuries continue to retain their Dalit identity. In the 1991 census, Dalits constituted more than 16% of India 's population, with the greatest numbers living in Uttar Pradesh , West Bengal , and Bihar . They are also found in Nepal . In Pakistan , more than 60% of all Hindus are Dalits, keeping in mind that Pakistan is predominantly Muslim.

Dalits and Indian Politics

M.K. Gandhi made it part of the Indian National Congress 's mission to eradicate untouchability. For this reason, untouchability has been officially abolished in India, although social practice has lagged behind, particularly in rural villages. In a few of these extremely traditional villages, Dalits are still not allowed to let their shadows fall upon Brahmin s for fear of ritually contaminating them; and they are still required to sweep the ground where they walk to remove the 'contamination' of their footfalls.

In some of these villages, rural Dalits are forbidden to worship in temples or draw water from the same wells as caste Hindus, and they usually live in segregated neighbourhoods outside the main village. In urban areas and most villages the old concepts of a rigid caste system and untouchability usually no longer exist, though most Indians still voluntarily hold on to their caste origins.

Some seats in the National and State Parliments are reserved for Scheduled Caste and Tribe candidates, a measure sought by B.R. Ambedkar and other Dalit activists in order to ensure that Dalits would obtain a proportionate political voice.

Dalits and Religion

One of the tougher questions in modern Indian society is whether the Dalits are really Hindus . Traditionally, Dalits have been barred from many activities that were seen as central to Vedic religion and Hindu practices. The wide variety of practices and beliefs observed in Hinduism makes any clear assessment difficult. Defined narrowly as the practice of rituals associated with the Vedic teachings and Brahmin-centered orthodox religious complex, then many Dalits would be classified as non-Hindus. But if ' Hinduism ' is viewed in wider terms as simply a convenient label for the full range of Indian religious practices, then most Indians- including Dalits- would fit into that category.

Many Dalits continue to debate whether they are 'Hindu' or 'non-Hindu'. Some have succesfully integrated into urban Indian society, where caste origins are less obvious and less important in public life. In rural India, caste origins are more readily apparent, and Dalits remain excluded from local religious life.

DALIT LITERATURE

Dalit Literature, literature about the Dalits, the oppressed class under Indian caste system forms an important and distinct part of Indian literature.

Though Dalit narratives have been a part of the Indian social narratives since 11th century onwards, with works like Cekkilar's Periya Puranam documenting Dalit life, Dalit literature emerged into prominence and as a collective voice after 1960, starting with Marathi, and soon appeared in Hindi, Kannada, Telugu and Tamil languages, through Self narratives, like poems, short stories and most importantly autobiographies known for their fierce and often stark realism, and for its contribution to the Dalit politics.

It denounced as petty and false the then prevailing romanticism with the bourgeois Sadashiv pethi literature treated the whole Dalit issue, ignoring the social reality of appalling poverty and oppression of caste Hindus which was the result of the bourgeois character of this culture. It is often compared with the African-American literature especially in its depiction of issues of racial segregation and injustice, as seen in Slave narratives One of the first Dalit writers was Madara Chennaiah, an 11th-century cobbler-saint who lived in the reign of Western Chalukyas and who is also regarded by some scholars as the "father of Vachana poetry". Another poet who finds mention is Dohara Kakkaiah, a Dalit by birth, six of whose confessional poems survive.

In the 20th century, the term "Dalit literature" came into use in 1958, when the first conference of Maharashtra Dalit Sahitya Sangha was held at Mumbai, a movement driven by thinkers like Jyotiba Phule and Bhimrao Ambedkar. Baburao Bagul was pioneer of Dalit writings in Marathi. His first collection of stories, Jevha Mi Jat Chorali, published in 1963, created a stir in Marathi literature with its passionate depiction of a crude society and thus brought in new momentum to Dalit literature in Marathi; today it is seen by many critics as the epic of the Dalits, and was later made into a film by actor-director Vinay Apte. Gradually with other writers like, Namdeo Dhasal, these Dalit writings paved way from strengthening of Dalit politics.

POLITICS, AND INTERESTS AND WAVE OF THE DALIT-HNDUTVA UNITY

In addition to the politics of collective interests, the politics of individual interests too has found a space in this formation. Often in political parties such as the BJP, Congress, Left parties and even Shiv Sena, political activists either come from stable independent economic background, or the parties create sources of empowering political activists. Some of these parties even have full-timers whose day-to-day needs are taken care of. As a result, activists are not all the time pressed for day-to-day survival, and are free and committed to work for party's ideological persuasions. Compared to this, activists in Dalit politics have been drawn from the Dalit movement.

The activists of Dalit movement in Maharashtra, many of whom are drawn from Dalit Panthers, have generally been drawn from very humble economic background. As youths inspired by Ambedkarite consciousness, and participating in struggle against Dalit atrocities, these activists left college and other professional education incomplete, and hence are without any source for day-to-day existence. Further, activists in Dalit struggle have often been elder sons of homes that have spent meagre family earnings on their education. When dreams of changing the order become more distant and inability to help even to their families that need them is an immediate and continuous experience, these activists tend to get frustrated. In addition to this the lack of any political recognition, despite long participation in the struggle leads them to feeling of dejection.

The author personally knows many such activists who have undergone this experience. Of course this fate of activists is indeed true of other social movements too. Many communists, for instance, too have faced this. The communist movement has had sizable number of activists, women and men, who have remained unsung and gone into oblivion. However, the point here is about the politics of recognition. While the contribution to the left movement is recognised as a contribution to the people's cause, that of Dalit movement seen as to the specific issues. Moreover, Dalit masses too, because of being powerless in all spheres of life, have tended to socially recognise those who assume some political office, be that power more rhetorical than real. As a result Dalit activists have experienced non-recognition from both broader structures of recognition and Dalit masses. Of course, on the other hand, like other political formations such as Congress or Hindutva parties, Dalit politics too has attracted people who harbour the wish to pursue political careers. When, despite working for the party for long time, they become unsuccessful in getting elected to a political office, they tend to look for new areas political habitation.

Of course though the move of unity of Dalit-hindutva sounds alluring to 'dissenting' and politically 'eager' voices among Dalit communities, its implications for long-term politics are full of perils rather than promises. For, though 'empowering' some with political office, it has dangers of new patron-client formation, ironically, emerging even in urban and modern conditions. Moreover, it also has serious implications for recovery of Dalit subjectivity and autonomy, not only in the realm of the politics but identity, culture and economy. In recent history one such formation of Dalit-Hindutva alliance was sought. But the unity with Bhimshakti was the need of the 'hour' for the new Shiv Sena; it was Shiv Sena's project that sought to decide the nature, development and outcome of the project. Such a move is dictated by the compulsions of politics of numbers encounters by the Shiv Sena and the BJP, and it is these forces that determine and direct the discourse and the agenda. Thus, not only is the autonomous voice of the Dalit critique is lost in such formulation, there is a danger of the Dalit remaining a perennial marginalized 'other' of the Brahminic 'centre'. Hence, the Dalit movement asserting for autonomy of the Dalit voice in the socio-political sphere cannot be a long-term ally to the Hindutva forces. At this juncture, let us try to understand as to why the developments within the Dalit movement have led to attempts of collaboration with ideological adversaries such as the BJP and Shiv Sena.

It is also necessary to note that the political aspirations of Dalit communities outside the Ambedkarist fold, the perception of the Dalit question shared by forces advancing politics of issues such as the Left, and the feeling of loss of possibilities of sharing political power among Dalit activists, will have to seen as factors contributing to the attempts of alliances with the ideological adversaries like the BJP and the Shiv Sena. Earlier, we noted that the Dalit assertion in the beginning of the twentieth century was expressed in the form of assertion of Dalit humanity in terms of the right to dignity and equal humanity. Thus, various ideological 'adi' movements sought to recover Dalit history as rooted in non-brahminic egalitarian framework. However, the rise of Ambedkarism saw the question of Dalit humanity as rooted in the oppressive and exploitative structures of domination; hence, the Dalit movement during the Ambedkarist phase pursued the politics of issues, and attempted to extend this concern to the politics of issues of the larger marginalized categories. However, in the post-Ambedkar phase the focus of the Dalit movement came to be restricted in achieving spaces of political offices and issues of identity. As a result, the Dalit movement lost connections with the issues confronting both Dalit masses and other marginalized sections. Here it should be highlighted that the efforts and strength of the Dalit movement was spent on struggling with the traditional issues of the practice of untouchability and caste discrimination. The growing consciousness among Dalit masses, both in rural and urban areas, and assertion against the oppressive caste system gave rise to further cases of atrocities, caste discrimination and social boycott. Thus resulting in Dalit struggle was forced to engage with the issues of discrimination resulting from traditional social order. This is also a telling comment on the nature of caste rigidities and prevalence of caste consciousness even in Maharashtra that is seen as a land of rationalist, reformist and even working class movement and consciousness.

Indeed the Dalit Panthers did try to infuse a new consciousness and attempted to provide a broader content to the category 'Dalit'. However, in the absence of a stable organized structure, the Dalit Panthers also become willing victims of tactics of the politics of appropriation.

Some of its leaders of DP tried to share political space with the Congress, whereas others, that too leading ideologues, have ironically, seen possibilities of politics of masses in formations such as Shiv Sena. Of course, political parties such as Congress, Shiv Sena and BJP are keen to share a political space with the Dalits. Such a concern however, emanates more from claiming Dalit votes rather than commitment to annihilate traditional caste order and ushering of progressive social change.

Moreover, it has contributed to creation of claimants for political power among Dalit communities, which in turn has led to further fragmentation of the Dalit movement and the weakening of the possibility of the politics of issues and politics of emancipation. On the other hand, political formations claiming allegiance to left ideology and attempting to articulate the politics of issues have shared a problematic relationship with the Dalit movement. Though many Dalit youth are active in Left political formations and Left ideologues have now 'recognized' caste as context of oppression, Left politics have traditionally seen Dalit movement as sectarian, pro-British and divisive in character.

Moreover, ideologically left parties have privileged the category of class over that of caste as sites of exploitation and oppression; and also as a source of revolutionary politics. Thus left formations saw class as a subsuming category and held that the class struggle alone would lead to revolutionary emancipatory politics.

There is ground to believe that such a denial of caste as a site of oppression and exploitation was a result of the left ideologues' social location. On the other hand, Dalit activists encountering discrimination ignored the fact that such discrimination was also emanated and reiterated in exploitative and oppressive structures of economic domination. One of the most serious challenges that the politics of accommodation throws before Dalit movements is the growing atrocity against Dalits. The politics of unfair 'inclusion' (practices of inclusion in which Dalits are denied any say as active agents of change) and politics of 'accommodation', which creates possibilities of "sharing" of power at the behest of the ruling class interests, do not allow struggle against atrocities, as perpetrators of atrocities could be "sharing" power with the accommodated Dalit leadership at local levels. During the last two decades brutal atrocities have been encountered by the Dalits who are gradually assuming self respect and resisting discrimination at the hands of the dominant castes.

The lynching of Dalits in Jajjhar in Hariyana, the perpetual on going Dalit carnage in the Tamilnadu since the eighties, not to mention the caste "conflicts" in UP and Bihar, have been part of traumatic Dalit public memory. While the spurt of brutal atrocities against Dalits during the last two decades in Tamilnadu, Hariyana, and other parts of the country could be understood on account of relatively recent awakening of assertive Dalit consciousness leading to assertion for social mobility and equal humanity, in Maharashtra, due to a long history of Dalit revolt, Khairlanji kind of atrocities, public humiliation, rape and brutal killing of a Dalit family, were unexpected and hence shocking. Of course in Maharashtra too we find new spurt of atrocities against Dalits since the nineties taking place in regions such as Marathwada, where, however, the targets of violence are not necessarily erstwhile Mahras, but the Matangs. The cruel burning of a Matang youth Dilip Shendage and hacking of Dadaroa Dongre, came fore as new phase in atrocities against Dalits.

THE DALIT POLITICAL STRATEGY

Both historically and currently Dalits have adopted four strategies, singly or in combination, in order to attain these ends. The first and most dominant has been the political strategy of gaining power either as an end in itself (if you have power, others come to you and you do not have to go begging to them) or as a means to other ends (*e.g.*, greater economic and educational opportunities).

However, Dalits have been divided over whether to pursue political power independently of other castes or in alliance with those members of other castes and communities whose interests and ideals are close to their own. For example, there are at present Dalit members of Parliament and of State Legislative Assemblies, as well as Dalit party workers, in virtually all the major political parties, including the Prime Minister's Bharatiya Janata Party, which in its traditionalist Hindu ideology, is quite anti-Dalit.

There are also exclusively Dalit political parties at the regional level and two Dalit-led political parties, the Bahujan Samaj Party of Kanshi Ram and Ms. Mayawati as well as the Republican Party of India, have members of Parliament as well. The Dalit debate within and between the various parties over whether to get whatever share of power Dalits can through whatever alliances are most expedient or to maintain pressure from outside on those in power by maintaining some ideological and programmatic unity, at least among Dalits themselves if not with other disadvantaged groups (tribals, religious minorities, women, the poor in general) as well, has yet to be resolved.

As this brief description suggests, there is little political unity among Dalits at the present time and many are wondering out loud whether the political process can deliver what Dalits have every right to expect from it.

THEIR ECONOMIC STRATEGY

The second strategy has been economic. Not only are Dalits extremely poor (almost half of them living below the poverty line as compared to less than one-third of the rest of the population) but they are also almost totally dependent upon the dominant castes for their livelihoods as agricultural or urban labour.

Thus many Dalits have sought greater economic independence, both as an end in itself and as a means to other ends (*e.g.*, political power, educational opportunity). During the past decade a good number of international development agencies, both religious and secular, have also adopted this strategy by funding a variety of grassroots Dalit organizations engaged in a range of community development activities. These activities focus on such things as small-scale industries, teaching new skills, educating Dalits on how to take advantage of government development assistance, developing cooperatives.

The task is enormous. Over 75% of the Dalit population is still rural and so these activities have to be carried out village by village. They also face opposition within each village from members of the dominant castes who want to keep Dalits as an impoverished and dependent source of cheap labour.

THE SOCIAL STRATEGY

A third strategy, which can be described as social, has two components. Education is one. If Dalits become literate or even educated, they can move beyond unskilled labour, earn more money, and so gain greater respect. The other is making life-style changes which get rid of those practices considered especially "low" or "polluting" and substituting those of the "higher" castes instead.

For example, they should give up eating certain meats and cease working at certain jobs (*e.g.*, cleaning latrines). The aim of education and life-style change has been to remove some of the more obvious reasons for anti-Dalit prejudice. The social strategy was adopted by the Christian missions over a century ago and it still dominates the churches' thinking about improving the Dalits' lot. Today there are churches which are not only giving special priority to Dalits in some of their institutions of formal education, but are also developing joboriented, nonformal educational projects to enhance skill development. The social strategy has also undergirded much of the affirmative action policy built into India's constitution. The assumption is that if Dalits get educated, get better jobs, and earn more money so as to raise their class status, then their caste status (measured in terms of mutually respectful and friendly relations with members of "higher" castes) would improve also.

The problem has been that the government (controlled by the dominant "higher" castes) has never fully implemented all the progressive affirmative action legislation it has passed into law. This is a source of great resentment, especially among educated Dalits.

THE RELIGIOUS STRATEGY

The fourth strategy has been religious in nature. Its moderate form involves reform from within one's own religious tradition. For example, some Hindu sects have renounced caste hierarchy and some Hindu reformers, Gandhi being the best known, have sought to "uplift" the Untouchables. The more radical religious option, however, has been conversion to another, more egalitarian religion. For example, over the past 125 years, so many Dalits have converted to Christianity that today the majority of the Christian population of India is Dalit!

Following the induction of their great leader, Dr. B. R. Ambedkar, into the Buddhist Sangha in 1956, several million Dalits have become Buddhists. What a new religion offered to the Dalits was a new identity defined by religion rather than by caste, as well as a more egalitarian religious counterculture. This has been only partially successful. No matter what goes on in Christian or Buddhist circles, most Indians still think in terms of caste and so simply assume that anyone who is a Christian or Buddhist is a Dalit. Moreover, both Christian and Buddhist Dalits were denied the affirmative action benefits and protections granted to other Dalits; in 1990 the Buddhist Dalits became eligible and Dalit Christians are still ineligible. By denying these to Christian (and Muslim) Dalits the government is in fact providing strong economic disincentives to conversion and strong economic incentives to Christian Dalits to return to the Hindu fold.

THE CHRISTIAN DALITS

As this brief analysis suggests, the present situation of Dalits in India is complex and confusing. There are no obvious, agreed upon solutions to the problems which the Dalits face; the way forward in the Dalit struggle is by no means clear. However, there are a few trends visible among Christian Dalits which are quite important for Christian thinking on this subject. First and foremost among these is a growing acknowledgment that they are Dalits and that conversion to Christianity has not really changed that significant fact of their lives, despite hopes and promises to the contrary. Most Christian Dalits thus have a dual social and psychological identity, Christian as well as Dalit, and have to live with the tensions built into that dual identity.

A second trend is an increasing assertion of Dalit identity as a positive thing, a source of pride rather than of shame. In this they (rightly) challenge pervasive cultural norms. One expression of this assertiveness is Dalit Theology; another is a harsh critique of those missionary and Indian Church leaders who, in their efforts to "Indianize" the Church, have equated "Indian" culture with Brahmanic instead of Dalit culture. (One reason why Dalit Christians have resisted a lot of efforts to "Indianize" the theology and liturgy of the Church is because they are fed up with the Brahmanic culture which they converted to get away from!)

Perhaps most obvious of all are the persistent efforts to "raise the caste issue" and exorcise the demon of caste discrimination (which is "Legion" and takes many forms) within the churches themselves. Until this is done, the churches cannot embody much "good news" for their own Dalit members, let alone for other Dalits. Finally, there are Christian Dalits who are staunch advocates of each of the four Dalit strategies and are working hard at implementing those strategies. We see no evidence that one strategy, or even one combination of strategies, has become clearly predominant in Dalit Christian circles.

What does seem evident, however, is that over the past two decades Christian Dalits are working more closely with other Dalits to achieve common aims and objectives than was true earlier. "Dalit Solidarity" is an end and means much desired but difficult to achieve; yet many Dalit Christian leaders have come to the conclusion that their Christian hopes for their own people cannot be realised in isolation from the realisation of the hopes of all the Dalit people.

POLITICS OF ACCOMMODATION

Despite these early concerns with the politics of the issues of the broader marginalized constituency, the post-Ambedkar Dalit movement, with an exception of the Dadasaheb Gaikwad led satyagraha of landless agricultural labour, came to be entrapped in the politics of accommodation.

The educated leaders of the Dalit movement during the post-Ambedkar era pursued the dream of political power as a panacea for addressing the Dalit question. They deliberately vulgarized Ambedkar who had exhorted them to be the ruling community in the particular context of emphasizing the importance of political power as 'a key to all problems'.

Running after the mirage of political power through electoral process, necessarily led the Dalit leaders astray from meaningful emancipatory politics of the oppressed and trapped them into the ruling class net. Ruling class politics thus largely subsumed Dalit politics and the Dalit movement. The sole expressions of radical Dalit assertion for dignity and some possibilities of engaging with broader emancipatory struggles of the marginalized could be seen in the agitations launched by Dadasaheb Gaikwad. He led the Satryagraha of The Bhumihinas or the landless and worked on concrete issues of marginalization.

Absorbed in the Congress politics of accommodation, the Dalit movement lost its edge as a possible vehicle of the politics of the marginalized. Thus the Republican Party of India, with a tie up with the Congress, resulted in both accommodation of Dalit politics and marginalization of Dalit politics from its larger focus. This continues to be one of the faces of Dalit politics even today. Indeed, the emergence of Dalit Panthers led to a resurgence of the Dalit consciousness.

Dalit youth, inspired by Dalit Panthers, criticized 'accommodated' Dalit leadership that was ineffective in addressing the atrocities the Dalits encountered. They sought to damn the brahminical social order and dreamt of radical change leading to a just India. Moreover, as pointed out earlier, Dalit Panthers attempted to provide a broad content to the category Dalit by articulating the concerns of Dalits, landless agricultural labourers, marginalized peasantry, toiling working masses and women, as represented by the term 'Dalit', and attempted to provide a broader conception of struggle.

However, despite this, Dalit Panthers too were soon to be trapped in the politics of accommodation. Thus, though Dalit Panthers presented an ideologically conscious Dalit rebel, who challenged the existing Dalit leadership for being ineffective in arresting growing atrocities on Dalits and also succumbing to politics of accommodation, they themselves were soon to be accommodated and contained in the gamut of politics of interest. Moreover, despite contributing to the resurgence of Dalit consciousness that gave rise to Dalit revolt in other parts of India, in terms of acquiring political power through electoral politics, Dalit Panthers too were unsuccessful.

This marked the shift in the Dalit agenda: from social movement of the marginalized to political formation to achieve political power through electorates for some Dalit castes. Further, this also marks the beginning of politics of interest in Dalit politics and the new equation: The political power is controlled by dominant political parties that represent dominance of the upper and dominant castes even in the democratic set up. And such oppressive power is based on appropriated Dalit votes. Hence, it was felt that Dalits should politically consolidate their votes and also articulate *Bahujanwad* in the realm of electoral politics. Furthermore, it was felt that only through political power that is gaining seats in assemblies and parliament could the Dalits hope to change the oppressive order of Manuwad.

DALIT MOVEMENT AND POLITICS OF IDENTITY

The initial concern of the Dalit movement for securing dignity and justice was expressed as the Dalit assertion for human rights. Dalits sought to enter Hindu temples in order to assert that as human being they too had equal rights to temple-entry, which was denied to them by the system of Untouchability. The Mahad Temple Entry Satyagraha, the Nasik Kalaram Mandir Satrygraha, and Parwati Temple Entry in Poona were some examples of these struggles. Another expression came in the form of assertion for Dalit identity, which was to be constructed defiantly outside the framework of Brahmanism, through a rediscovery of Dalit history and culture located in an egalitarian order, real or imaginary, as opposed to the iniquitous brahminical social order. This ideological assertion reflected in various 'adi' movements in India, namely, 'adi-Dharam' movement in Punjab, and 'adi-Dravida', 'adi-Andhra', 'adi-Kannada' movements in South India advanced an ideological claim that Dalits were the original inhabitants of this country—*a la* sons of the soil—and belonged to a superior egalitarian cultural tradition. In Uttar Pradesh, for instance, Dalit groups such as Mehtars, Bhangis, Chamars, Doms, and Jatvavs claimed that they were Buddhists, questioned caste discrimination against them and asserted that they were the original inhabitants of India who were conquered by deceit and manipulations by the Brahmins coming from outside. In the south the ideological assertion was seen in Iyoti Thass' attempts of conversion to Buddhism. From 1870s he had initiated movement of Buddhist conversion among the untouchables.

Of course, apart from this assertion of human identity in the traditional and religious framework, rediscovery of traditions and religiosity, the Dalit movement in later years approached the question of justice in the modern secular context. During the Ambedkarian struggle the ideological basis for Dalit assertion came from ideals of justice, liberty, equality and fraternity based these ideals. He engaged with the colonial state in the ideological framework of modernity and advanced the untouchables' claims for dignity in the language of rights. This was seen in Ambedkar's continuous critique of Brahmanism, its philosophical foundations, its ideal of Chaturvanya, in the language of denial of Untouchables and women into the membership of community of humanity. Even Ambedkar's articulation and reconstruction of Buddhism, to which he converted with his five lakhs followers in 1956, exhibits both critique of Brahmanism and socially embedded character of Buddhism. Buddha's Dhamma for instance was fundamentally social and that Buddha advocated reconstruction of society on the principles of justice, equality and reason as guiding principles of social organization. The democratic values that Dr. Ambedkar adhered to and the parliamentary form of governance that he advocated had roots in Buddha's Sangha. Further during 1930s Ambedkar was working towards a broader unity of the oppressed based on their social and economic experiences of marginalization. While speaking before the G.P.I railway workers he had pointed out that the oppressed in this country have to struggle against two enemies: Brahmanism and Capitalism. Through the Independent Labour Party he had advanced a broad category of the oppressed–—Dalits, marginalized peasantry and unorganised sector working classes.

This ideological legacy was later reinvented during the radical assertion of Dalit youth during early 1970s. Following the Black Panthers of America, these creative writers named themselves as Dalit Panthers. The panthers who experienced alienation from the ruling class oriented post-Ambedkarite Dalit politics, were disturbed on the issue of growing atrocities on Dalits in rural areas and sought to radicalised culture and politics as tools of resistance. It is they who gave currency to the term Dalit and also posited it with the new broad content—the referring to untouchables, landless agricultural labours and urban working classes and women. The panthers stormed the sites of atrocities and sought to reinvent self-respect and struggle as means of addressing faced by Dalits. Despite the fact that Panthers were to later split on egoistic expressions of right interpretation of Ambedkarism, Dhasal going the Marxist way and Dhale sticking to Buddhism seen as opposed to Marx, the movement gave rise to new literature that brought with it expressions of altogether different world unknown to the middle class Brahmanical taste, and one that depicted pain, oppression and resistance. This literary movement inspired political and literary movements in other parts of the country. This was very briefly in seen Gujarat and later in Karnataka in the form of Dalit Sangharsha Samiti. During the last two decades Dalit Panther is once again being reinvented in Tamilnadu as aggressive stance towards Dalits atrocities by the dominant land owning backward classes.

DALIT MOVEMENT AND POLITICS OF ISSUES

The Dalit movement in the 1930s saw a shift from temple-entry satyagrahas to rights to education, employment and political representation as necessary prerequisites for securing justice. Concluding the temple-entry satyagraha, Dr. Ambedkar pointed out that Dalits were not interested in entering temples of a religion that teaches inequality and injustice as part of religious duty, that they carried out temple-entry satyagrahas only to assert their equal humanity. He also pointed out that justice could be ensured only through struggle for education, employment and political representation. Thus Dalit movement articulated the question of justice and dignity in the context of a modern secular framework, rather than the traditional religious mode. Thus Dalits campaigned for education of Dalit children, and had to struggle to end discriminatory attitude of teachers and school authorities. However, the question of political representation, the question of separate electorate for Dalits, brought Ambedkar to the bitter and well-known controversy with Gandhi and the Congress. This also shows that perhaps caste Hindu hegemony would have 'tolerated' Dalits entering temples, and occupying a designated space in religious structures, but Dalit assertion for a share in modern resources capable of initiating social change and thereby undermining the authority of Brahminism was visualized as a real threat to brahminical hegemony.

Thus the politics of issues, a concern for a share in the resources in modern structures (not mere acceptance and benevolence) as possible mechanism of empowerment and change was the focus of the Dalit movement. Of course, the Dalit concern for politics of issues also saw the other oppressed such as marginalized peasantry and unorganized working class as victims of exploitation and oppression. It is important to note that while other working class struggles, especially in Bombay, were campaigning for concerns of workers in formal organized sectors, Ambedkar's Independent Labour Party (ILP) focused on unorganized sector working classes. Thus with the formation and struggles led by the ILP, the Dalit movement exhibited a concern for politics of the issues of the larger marginalized constituency, which also presented a possibility of the broader conception of politics of emancipation.

Further in addition to these struggles Ambedkar also stressed on education as a possible vehicle of social change and life with dignity. Towards this end he initiated a people's Education Society that stated colleges in Bombay and later an institutional campus in Aurangabad (Nagsenvan). These institutions, during his lifetime, were best centres of learning. They attracted best teachers and zealous students. It is through these efforts that educated youth, which were to occupy positions in government employment, was trained. In Marathwada, the PE Society's campus was to later become a centre of literary movement in the form of 'Asmitadarsha'. Of course in contemporary times the glory of PE society has vanished thanks to the inefficient and irresponsible administration.

LIMITS OF AMBEDKAR'S QUEST FOR LIBERATION

In a limited sense, Ambedkar's conception of equality and justice derive from the liberal vision and tradition. But given the context of the colonial state, he departs from that tradition and innovates thinking about justice in a remarkably novel way. There are three components of Ambedkar's theory of distributive justice:

(a) equality of opportunity for all citizens
(b) critique of Hindu society based on an autonomous ideology, and
(c) establishment of a casteless society by removing oppression and domination.

Ambedkar accepted a legal and social conception of equality, which call the formal principle of a liberal conception of equality. It entails the elimination of arbitrary advantages in a social and economic system, irrespective of whether the inequality results from one's choice or that of another.

What he also found desirable was the idea of equality of opportunity for all human beings in the social and political sphere. It was further linked to his argument for more abundant political and civil liberty for dalits. On his account this requires that any government treat all those in its charge as equals, that is, as entitled to equal concern and respect. This idea of equality of opportunity as an example of the maximisation of equal liberty. In this view, to demand equality of opportunity is to demand the removal of obstacles that stand in the way of an individual realising his potential.

Ambedkar's initial programmes attempt to integrate the dalits into society and politics through 'modern' political institutions. He put his faith in the constitution and the legislative process, as well as the representative bodies to correct social and economic injustice. Ambedkar's ideal for the low caste groups was to raise their educational standard so that they may overcome the social disadvantages imposed by their birth, and be in a position to use political power in resolving problems of injustice. His adaptation of western concepts is reflected in the way he used to justify political rights of the dalits based on democracy, fraternity and liberty, in Marathi speeches; he conveyed the implication of these concepts in a single word, manuski which means 'humanness'.

While Ambedkar saw the prescriptive uses of the concept of equality in moral and political arguments as quite useful, he was conscious of the inequality of treatment based on caste and tradition. To bring about a more substantial equality must involve treating people differently which is contrary to the formal principle. For such reasons he advocated a separatist policy for the dalits which might accentuate caste distinctions at an initial stage but eventually make these identities unimportant. Therefore, Ambedkar insisted on the right to take into account the special claims of certain communities which had for centuries been excluded from position of equality and respect.

Departing fundamentally from the individualist premise of the equality principle he proposes:

(1) A theory of rights as legal entitlements casting obligations on the members of civil society. The 'untouchables' had a set of rights and the state a duty to eradicate discriminatory practices. Norms of nondiscrimination apply not only to government but also to civil society–corporations, schools, places of worship, etc.

Where the rights theorists of the 17th and 18th century tended to regard right as a faculty of possession, Ambedkar encourages us to stress the relational aspect of rights. The important point here is that these rights are put forward as important elements or vital ingredients in a fully realised human life. The core argument is that members of the group suffer because they are neither accorded the same respect nor afforded the same opportunities as other persons or groups. They are prevented from realising their capacities, in other words, they are not treated with full respect and dignity.

(2) The basic human needs of the dalits were not only material (wealth, occupational mobility) but non-material; all have the right to be human and the right to live with dignity and self-respect. Although, he stressed the need for reservation in representative institutions, this is only to acquire equality in other goods. For such reasons, he extended his theory to cover such goods as self-respect, power and honour.

Therefore, Ambedkar accepted the premise of equality but advocated group-based politics to achieve that goal. The first is constitutive and the second derivative. Ambedkar eloquently pleaded the case the necessary priority of community claims over individual rights on the grounds that these departures from formal equality could be justified in the following way:

The Anti-discriminatory Theme: The anti-discriminatory principle's main purpose is to prevent private practices and legal procedures from stigmatising the individuals involved. This was viewed as necessary given that structural forms of oppression against the dalits were well entrenched. To remedy this social malaise Ambedkar raises the possibilities for political participation of dalits through reservations. It was his view that a legislature 'mainly composed of high caste men, will not pass a law removing untouchability, sanctioning inter-caste marriages, removing the ban of the use of public streets, public temples, public schools.'

The Reparation Theme: The other idea was that of historic injustice suffered by the dalits. This theme was proposed to offset the systematic and cumulative deprivations suffered by lower castes in the past. Ambedkar argues that some oppressive cultural practices and social institutions result in injustice and accumulated disabilities for untouchables. He was aware of the conceptual incoherence these themes gave rise to when applied to policy issues. But this is a derivative political position. In fact, he was to warn of the possibility that these special claims might eat the general rule of equality altogether. Unlike anyone else, he pursued the argument that "the constitution should not only declare that we shall have specific rights that every community will have, but that the constitution should provide ways and means by which we shall be protected in the exercise of these rights".

The second component of Ambedkar's theory of distributive justice was the construction of an 'autonomous' ideology opposed in fundamental respects to the traditional ideology of varna. The central problem, for him, in this regard was the formulation of a counter-ideology which can bring about radical social change; he was concerned to fight for a new society based on equal concern for all. This is evident from his critique of the Hindu community on the following basis:

(1) the community as unequal;

(2) the community as based on segregation both territorial and ideological;
(3) the closed nature of the community; and
(4) the distinction between the public and private sphere.

The first aspect of his critique was directed at the theory of 'chaturvarnya' which makes the principle of graded inequality 'the basis for determining the terms of associated life as between the four varnas'. This is not merely notional, but legal and penal: under this system the sudra is subjected to innumerable ignominies and disabilities so as to prevent him from raising above the conditions fixed for him by law. The second aspect draws attention to the permanent segregation of people in the Hindu community based on the ideological principle of purity and impurity. He rejects the territorial segregation which accompanies this. While distinguishing between the rights of untouchables and the pure he raises some fundamental questions of citizenship: "But the impurity of the 50-60 million of the untouchables of India, quite unlike the impurity arising from birth, death, etc., is permanent: The Hindus who touch them and become polluted thereby can become pure by undergoing purificatory ceremonies. But there is nothing which can make the untouchables purer... It is a case of permanent, hereditary stain which nothing can cleanse".

The third aspect of his critique is directed at the nature of closed religious communities without entry points. In 'Mr. Gandhi and the Emancipation of Untouchables' (1945), he points out that the legislative majorities and minorities are political categories which are fluid subject to the process of party formation and electoral practices. But the Hindu and the untouchable relationship cannot be captured by these categories. Their difference is that 'they are separated by a fundamental and deadly antagonism'. Hindus and untouchables are not fluid categories but they are 'fixed as permanent communities'.

He argues against nationalist attempts to define what it means to have equal opportunities – in terms of having the same distribution of results for major social groups in the public shaper. He revealed the inequality in the social sphere arising out of the nature of closed religious communities, because "most people do not realise that society can practise tyranny and oppression against an individual in far greater degree than a government can... What punishment in the penal code is comparable in its magnitude and its severity to excommunication?"

On the basis of these propositions, Ambedkar's solution for the dalits – the establishment of a casteless society – went beyond the liberal framework he was located in.

From a liberal point of view, Ambedkar was arguing for an individual's freedom to associate; to form communities and to live by their own terms based on equal concern. A corollary of this is that the individuals should be free to dissociate from such communities. Again, his view placed great weight on the nature of communities as voluntary associations. But, since membership is determined by birth in a Hindu community, rather than by deliberate choice, it is a coercive association.

There is no option of entry for those born outside–even though groups might seek to redefine their boundaries. While superficially attractive, the liberal view of the self as a totally unencumbered and radically free subject seemed plagued with difficulties.

This eventually led Ambedkar to locate the distinction between a (voluntary) political community within which an individual exercises his legal rights, and a (coercive) cultural community within which individuals could not even formulate their aims. People who have the same rights to citizenship may not have the same cultural rights. A political community, argued Ambedkar, may not be coextensive with one cultural community, as is envisaged by the nation state. For Ambedkar the two forms of community do not always coincide. This distinction leads him to argue that individuals are free to leave–to renounce– membership and to reconstitute their own community. Here Ambedkar was mistaken in his assertions about liberalism's implications: there was no good reason for any liberal to support him in this. But, it is this very justification that inspired him to seek conversion to Buddhism.

In Ambedkar's opinion the transition from British to Hindu masters signified no emancipatory potential for the masses. The fight for a national cause, according to him, misconstrues the role of Swaraj: "In the fight for Swaraj, you fight with the whole nation on your side. In this, you have to fight against the whole nation and that too, on your own... In my opinion, only when the Hindu society becomes a casteless society that it can hope to have strength enough to defend itself. Without such internal strength, Swaraj for Hindus may turn out to be only a step towards slavery."

It is this total programme of societal transformation which constituted his conception of Swaraj. Swaraj was not just freedom from the British, it was a freedom based on distributive justice.

Ambedkar's critical dialogue with some Congress leaders and his struggles to reform Hindu society occurred within a colonial context. His struggle is not with faith but with false brahmanical beliefs, not with religion but with Brahmin domination of Indian society. He portrays the nature of the caste system in our society in particular using it to show that Hinduism was incapable of establishing a just political and social order. His view differed from other nationalist leaders and social reformers in that he never claimed higher caste status for untouchables, nor did he ever invoke another claim – that untouchables were pre-Aryan, the original settlers of the land or claimed spiritual equality for lower castes within the Hindu tradition. And most importantly his reforms were not directed towards the caste- Hindus. Unlike other critiques of Brahmin domination and caste hierarchy which focus on the unity argument, Ambedkar's critique provides a justice argument against the caste system.

Most nationalists argued that their country was fragmented, deeply divided into a large number of castes, sub-castes and local communities; that is why the Hindus had failed to develop a sense of mutual concern and social compassion. Ambedkar's theory of caste oppression focuses not only the distributive paradigm (allocation of material goods such as resources, income, wealth or the distribution of social positions, such as jobs) as many contemporary liberal theories do, but also brings out the issues of decision-making (representative institutions for the dalits) division of labour (occupational mobility), and culture that bear on distributive justice but were often ignored in national assessments of their social structure.

This argument was premised on two views: (a) the problems of dalits would always have a particularity that could not be subsumed under class or national mobilisation; (b) the status of the dalits was 'irreversible' if they remained isolated within Hinduism. Therefore, he formulated Dalit liberation in terms of two solutions–political assertion through separate electorates and ideological liberation from Hinduism by converting to Buddhism.

Unfortunately, the very cogency and persuasiveness of his arguments raise questions as to the broader contours of his thesis. Dissatisfied with the dominant proposals for the reform of the caste system, Ambedkar undertakes a recovery of Buddhism as a religion that relates to individuals with dignity and respect. However, Ambedkar's point that Buddhism provides the needed theoretical framework to understand Indian politics has its weaknesses. Indeed, by spending considerable energy exploring key conceptions in Buddhism such as Ahimsa, rebirth, karma, etc., Ambedkar leaves us wondering how helpful Buddhism is if the terminology is so open to interpretation. Behind this solution lay the laudable ideal that responsibility for removing group identity status lies with the dalits themselves, not with the larger dominant society. But it is an explanation that completely ignores the pernicious effects of casteism in the Indian social fabric. On the flip side, Ambedkar's 'self-help' ideology perpetuates the mythical notion of a 'monolithic' Dalit community which made it possible for them to confront other parties. But this political legitimisation also pre-empts questions of interest differentiation among the dalits. This takes us to my final observations. All this is not to deny that in his critique of the caste system, Ambedkar is clearly arguing for expanding the rights of citizenship to the 'untouchables'. At a more substantive level he is pushing the case for a casteless society without oppression. How was this possible in practical politics?

These two perspectives are contradictory if the objectives they focus upon – the promotion of political and social equality, the abolition of the caste system – are conceived as aims in themselves.

But unlike the abolition of the caste system, in Ambedkar's writings, that liberal politics with their emphasis on rights, equality of concern and respect, or freedom to associate can sensibly be defended as more than an instrumental objective. He believed that the more an individual's rights are restricted due to his caste location–for example by constricting the mobility in occupation, of residence, of religion, etc.–the less possibility is there of social and distributive justice.

The principles underlying the caste system unlock the mystery to the inegalitarian distributive outcomes in other spheres. It is an important consideration and one that plays a key role in what is regarded as the only cogent justification for removing caste system in Ambedkar's work. He poses the question whether separation, in some fashion, from the larger body politic, may produce more tangible results than have previous strategies (Gandhi's and Shinde's) aimed at integrating them into the system. Hence, his arguments for separate electorates for dalits should be seen as derivative; equal opportunity in liberal politics was not his ultimate goal. In fact, he wishes to achieve much more.

In the most general sense, the Dalit community is reconstructed by analysing the structural antagonism and conflict within the Hindu community: the idea of shared meanings, of normative frames and cultural values is questioned. By developing a theory of oppression of the untouchables by locating their exploitation, marginalisation and powerlessness, he highlights the structural and institutional relations that delimit the lives of the dalits. He also gives prominence to their cultural oppression which means how the dominant meanings of our society stereotype one group. Ambedkar always thought his account of the role of caste system and its ultimate demise was superior to any other. And as history has shown, he was too optimistic in his predictions and not clear enough in this vision. However, mistaken he was in this analysis and however short-sighted he might appear to many scholars, with respect to the discourse of nationalism, the chief application of Ambedkar's political thought may be seen today to reside in his reflections on social and distributive justice. The subsequent course of Indian politics was to prove him correct; it was not the nation state but its opposite, – irreconcilable political clashes between religious communities and caste-wars that would become the order of the day.

AMBEDKAR'S REPLY TO GANDHI

A village was on fire, and the wind that swirled the flames high above the ancient banyan tree carried with it an unmistakable sound: a lone woman crying over a corpse. It was grief at its most elemental, purer than the wind and fire devouring this village in the dark night of southern India. The woman wailed and shuddered while cradling her dead husband. She is an untouchable, and so was her young husband, Perumal Radhakrishnan. An invisible line divides this village, called Karisakulam, and thousands of others like it across India, separating the untouchables—those beneath Hinduism's rigid caste hierarchy—from the upper-castes. Radhakrishnan had crossed that line. As a leader of the village's untouchables, he had dared to defy the higher-caste community of Thevars.

That evening, Radhakrishnan, a thin and bare-chested man, had ambled over to the upper-caste side to watch the evening news on the village's only TV, rigged up under the stars. While he sat there, four men from the Thevar caste pinned him to the dirt while a fifth man pulled out a sword and butchered him. Enraged by the killing, the untouchables burned down the houses of all the Thevars in the village and slaughtered their animals. They even smashed the TV; its fragments lay scattered next to Radhakrishnan's corpse. Then the untouchables took fright—they were afraid the Thevars would rouse the upper-castes from nearby villages and seek revenge—and so they fled into a wasteland of thorn bushes, leaving Radhakrishnan's widow alone, silhouetted against the flames as she rocked her husband's corpse.

A few years ago, these untouchables would have dragged away Radhakrishnan's body and cowered in their mud-huts, resigned to their subhuman status. But now, scenes of defiance like the rampage at Karisakulam are taking place throughout India. The country's more than 150 million untouchables (who prefer to call themselves Dalits, Hindi for "the oppressed") are striking back. They are instigating a social revolution that is long overdue, one whose aim is to topple the 2,500-year-old juggernaut of the Hindu caste system. Increasingly, Dalits are challenging Hinduism's tenets that a person is condemned to his caste—determining whether he becomes a doctor or a scavenger, whom he marries, which village well he drinks from, and his social standing in a complex, ordered hierarchy—all by his actions in a past life. In this rebellion, the Dalit's main weapons are education and the vote. But in some rural areas, where resistance to their demands for equality is entrenched, they are taking up the gun. "Power was gradual

By slipping through the hands of the dominant castes for several decades," says Ashis Nandy, director of the Centre for the Study of Developing Societies in New Delhi. "It had already slipped down to the lower castes and is now reaching the Dalits. This will help democracy." Or will it? Consider the caste warfare and chaos now engulfing the northern states of Bihar and Uttar Pradesh, where Dalits are trying to grab what they believe is theirs after so many centuries.

Dalits make up one-sixth of India's population, yet only a few have managed to occupy top places in society as politicians, lawyers and scientists. A poor Dalit from Kerala, Kocheril Raman Narayanan, encountered discrimination in school and work. And yet this year he rose to become India's President, the first untouchable to hold that post. Before, Dalits had to support their landlords' candidates or they were beaten away from the polling booths when they tried to vote; now they are asserting themselves with the ballot, and their newfound power has jolted all of the national political parties, especially the long-ruling Congress. Ram Vilas Paswan, a Dalit member of the Janata Dal Party, is now serving in the United Front cabinet. Twice now, a Dalit woman, Mayawati, has been elected Chief Minister of populous Uttar Pradesh state, though her last six months in office were squandered in a vendetta against high-caste rivals. Says Mayawati: "Earlier I had thought it would take longer, but change is now so rapid that in a few years we will have a Dalit Prime Minister in New Delhi."

Politicians and their promises offer little, however, to the most radical Dalits. They would prefer an armed insurrection, and they are willing to settle scores with higher-caste landlords using guns and home-made bombs. Says Ram Prit, a 75-year-old Dalit labourer in Bihar: "If you keep pouring water into a rat hole, the rats will come out fighting."

Religious sanction has allowed this apartheid to survive Muslim invasions, British colonialism and even 50 years of democracy. Defenders of the caste system usually cite a verse from the Upanishads, Hinduism's ancient sacred texts: "Those whose conduct on earth has given pleasure can hope to enter a pleasant womb, that is, the womb of a Brahman or a woman of the princely class. But those whose conduct on earth has been foul can expect to enter a foul and stinking womb, that is the womb of a bitch, or a pig, or an outcaste." A hymn from the sacred Rig Veda describes how this human stratification came about: a cosmic giant, Purusha, sacrificed parts of his body to create mankind. "His mouth became the Brahman, his arms were made into the Warrior (Kshatriya), his thighs the People (Vaishiya) and from his feet the Servants (Sudra) were born." Through the centuries, these four main divisions (called varnas), were silvered into more than 3,000 sub-castes, based on the purity of their professions. A goldsmith is higher up the ladder than a blacksmith, and a priestly Brahman, whose rituals bring him in touch with the gods, is highest of all. The untouchables, however, are off the ladder completely. By origin, many were India's dark-skinned first inhabitants, conquered by Aryans and assigned such awful tasks as burning bodies, skinning carcasses and removing "night soil"—human excrement—from latrines. For thousands of years, outcastes were burdened with these denigrating chores.

In many villages, untouchables still live in poverty and subjugation. They are forbidden from entering temples or drinking from the same wells as upper-castes. It was customary for higher-caste landlords to deflower a Dalit bride on her wedding night, before her helpless groom. (To cleanse himself after such a dalliance, according to the more than 2,500-year-old Laws of Manu, an upper-caste man must give alms and make "daily mutterings" of prayers.) These Hindu rules are far from evenhanded: even today in some parts of India, if an untouchable is caught sleeping with a high-caste woman, both he and the woman are executed. A Dalit also can be considered too uppity, and risks a beating, if he wears a wristwatch or trousers instead of a traditional dhoti or loincloth. In some places in the south, Dalits aren't allowed to use an umbrella. Some roadside tea stalls refuse to serve them out of ordinary cups, and often Dalit children are warned not to try sharing classrooms with upper-caste kids. In some villages like Vembakkotai, in Tamil Nadu, the Dalits are forced to live on the leeward side to prevent the wind that touches their bodies from defiling the upper-castes.

Faced with such persecution, Dalits are finally running out of patience. What's surprising is that it took them so long, Their emancipation began only in this century, behind the efforts of India's two great social reformers, Mahatma Gandhi and Bhimrao Ramji Ambedkar, an angry, brilliant Dalit lawyer and politician. Through a scholarship from the Maharajah of Baroda, Ambedkar, an impoverished village boy, was able to study abroad and eventually earned several degrees. He worked as a financial adviser to the Maharajah but quit in disgust because the prince's upper-caste servants would fling documents onto his desk, rather than hand them to him, for fear of contamination. Yet his genius was unstoppable, as was his grit. "Nothing can emancipate the outcaste except the destruction of the caste system," Ambedkar once declared. "Nothing can help to save the Hindus and ensure their survival in the coming struggle except the purging of the Hindu faith of this odious and vicious dogma." As an author of the Indian constitution, he secured guarantees for the advancement of outcastes. For decades, these promises were often blocked by upper-caste bureaucrats, but a new generation of Dalits inside the civil service is helping their downtrodden people. In Uttar Pradesh, for example, 150 positions are held by Dalits in the elite 540-member Indian Administrative Service. The government gives Dalits a lift by reserving 15% of all government jobs and college places for them.

Many of these educated Dalit bureaucrats are infuriated when, on visits to their villages, they are mistreated by upper-caste neighbours poorer and less educated than they. Man Dahima, a Dalit who is one of the most senior civil servants in Bhopal, capital of Madhya Pradesh state, says he still encounters "feudal harassment" when he goes back to his village. "Even today, we're not allowed in some temples," he says. "There are no signs outside, but these things are well understood." Other urbanized Dalits seethe when being served out of coconut shells instead of teacups or when forced to sit at a village Brahman's feet. Says Ezhilmalai, a Dalit politician in Tamil Nadu: "The Dalit would rather die than live without self-respect. And when he prefers to die for honour, what is there to care for?"

Ambedkar wanted to destroy the caste pyramid through democracy, but the rule of law has been slow in reaching many villages where upper-caste landlords, often in league with local police, are keeping the Dalits down. In such places, many Dalits are opting for armed resistance. "The condition of the Dalits in the villages is so bad that the concern for most is how to gain minimum self-respect and security," says a senior state official in Uttar Pradesh. "What they want today is not jobs, but to be able to live without being humiliated and harassed." In Uttar Pradesh, Bihar, Tamil Nadu and Andhra Pradesh, caste conflict is rife, and it has spread to other states such as Madhya Pradesh and Maharashtra. Many Dalits, along with forest-dwelling tribals, have signed up with armed leftist groups like the Maoist Communist Centre, Liberation and People's War Group, which go around shooting or slitting the throats of feudal upper-caste landowners and policemen. This communist insurgency, which flared in the 1970s, still rages in the backward regions of central and eastern India.

Not surprisingly, the upper-castes are hitting back. In Bihar, high-caste landowners raised a private army called the Ranvir Sena, and hardly a day goes by without caste killings. Even Rabindra Chowdhary, a Ranvir Sena leader, concedes that the landlords had cruelly exploited the Dalits. "We were abusive and did not treat these people well," he says. "We do not believe in killing. But if we do not kill, they will think that we are weak." Tension runs high, and even the most nonsensical incident can trigger a bloody outburst. In Tamil Nadu, a game of tag between Thevar and Dalit schoolboys led to the beheading of a Dalit and the revenge killing of 13 people, both Thevars and Dalits, many of them dragged off a bus and hacked to death. In Bihar's Belaur village, a tiff over a pack of cigarettes led to a mini-war between Dalits and the upper-caste Bhumihars that ultimately left 16 dead and dozens wounded. Even today, that feud festers: more than 350 Dalit families have deserted the village, and the Bhumihars—who patrol their village at night with guns and spears, ready for attack—cannot hire labourers for their fields. Some Dalits are even refusing to carry out their repugnant jobs. "My generation is fighting," says Sri Prakash, a Dalit whose house was set ablaze in a caste feud. "We've told the Thevars we're not going to cremate their dead any more. Let them do it themselves." Says Sociologist Nandy: "The Dalits are much more aggressive. Now that they have tasted power, they don't want to be denied it."

A mini-partition based on caste lines is taking shape in areas where Dalits are especially politicized. In some districts, police say, Dalits are probably better armed and organized than their upper-caste adversaries. It has become too dangerous for a Thevar family to live among the Dalits. Thevars are migrating to villages where they are in control, while Dalits are moving to places where they are in the majority. A Thevar knows better than to wander into some villages in the Srivilliputhur district, where Dalits humiliate upper-caste strangers by making them walk through the village with their sandals on their heads, ridiculing Vedic order by putting the lowliest on top. Dalits toiling in stone quarries and match factories have allegedly pilfered enough explosives to gain a lethal edge. Says Mahboob Batacha, a Tamil social worker in Madurai: "There's no village around here where the Dalits aren't armed. Now, more Thevars are getting killed than Dalits."

Envy is often the spark for caste warfare. It is not usually the top-rung Brahmans and Kshatriyas who clash with the Dalits but rather the castes lower down: those slightly above the untouchables, such as the Thevars in Tamil Nadu and the Yadavs in Bihar and Uttar Pradesh. As Dr. K. Krishnaswamy, a prominent Dalit politician in Tamil Nadu, explains, "Some Dalit youth are climbing fast through reserved government jobs. Others have gone to the Gulf for employment, and they are all bringing back TVs, refrigerators and vcrs. This is causing a lot of heartburn among the other castes." Krishnaswamy's own life is an illustration of this jealousy. When he was granted a scholarship to a prestigious college, the upper-caste postman pocketed his admissions letter, and Krishnaswamy never found out that he was accepted until too late.

Eventually he made it to medical school and, after leaving, set up practice near his village. Many of his patients were Dalit women who wanted abortions after being raped by upper-caste landowners. "I went to the upper-caste men and told them this wasn't right. They should marry these girls," he says. It was not a popular idea; a mob of 1,000 upper-caste men besieged the doctor's house one night, attacking him and his family. After a month in the hospital, he returned, full of fight. "It made me angry, more determined than ever," he says. Today, Krishnaswamy is one of only a few Dalits elected to Tamil Nadu's assembly, even though Dalits comprise about 20% of the state's voters.

His life has been threatened so often that, while driving through upper-caste-dominated areas of the state, he is accompanied by two armed bodyguards. Says Krishnaswamy: "The political parties are the real culprits for keeping the caste conflict going." But caste politics is alive and well, and is contributing to a stirring-up of anti-Dalit sentiment in Bombay. In July, slum-dwellers awakened to find that their statue of the bespectacled Ambedkar had been garlanded not with the customary flowers but with a wreath of dirty sandals. That was all it took to start a riot. Hundreds of angry Dalits poured onto the streets, hurling stones and setting up roadblocks with burning tires. Fearing the rioters would set fire to a parked gas tanker, police started shooting in the shanty lanes, killing about a dozen people. Once news of the deaths spread, Dalits began protesting in the neighbouring states of Gujarat, Karnataka and in the capital, New Delhi.

The police shootings also revived antagonism between the Dalits and Maharashtra's ruling Shiva Sena party. Its militant Hindu leader Bal Thackeray has often attacked job reservations and the renaming of a university after Ambedkar. The Bombay incident also revealed the Dalits' disillusionment with their own leaders. When a former State Minister and Dalit leader visited the shantytown the day after the killings, he was attacked and had to run for his life. The funeral procession for those shot by police was attended by 150,000 Dalits, but not one Dalit politician dared to show up. Says Savita Ambedkar, the 81-year-old widow of the Dalit leader: "If we can stay together, we have the power to make a party succeed. But it's a great disappointment that the movement has been captured by people who cannot really lead it properly." A doctor and a Brahman who became Ambedkar's second wife, Savita now lives alone in a shabby house in central Bombay. She has written a biography of her late husband, but because of her high caste, she was never really accepted by Dalits. Ambedkar's grandson Prakash hasn't fared much better. Ambedkar died in late 1956, soon after founding the Republican Party of India, but grandson Prakash, who now leads one of its many factions, lacks his visionary fire.

Desperate, the Dalits in Bombay's slums are flailing for an alternative leadership—or at least a godfather. Shortly after the funeral of the slain Dalits, a lower caste Bombay underworld chieftain named Arun Gawli offered himself as their saviour. When the gangster called a Bombay rally, thousands of Dalits flocked to it. Says social worker Sushoba Barve: "After the killings, many Dalit youth felt that the only way to protect themselves was to ally with someone who could give them protection."

Elsewhere in India, Dalits are feeling equally deceived by the national parties, which are top-heavy with high-caste politicians. Dalits have yet to unite. "All that keeps India from having a bloody revolution is that we Dalits are a divided lot," says civil servant Dahima. Even among the Dalits, strong caste rivalries exist; one study discovered 900 Dalit "sub-castes" in the country. Basically, everyone is squirming not to fall to the bottom of India's massive pile of humanity. Predicts one Dalit official: "As benefits trickle down, the conflicts between sub-castes are bound to sharpen." Lately, a number of regional leaders have been trying to bring unity to lower-caste aspirations. Several could easily cripple their state capitals with 100,000-strong demonstrations. So far, the only Dalit politician to challenge the mainstream parties is Kanshi Ram, a former technician at a government defence laboratory. Armed with wiliness and an ability to survive in the venal world of Indian politics, Ram has no qualms about forming alliances with his high-caste adversaries if it brings his Bahujan Samaj Party to power. His abrasive protege Mayawati governed Uttar Pradesh for six months in alliance with the Hindu nationalist Bharatiya Janata Party, many of whose followers adhere stoutly to Manu's ancient law.

DISTRIBUTIVE JUSTICE: DEBATE WITH GANDHI

The conflict between Gandhi and Ambedkar in terms of their ideological difference on the caste system. Both the thinkers approach the matter from quite different angles. There are real and serious disagreements between them, especially regarding the conclusions that each of them draws from their premises.

Gandhi had two arguments against untouchability: the unity or the political argument and the ethical argument.

As a leader working for a national goal, Gandhi argued for removing injustices faced by 'untouchables' because he felt the need to weave the divergent interests in India into a unified opposition to the British; he argued for pursuing this course of reform without challenging the social fabric of Indian society. He emphasised that a political separation of untouchables from the rest of the Hindu population would reduce Hindu plurality vis-a-vis other minority groups, in part, the Muslims. The ethical argument is premised on the view that Hindu society must rest on moral consensus, that political conflict can only be kept within bounds if there is a moral consensus on the caste system. Gandhi's ethical argument rested on two claims. First, he claimed that the heart of the caste Hindu could be changed by applying moral pressures within the framework of the Hindu tradition. Second, there was an obligation on the caste Hindu to be individually responsible towards the lower caste groups. In his conception of the moral or perfect society, Gandhi maintained that its enduring basis can only be the moral calibre of the individuals who constitute it. Although Gandhi's views changed over the years, he always believed in the *varnashrama dharma,* the divinely ordained division of society into four defined groups according to duty: Brahmin, Kshatriya, Vaishya, Sudra. In an exchange of views on this problem, he said:

> *I do not believe the caste system even as distinguished from varnashrama to be an 'odious and vicious' dogma. It has its limitations and defects but there is nothing sinful about it, as there is about untouchability, and, if it is a bye-product of the caste system, it is only in the same sense that an ugly growth is of a body or weeds of a crop. It is wrong to destroy caste because of the outcaste, as it would be to destroy a body because of an ugly growth in it, or of a crop because of its weeds...*

Later, he distinguished between caste and varna. In his response to Ambedkar's undelivered speech titled: 'Annihilation of Caste' (1936), he said:

Caste has nothing to do with religion... it is harmful both to spiritual and national growth. Varna and Ashram are institutions which have nothing to do with castes. The law of varna teaches us that we have each one of us to earn our bread by following the ancestral calling. It defines not our rights but our duties... The callings of a Brahmin– spiritual teacher–and a scavenger are equal, and at one time their due performance carries equal merit before god and seems to have carried identical reward before man.

To this Ambedkar replied, questioning the logical conclusions of his doctrine: "When can a calling be deemed to have become an ancestral calling so as to make it binding on a man? Must man follow his ancestral calling even if it does not suit his capacities, even when it has ceased to be profitable? Must a man live by his ancestral calling even if he finds it to be immoral?"

Following arguments from justice, rather than arguments for unity, Ambedkar states that existing inequalities cannot be morally defended: to avoid the morally illegitimate exclusion of untouchables one would have to differentiate conceptually and practically between different levels of citizenship. Ambedkar proposed these arguments when he came into conflict with the Congress, and with Gandhi in particular, on two occasions – the temple entry attempts and separate electorates. Ambedkar put forward arguments based on the principle of liberal equality and distributive justice to sustain his case. Equality meant not the equal status of varnas, but equal social, political and economic opportunity for all.

At first, he made several attempts to gain religious and social rights for the untouchables, by using the Gandhian technique of satyagraha; drinking water from a public tank in Mahad (1927), temple entry to the Parvati temple at Poona (1929), and then the Kala Ram temple at Nasik (1930-35). The failure of temple entry movements demonstrated, according to Ambedkar, that the untouchables were not really a part of Hindu society and would never be accepted as equals by Hindus within that framework. It was quite obvious that this low threshold concept of a legal conception of equality allows for different degrees of political participation.

In short, it does not allow for a corresponding conception of political citizenship. Thus, from a position of questioning the brahmanical social order, Ambedkar moved towards its rejection: raising the issue of conversion by the untouchables in 1935. But there was another reason. The second occasion was the Round Table Conference held in 1930 at London, where both leaders confronted each other on the issue of the political rights of depressed classes.

Earlier, in the 'Evidence before the Southborough Committee on Franchise' (1919), Ambedkar (invited as a delegate of the depressed classes) had argued eloquently for uniform franchise, for securing access for the depressed classes to the public sphere–to public wells, roads, schools, temples, and cremation grounds–and for special provisions for their adequate representation of their interests and opinions.

Untouchability constitutes a definite set of interests which the untouchables alone can speak for. Hence, it is evident that we must find the untouchables to represent their grievances which are their interests, and secondly, we must find them in such members as will constitute a force sufficient to claim redress.

After the Round Table Conference, (where he argued against a general territorial electorate for the untouchables), the communal award of 1932 gave the depressed classes, a double vote, one in a special constituency and one in the general electorate – a decision which appeared to recognise untouchables as a minority group outside of Hinduism. Gandhi's response was to enter fast unto death on September 20, 1932. He expressed his argument on the grounds for unity between the two:

A heart understanding between the two, the greatest opportunity of repentance and reparation on the part of the suppressors... I would therefore favour widest possible franchise for the suppressed and establish a convention between the two sections for securing proper election of representatives of the suppressed. Under great pressure from other political leaders, Ambedkar relented. However, the Poona Pact, which followed, recognised untouchables as a political category across British India by providing reservations of seats for the depressed classes in the central legislature and in the provincial legislature. Admittedly, all of these changes had hardly any effect on the economic conditions of the untouchables, but it did set in motion an important process of transformation at the level of ideology.

MANDAL COMMISSION

The Mandal Commission was established in India in 1979 by the Janata Party government under Prime Minister Morarji Desai with a mandate to "identify the socially or educationally backward." It was headed by Indian parliamentarian Bindheshwari Prasad Mandal to consider the question of seat reservations and quotas for people to redress caste discrimination, and used eleven social, economic, and educational indicators to determine backwardness. In 1980, the commission's report affirmed the affirmative action practice under Indian law whereby members of lower castes (known as Other Backward Classes (OBC) and Scheduled Castes and Tribes) were given exclusive access to a certain portion of government jobs and slots in public universities, and recommended changes to these quotas, increasing them by 27% to 49.5%.

Setting up of Mandal Commission

The plan to set up another commission was taken by Mr. Clooney and the Morarji Desai government in 1978 as per the mandate of the Constitution of India under article 340 for the purpose of Articles like 15 and 16. The decision was made official by the president on 1 January 1979. The commission is popularly known as the Mandal Commission its chairman being B.P. Mandal..

Criteria to identify OBC

The Mandal Commission adopted various methods and techniques to collect the necessary data and evidence. The commission adopted 11 criteria which could be grouped under three major headings: social, educational and economic in order to identify OBCs.

Social

- Castes/classes considered as socially backward by others.
- Castes/classes which mainly depend on manual labour for their livelihood.
- Castes/classes where at least 25 per cent females and 10 per cent males the state average get married at an age below 17 years in rural areas and at least 10 per cent females and 5 per cent males do so in urban areas.
- Castes/classes where participation of females in work is at least 25 per cent above the state average.

Educational

- Castes/classes where the number of children in the age group of 5–15 years who never attended school is at least 25 per cent above the state average.

- Castes/classes where the rate of student dropout in the age group of 5–15 years is at least 25 per cent above the state average.

Economic

- Castes/classes where the average value of family assets is at least 25 per cent below the state average.
- Castes/classes where the number of families living in kuccha houses is at least 25 per cent above the state average.
- Castes/classes where the source of drinking water is beyond half a kilometer for more than 50 per cent of the households.
- Castes/classes where the number of households having taken consumption loans is at least 25 per cent above the state average. Also known as "Creamy layer," this criteria of separation is ignored by the government which is known as the most controversial issue of reservation.

Weighting Indicators

As the three groups are not of equal importance for the purpose, separate weightage was given to indicators in each group. All the Social indicators were given a weightage of 3 points each, educational indicators were given a weightage of 2 points each and economic indicators were given a weightage of 1 point each. Economic, in addition to Social and Educational Indicators, were considered important as they directly flowed from social and educational backwardness. This also helped to highlight the fact that socially and educationally backward classes are economically backward also. It will be seen from the values given to each indicator, the total score adds up to 22.

All these 11 indicators were applied to all the castes covered by the survey for a particular state. As a result of this application, all castes which had a score of 50% (*i.e.* 11 points) were listed as socially and educationally backward and the rest were treated as 'advanced'.

Observations and Findings

The commission estimated that 54% of the total population (excluding SCs and STs), belonging to 3,743 different castes and communities were 'backward'. So the commission used 1931 census data to calculate the number of OBCs.

The population of Hindu OBCs was derived by subtracting from the total population of Hindus, the population of SC and ST and that of forward Hindu castes and communities, and it worked out to be 52 per cent. Assuming that roughly the proportion of OBCs amongst non-Hindus was of the same order as amongst the Hindus, population of non-Hindu OBCs was also considered as 52 per cent.

- Assuming that a child from an advanced class family and that of a backward class family had the same intelligence at the time of their birth, it is obvious that owing to vast differences in social, cultural and environmental factors, the former will beat the latter by lengths in any competitive field. Even if a backward class child's intelligence quotient was much higher as compared to the child of advanced class, chances are that the former will lag far behind the latter in any competition where selection is made on the basis of 'merit'.
- In fact, what we call 'merit' in an elitist society is an amalgam of native endowments and environmental privileges. A child from an advanced class family and that of a backward class family are not 'equals' in any fair sense of the term and it will be unfair to judge them by the same yard-stick. The conscience of a civilized society and the dictates of social justice demand that 'merit' and 'equality' are not turned into a fetish and the element of privilege is duly recognised and discounted for when 'unequal' are made to run the same race.
- To place the amalgams of open caste conflicts in proper historical context, the study done by Tata institute of Social Sciences Bombay observes. "The British rulers produced many structural disturbances in the Hindu caste structure, and these were contradictory in nature and impact .... Thus, the various impacts of the British rule on the Hindu caste system, *viz.*, near monopolisation of jobs, education and professions by the literati castes, the Western concepts of equality and justice undermining the Hindu hierarchical dispensation, the phenomenon of Sanskritization, genteel reform movement from above and militant reform movements from below, emergence of the caste associations with a new role set the stage for the caste conflicts in modern India. Two more ingredients which were very weak in the British period, *viz.*, politicisation of the masses and universal adult franchise, became powerful moving forces after the Independence.

Recommendations

The report of the commission was submitted in December 1980. Following are the recommendations as stated in the report. It may appear the upliftment of Other Backward Classes is part of the larger national problem of the removal of mass poverty.

This is only partially correct. The deprivation of OBCs is a very special case of the larger national issue: here the basic question is that of social and educational backwardness and poverty is only a direct consequence of these two crippling caste-based handicaps. As these handicaps are embedded in our social structure, their removal will require far – reaching structural changes. No less important will be changes in the perception of the problems of OBCs by the ruling classes of the country.

Reservations

One such change in the attitude of the ruling elite pertains to the provisions of reservation in Government services and educations institutions for the candidates of Other Backward Classes. It is generally argued that looking to the large population of OBCs (52%), recruitment of a few thousand OBCs every year against reserved vacancies is not going to produce any perceptible impact on their general condition. On the other hand, the induction of a large proportion of employees against reserved vacancies will considerably impair the quality and efficiency of the Government services.

It is also stated that the benefits of such reservations will be skimmed off by those parts of OBCs which are already well off and the really backward parts will be left high and dry. Another argument advanced against this approach is that the policy ot large scale reservations will cause great hurt burning to those meritorious candidates whose entry into services will be barred as a result thereof. All the arguments are based on fairly sound reasoning. But these are also the arguments advanced by the ruling elite which is keen on preserving its privileges. Therefore, like all such reasoning, it is based on partisan approach. By the same token, while illuminating some immediate areas of concern it tends to ignore much larger issues of national importance. It is not at all our contention that by offering a few thousand jobs to OBC candidates we shall be able to make 52% of the Indian population as forward. But we must recognise that as essential part of the battle against social backwardness is to be fought in the minds of the backward people.

In India Government service has always been looked upon as a symbol of prestige and power. By increasing the representation of OBCs in Government services, we give them an immediate feeling of participation in the governance of this country. When a backward class candidate becomes a Collector or a Superintendent of Police, the material benefits accruing from his position are limited to the members of his family only. But the psychological spin off of this phenomenon is tremendous; the entire community of that backward class candidate feels socially elevated.

Even when no tangible benefits flow to the community at large, the feeling that now it has its "own man" in the "corridors of power" acts as a morale booster. In a democratic set-up every individual and community has a legitimate right and aspiration to participate in ruling this country.

Any situation which results in a near-denial of this right to nearly 52% of the country's population needs to be urgently rectified. Apprehensions regarding drop in the quality of Government services owing to large-scale induction of S.C./S.T. and O.B.C. candidates against reserved posts may be justified only up to a point. But is it possible to maintain that all candidates selected on merit turn out to be honest, efficient, hard-working and dedicated? At present, top echelons of all the Government services are manned predominantly by open competition candidates and if the performance of our bureaucracy is any indication, it has not exactly covered itself with glory.

Of course, this does not imply that candidates selected against reserved posts will do better. Chances are that owing to their social and cultural handicaps they may be generally a shade less competent. But, on the other hand, they will have great advantage of possessing first hand knowledge of the sufferings and problems of the backward parts of society. This is not a small asset for field workers and policy makers even at highest level. It is no doubt true that the major benefits of reservation and other welfare measures for Other Backward Classes will be cornered by the more advanced parts of the backward communities.

But is not this a universal phenomenon? All reformists remedies have to contend with slow recovery along the hierarchical gradient; there are no quantum jumps in social reform. Moreover, human nature being what it is, a "new class" ultimately does emerge even in classless societies. The chief merit on reservation is not that it will introduce egalitarian amongst OBCs when the rest of the Indian society is seized by all sorts of inequalities. But reservation will certainly erode the hold of higher castes on the services and enable OBCs in general to have a sense of participation in running the affairs of the country.

It is certainly true that reservation for OBCs will cause a lot of heart burning to others. But should the mere fact of this heart burning be allowed to operate as a moral veto against social reform.... When the higher castes constituting less than 20% of the country's population subjected the rest to all manner of social injustice, it must have caused a lot of heart burning to the lower castes.

But now that the lower castes are asking for a modest share of the national cake of power and prestige, a chorus of alarm is being raised on the plea that this will cause heart burning to the ruling elite. Of all the specious arguments advanced against reservations for backward classes, there is none which beats this one about 'heart-burning' in sheer sophistry.

In fact the Hindu society has always operated a very rigorous scheme of reservations, which was internalised through caste system. Eklavya lost his thumb and Shambhk his neck for their breach of caste rules of reservations. The present furore against reservations for OBCs is not aimed at the principle itself, but against the new class of beneficiaries, as they are now clamouring for a share of the opportunities which were all along monopolised by the higher castes.

Quantum and Scheme of Reservations

Scheduled Castes and Scheduled Tribes constitute 22.5% of the country's population. A pro-rata reservation of 22.5% has been made for them in all services and public sector undertakings under the Central Government.

In the States also, reservation for SCs and STs is directly proportional to their population in each State. The population of OBCs, both Hindu and non-Hindu, is around 52% of the total population of India. Accordingly 52% of all post under the Central Government should be reserved for them, but this provision may go against the law laid down in a number of Supreme Court judgements wherein it has been held that the total quantum of reservations under Articles 15(4) and 16(4) of the Constitution should be below 50%. In view of this the proposed reservation for OBCs would have to be pegged at a figure which, when added to 22.5% of SCs and STs, remain below 50%. In view of this legal constrain, the commission is obliged to recommend a reservation of 27% only, even though their population us almost twice this figure. States which have already introduced reservation for OBCs exceeding 27%, will remain unaffected by this recommendation.

With the general recommendation regarding the quantum of reservation, the Commission proposes the following over-all scheme of reservation for OBCs:

- Candidates belonging to OBCs recruited on the basis of merit in an open competition should not be adjusted against their reservation quota of 27%.
- The reservation should also be made available to promotion quota at all levels. Nitika goyal (3) Reserved quota remaining unfilled should be carried forward for a period of three years and deserved thereafter.
- Relaxation in the upper age limit for direct recruitment should be extended in the same manner as done in case of SCs and STs.
- A roster system for each category of posts should be adopted by the concerned authorities in the same manner as presently done in respect of SC and ST candidates.

The scheme of reservations in its toto should be made applicable to all recruitment to public sector undertakings both under the Central and State Governments, as also to nationalised banks. All private sector undertakings which have received financial assistance from the Government in one form or the other should also be obliged to recruit personnel on the aforesaid basis. All universities and affiliated colleges should also be covered by the scheme of reservation. To give proper effect to these recommendations, it is imperative that adequate statutory provisions are made by the Government to amend the existing enactments, rules, procedure, etc. to the extent they are not in consonance with the same.

Educational Concessions

Our educational system is elitist in character, results in a high degree of wastage and is least suited to the requirements of an over-populated and developing country. It is a legacy of the British rule which was severely criticised during the independence struggle, and yet, it has not undergone any structural changes. Though it is least suited to the needs of backward classes, yet, they are forced to run the rat-race with others as no options are available to them. As 'educational reform' was not within the terms of reference of the Commission, we are also forced to trend the beaten track and suggest only the palliative measure within existing framework.

Various State Governments are giving a number of educational concessions to other backward class students like exemption of tuition fees, free supply of books and clothes, mid-day meals, special hostel facilities, stipends, etc. These concessions are all right as far as they go. But they do not go far enough. What is required is, perhaps, not so much the provision of additional funds as the framing of integrated schemes for creating the proper environment and incentives for serious and purposeful studies. It is well known that most backward class children are irregular and indifferent students and their dropout rate is very high. There are two main reasons for this. First, these children are brought up in a climate of extreme social and cultural deprivation and consequently, a proper motivation for schooling is generally lacking.

Secondly, most of these children come from very poor homes and their parents are forced to press them into doing small chores from a very young age. Upgrading the cultural environment is a very slow process. Transferring these children to an artificially upgraded environment is beyond the present resources of the country. In view of this it is recommended that this problem may be tackled on a limited and selective basis on two fronts. First, an intensive and time bound programme for adult education should be launched in selected pockets with high concentration of OBC population. This is a basic motivational approach, as only proper motivated parents will take serious interest in educating their children. Secondly, residential schools should be set up in these areas for backward class students to provide a climate specially conducive to serious studies.

All facilities in these schools including board and lodging, will have to be provided free of cost to attract students from poor and backward homes, separate Government Hostels for OBC students with the facilities will be another step in the right direction. A beginning on both these fronts will have to be made on a limited scale and selective basis. But the scope of these activities should be expanded as fast as the resources permit.

Adult education programme and residential schools started on a selective basis will operate as growing-points of consciousness for the entire community and their multiplier effect is bound to be substantial. Whereas several States are extended a number of ad hoc concessions to backward class students, few serious attempts have been made to integrate these facilities into a comprehensive scheme for a qualitative upgradation of educational environment available to OBC students.

After all, education is the best catalyst of change and educating the backward classes is the surest way to improve their self image and raise their social status.

As OBCs cannot afford the high wastage rates of our educational system, it is very important that their education is highly biased in favour of vocational training. After all reservation in services will absorb only a very small percentage of the educated backward classes and the rest should be suitably equipped with vocational skills to enable them to get a return on having invested several years in education.

It is also obvious that even if all the facilities are given to OBC students, they will not be able to compete on an equal footing with others in securing admission to technical and professional institutions. In view of this it is recommended that seats should be reserved for OBC students in all scientific, technical and professional institutions run by the Central Government as well as State Governments.

This reservation will fall under Article 15(4) of the Constitution and the quantum of reservation should be the same as in the Government services, *i.e.*, 27%. Those States which have already reserved more that 27% seats for OBC students will remain unaffected by this recommendation. While implementing the provisions for reservation it should also be ensured that the candidates who are admitted against the reserved quota are enable to derive full benefits of higher studies. It has been generally noticed that these OBC students coming from an impoverished cultural background, are not able to keep abreast with other students.

It is, therefore, very essential that special coaching facilities are arranged for all such students in our technical and professional institutions. The concerned authorities should clearly appreciate that their jobs is not finished once candidates against reserved quota have been admitted to various institutions. In fact the real task starts only after that special coaching assistance to these students, not only these young people will feel frustrated and humiliated but the country will also be landed with ill-equipped and sub-standard engineers, doctors and other professionals.

Financial Assistance

Vocational communities following hereditary occupations have suffered heavily as a result of industrialisation. Mechanical production and introductions of synthetic materials has robbed the village potter, oil crusher, blacksmith, carpenter, barber, etc. of their traditional means of livelihood and the pauperisation of these classes is a well-known phenomenon in the countryside. It has, therefore become very necessary that suitable institutional finance and technical assistance is made available to such members of village vocational communities who want to set up small-scale industries on their own. Similar assistance should also be provided to those promising OBC candidates who have obtained special vocational training. Of course, most State Governments have created various financial and technical agencies for the promotions of small and medium scale industries. But it is well known that only the more influential members of the community are able to derive benefits fro these agencies.

In view of this, it is essential that separate financial institutions for providing financial and technical assistance are established for the backward classes. Some State Governments like Karnataka and Andhra Pradesh have already set up separate financial corporations etc., for OBCs. Cooperative Societies of occupational groups will also help a lot. But due care should be taken that all office-bearers and members of such societies belong to the concerned hereditary occupational groups and outsiders are not allowed to exploit them by infiltrating into such cooperatives.

The share of OBCs in the industrial and business life of the country is negligible and this partly explains their extremely low income levels. As a part of its overall strategy to uplift the backward classes, it is imperative that all State Governments are suitably advised and encouraged to create a separate network of financial and technical institutions to foster business and industrial enterprise among OBCs.

Structural Changes

Reservations in Government employment and educational institutions, as also as possible financial assistance will remain mere palliatives unless the problems of backwardness is tackled at its root.

Bulk of the small land-holders, tenants, agricultural labour, impoverished village artisans, unskilled workers, etc. belong to Scheduled Castes, Scheduled Tribes and Other Backward Classes. "Apart from social traditions, the dominances by the top peasantry is exercised through recourse to informal bondage which arises mainly thorough money-lending, leasing out of small bits of land and providing house-sites and dwelling space to poor peasants.

As most of the functionaries of the Government are drawn from the top peasantry, the class and caste linkage between the functionaries of Government and the top peasantry remain firm. This also tills the socio-political balance in favour of the top peasantry and helps it in having its dominance over others."

The net outcome of the situation is that notwithstanding their numerical preponderance, backward class continues to remain in mental and material bondage of the higher castes and rich peasantry. Consequently, despite constituting nearly 3/4th of the countries population, Scheduled Castes, Scheduled Tribes and Other Backward Classes have been able to acquire a very limited political clout, even though adult franchise was introduced more than three decades back.

Through their literal monopoly of means of production of higher castes are able to manipulate and coerce the backward classes into acting against their own interests. In view of this, until the stranglehold of the existing production relations is broken through radical land reforms, the abject dependence of under privileged classes on the dominant higher castes will continue indefinitely. In fact there is already a sizeable volume of legislation on the statue books to abolish zamindari, place ceilings on land holdings and distribute land to the landless.

But in actual practice its implementation has been halting, half-hearted and superficial. The States like Karnataka, Kerala and West Bengal which have gone about the job more earnestly have not only succeeded in materially helping the Backward Classes, but also reaped rich political dividends into the bargains. It is the Commission's firm Conviction that a radical transformation of the existing production relations is the most important single step that can be taken for the welfare and upliftment of all backward classes. Even if this is not possible in the industrial sector for various reasons, in the agricultural sector a change in this nature is both feasible and overdue. The Commission, therefore, strongly recommends that all the State Governments should be directed to enact and implement progressive land legislations so as to effect basic structural changes in the existing production relations in the countryside. At present surplus land in being allotted to SCs and STs. A part of the surplus land becoming available in future as a result of the operation of land ceiling laws etc. should also be allotted to the OBC landless labour.

Miscellaneous

- Certain parts of some occupational communities like Fishermen, Banjaras, Bansoforas, Khatwes etc. still suffer from the stigma of untouchability in some part of the country. They have been listed as O.B.Cs. by the Commission, but their inclusion in the lists of Scheduled Castes/Scheduled Tribes may be considered by the Government.
- Backward Classes Development Corporations should be set up both at the Central and State levels to implement various socio-educational and economic measures for their advancement.
- A separate Ministry/Department for O.B.Cs. at the Centre and States should be created to safeguard their interests.
- With a view to giving better representation to certain very backward parts of O.B.Cs. like the Gaddis of Himachal Pradesh, Neo-Buddhists in Maharashtra, Fishermen in the Coastal areas, Gujjars in J&K., it is recommended that areas of their concentration may be carved out into separate constituencies at the time of delimitation.

Central Assistance

At present no Central Assistance is available to any State Government for implementing any welfare measures for Other Backward Classes. The 18 States and Union Territories which have undertaken such measures have to provide funds from their own resources. During the Commission's tours practically every State Government pointed out that unless the Centre is prepared to liberally finance all special schemes for the upliftment of OBCs, it will be beyond the available resources of the States to undertake any worthwhile programme for the benefit of Other Backward Classes.

The Commission fully shares the views of the State Governments in this matter and strongly recommends that all development programmes specially designed for Other Backward Classes should be financed by the Central Government in the same manner and to the same extent as done in the case of Scheduled Castes and Scheduled Tribes. Regarding the period of operation of the Commission's recommendations entire scheme should be reviewed after twenty years.

We have advisedly suggested this span of one generation, as the raising of social consciousness is a generational progress. Any review at a shorter interval would be rather arbitrary and would not give a fair indication of the impact of our recommendations on the prevailing status and life-styles of O.B.Cs.

Implementation

All the recommendations of the report are not yet implemented. The recommendation of reservations for OBC's in government services was implemented in 1993. As on 27 June 2008 there is still a backlog of 28, 670 OBC vacancies in government jobs. The recommendation of reservations in Higher educational institutes is implemented in 2008.

Criticism

The National Sample Survey puts the figure at 32%. There is substantial debate over the exact number of OBC's in India, with census data compromised by partisan politics. It is generally estimated to be sizable, but lower than the figures quoted by either the Mandal Commission or and National Sample Survey. There is also an ongoing controversy about the estimation logic used by Mandal commission for calculating OBC population. Famous Indian Statistician, Mr. Yogendra Yadav who supports Reservations agrees that there is no empirical basis to the Mandal figure. According to him "It is a mythical construct based on reducing the number of SC/ST, Muslims and others and then arriving at a number." National Sample Survey's 1999-2000 round estimated around 36 per cent of the country's population is defined as belonging to the Other Backward Classes (OBC).

The proportion falls to 32 per cent on excluding Muslim OBCs. A survey conducted in 1998 by National Family Health Statistics (NFHS) puts the proportion of non-Muslim OBCs as 29.8 per cent L R Naik, the only Dalit member in the Mandal Commission refused to sign the Mandal recommendations. He said that there are two social blocks among the OBCs: upper caste (Jat and Gujjar) and upper OBCs (Yadavs, Kurmis, etc.) and Most Backward Classes (MBCs). He feared that upper OBCs would corner all the benefits of reservation. Here we shall present the study of the Mandal Commissions's list of the OBC for the state of West Bengal only for the sake of brevity. In this list, Urao (along with its synonyms Bandot, Haro, Karkata, Luidu, Shitheo, Tigga and Tirki) has been listed as an OBC (OBC No.176). On the other hand, it is already in the list of Scheduled Tribes for the state with a slight difference of spelling "Oraon" (ST 33).

Similarly, Scheduled Tribes Kharia (OBC 105; synonym of Lodha, ST 23 in the ST List), Kherwar (OBC 107; ST 17, with a spelling Kharwar), Koda (OBC 113; ST 20, spelled Kora), Bhotia (OBC 33; ST 5, spelled Bhutia), Brijia (OBC 39, ST 7, with a spelling Birjia), Gonda (OBC 68; ST 12, spelled Gond) and Lakra (OBC 123, and Lakar OBC 122, which is actually a surname adopted by many members of the Scheduled Tribe Munda), which are already declared STs for the state.

Tharu (OBC 171) is a widely studied scheduled tribe. Thapa (OBC 170) is a synonym of ST Sherpa (ST 5, same as Bhutia, Tota, Dukpa, Kagatay, Tibetan, Yolmo). Many famous ST surnames have been listed as OBC Mahato (OBC 129), etc. Other anthropologically famous scheduled tribes listed as OBC are Kuki (OBC 118), Lushei (actually Lushai; OBC 124), Koli (OBC 116) and Rohangia. Similar manipulation has been done with many Scheduled Castes also. For example in the state of West Bengal, Bhangi has been listed as OBC (No. 26), with a rider "excluding those in the Scheduled Caste".

On the other hand the SC list for West Bengal shows that Bhangi (at place no. 22 in the SC list) is an unconditional SC for the whole of the territory of the state. Halalkhor has also been listed as an OBC (No. 73) with a similar condition but this caste is also an unconditional SC (No. 21, spelled Halelkhor).

A sub-caste of Dom (Maghaiya-Dom) has been listed as OBC at place No. 126. Dom as a whole has been a Scheduled Caste (No.17 in West Bengal SC list) for ages. Bahelia (SC No. 2) has been listed by its synonym Chirimar (OBC 45). Bagal (OBC 11) is already there in the SC list at place number 1, with a spelling Bagll. Although Nat is an SC (No. 47), its sub-caste KarwalNat has been made an OBC (OBC 97).

Jaliya Kaivartta (SC 23) is just the Sanskritized name of Machua listed as OBC (OBC 125). All the Nav-Buddhists (Neo-Buddhist) have been include in the OBC list, which is again an anomaly, because the Nav-Buddhists enjoy their SC status. Not only synonyms or alternative spellings of the SCs and STs have been recorded as OBC, but also there are other types of manipulations like same OBC caste has been listed twice or sometimes thrice in the list of the same state.

An example of this type of manipulation is Kahar in Bihar list (No. 23 as well as No. 70), Kewat (at no. 115 as well as 84.) At any rate the list is vitiated by such inclusions. The Kuki tribes (ST) actually live in Nagaland, Meghalaya, Mizoram and Tripura, none of which are neighbouring to West Bengal. Even if any member of the tribe migrates to West Bengal or anywhere else in India, either it retains its ST status of the mother state or becomes General population.

It is difficult to believe that some Kuki tribes live in West Bengal as OBC. Lushai tribe (ST) live mainly in Mizoram and are the principal Mizo tribe. They are also found in Manipur as ST. Koli (ST) are found in a widespread area ranging from Orissa to Rajasthan up to Karnatak. Rohangia ((OBC 158) are actually a distant tribe which mainly live in Myanmar but are also found in Bangla Desh-Myanmar-Tripura border areas). Introduction of such castes to the West Bengal OBC list seems to be an act of fertile brain and raises doubt whether any actual survey was done at all.

At any rate a small number of these tribes could be present in the former East Bengal (now Bangla Desh) in areas adjoining former state of Assam and Myanmar before partition. Some OBC caste names given in the list are obsolete of forward castes. Tyagi is an upper caste, which lives in UP, Haryana and Delhi. This caste was earlier called Taga. But with a general trend of all the North Indian castes to Sanskritize their names, Taga people adopted a new name Tyagi which was similar to Taga.

But still in the remote village especially by the illiterate people Tyagis are often called Taga. We find the name of Taga in Haryana Mandal list (OBC 74), Delhi (OBC 81) and Uttar Pradesh (OBC 109, as Taga-Bhat). The principles and norms set in the very beginning regarding the criterion for the Non-Hindu communities have been violated flagrantly, hence now the Roman Catholic is not a religion but a caste in the eyes of the Mandal Commission (Latin Catholic, OBC 106, Kerala). Anglo-Indians, who are the off-springs of the British rulers, have also been made an Other Backward Caste (OBC 6, Kerala).

Although it has been decided at the outset that only occupational castes among the Muslims and Christians and the castes bearing the same name as a Hindu OBC or SC will be included as a Muslim or Christian OBC caste, the set rule was violated wherever political expediency dictated. For example Kayastha (Muslim) has been made an OBC (OBC 93, Uttar Pradesh) which does not fulfill the criteria set for inclusion of non-Hindu castes. A last word about credibility of the Mandal survey.

Presence of obsolete and archaic caste names like Taga (for Tyagi in Haryana, Delhi and UP), Bhuihar (for Bhumi-har in Bihar), Domb (for Dom in all the southern states), listing of Kuki, Lushai, Rohangia tribes in West Bengal which are not found in West Bengal today but actually some of each of them lived in East Bengal in undivided India neighbouring Tripura, Meghalaya etc., and many such factors cannot be explained unless it is assumed that the Mandal list is not result of a recent survey, but it has been compiled by editing the caste list of 1931 census.

But the editing was most inefficient. These names could not have crept in unless the old united Bengla caste list of 1931 was just copied and some named SC & ST, as well as well known forward caste names were just deleted, to arrive at the current OBC list of Mandal. Every state's OBC list has the same story. The entire list seems to be manipulated, but most carelessly and inefficiently manipulated. Most famous scheduled castes like Dusadh (Dhari), Mochi, Domb (Dom) and Bhangi have been put as OBCs in many states. If the Government does not reject this whole Mandal list, all the SCs and STs listed as OBC will have to be deleted from the respective SC and ST lists.

Because the Mandal Commission was a constitutional body which had done a survey and this survey was done at a later date than the surveys for the SC and ST, which were done during the British period without the authority of our present Indian Constitution. Indeed any act (or survey) done under the authority of Indian Constitution automatically supersedes any act (or survey) of the British administration if there is an overlap or confusion.

Protest

A decade after the commission gave its report, V.P. Singh, the Prime Minister at the time, tried to implement its recommendations in 1989. The criticism was sharp and colleges across the country held massive protests against it. Soon after, Rajiv Goswami, student of Delhi University, committed self-immolation in protest of the government's actions.

His act further sparked a series of self-immolations by other college students and led to a formidable movement against job reservations for Backward Castes in India. First student to die due to self immolation was Surinder Singh Chauhan on Sep 24, 1990.

Arguments against Reservations

The opponents of the issue argue:

- Allocating quotas on the basis of caste is a form of racial discrimination, and contrary to the right to equality. Although the exact relation between caste and race is far from well established
- As a consequence of legislating to provide reservations for Christians and Muslim, religious minorities in all government education institutions will be introduced which is contrary to the ideas of secularism, and is a form of antidiscrimination on the basis of religion.
- Most often, only economically sound people (and rather rich) from the so-called lower castes will make use of most of the reserved seats, thus counteracting the spirit of reservations. Political parties know reservations are no way to improve the lot of the poor and the backward. They support them because of self-interest of the "creamy layer", who use the reservations to further their own family interests, and as a political flag of 'achievement' during election campaigns. In fact, several studies show that the OBC class is quite comparable with the general caste in terms of annual per capita consumption expenditure, and the top strata of OBC is ahead in a host of consumption areas.
- The quality of these elite institutes may go down, because merit is severely being compromised by reserving seats for certain caste-based communities.

- There are no efforts made to give proper primary education to truly deprived classes, so there is no need to reserve seats for higher studies. The government schools in India have absolutely no comparison to the public schools in the developed countries, and only about 65% of the Indian population is literate. The critics argue that "reservation" only in higher institutions and jobs, without improving primary and secondary education, cannot solve this problem.
- The government is dividing people on the basis of castes for political advantages.
- The caste system is kept alive through these measures. Instead of coming up with alternative innovative ideas which make sure equal representation at the same time making the caste system irrelevant, the decision is only fortifying the caste system.
- The autonomy of the educational institutes are lost.
- Not everyone from the so-called upper classes are rich, and not all from so called lower classes are poor.
- The reservation policy of the Indian Congress will create a huge unrest in the Indian society. Providing quotas on the basis of caste and not on the basis of merit will deter the determination of many educated and deserving students of India.
- Multi-national companies will be deterred by this action of the government, and foreign investment in India may dry down, hurting the growth of the Indian economy. Doubtless, urgent actions to improve the lot of the majority, which has not benefited from development—not achieved after 55 years of reservations for scheduled castes—are essential. But this must not hazard improving the economy's competitiveness in a very competitive world.
- There are already talks of reservations in the private sector. If even after providing so many facilities to reserved categories during education, if there is no adequate representation of those people in the work force, there must be some problems with the education system.

Critics of the Mandal Commission argue that it is unfair to accord people special privileges on the basis of caste, even in order to redress traditional caste discrimination. They argue that those that deserve the seat through merit will be at a disadvantage. They reflect on the repercussions of unqualified candidates assuming critical positions in society (doctors, engineers, etc.).

As the debate on OBC reservations spreads, a few interesting facts which raise pertinent question are already apparent. To begin with, do we have a clear idea what proportion of our population is OBC? The Mandal Commission (1980) it is 52 per cent. The 2001 Indian Census, out of India's population of

1,028,737,436 the Scheduled Castes comprise 166,635,700 and Scheduled Tribes 84,326,240, that is 16.2% and 8.2% respectively. There is no data on OBCs in the census.

However, just as to National Sample Survey's 1999-2000 round around 36 per cent of the country's population is defined as belonging to the Other Backward Classes (OBC). The proportion falls to 32 per cent on excluding Muslim OBCs. A survey conducted in 1998 by National Family Health Statistics (NFHS) puts the proportion of non-Muslim OBCs as 29.8 per cent. The NSSO data also shows that already 23.5 per cent of college seats are occupied by OBCs.

That's just 8.6 per cent short of their share of population just as to the same survey. Other arguments include that entrenching the separate legal status of OBCs and SC/STs will perpetuate caste differentiation and encourage competition among communities at the expense of national unity. They believe that only a small new elite of educated Dalits, Adivasis, and OBCs benefit from reservations, and that such measures do nothing to lift the mass of people out of backwardness and poverty.

Arguments Offered in Support of Reservation

- Affirmative Action has helped many—if not everyone from under-privileged and/or under-represented communities to grow and occupy top positions in the world's leading industries. Reservation in education is not the final solution, it is just one of the many solutions. Reservations is a means to increase representation of hitherto under-represented caste groups and thereby improve diversity on campus.
- Although Reservation schemes do undermine the quality of education but still affirmative Action schemes are in place in many countries including USA, South Africa, Malaysia, Brazil etc. It was researched in Harvard University that Affirmative Action programmes are beneficial to the under-privileged. The studies said that Blacks who enter elite institutions with lower test scores and grades than those of whites achieve notable success after graduation. They earn advanced degrees at rates identical to those of their white classmates. They are even slightly more likely than whites from the same institutions to obtain professional degrees in law, business and medicine. They become more active than their white classmates in civic and community activities.
- Although Reservation schemes do undermine the quality of education but still they are needed to provide social justice to the most marginalized and underprivileged is our duty and their human right.

Reservation will really help these marginalized people to lead successful lives, thus eliminating caste-based discrimination which is still widely prevalent in India especially in the rural areas. (over 60% of Indian population stays in Villages).

- But meritrocracy is meaningless without equality. First all people must be brought to the same level, whether it elevates a part or delevels another, regardless of merit. Only after that merit becomes meaningful. Privileged people have never known to go backward due to reservations or lack of "meritrocracy". Reservations have only slowed down the process of the 'forward' becoming richer and backward becoming poorer.
- In a perfectly functioning society the institutions and various walks of life must represent the many parts roughly in proportion to their share in population. In India it is clearly not the case and hence the need for reservations.
- India does not have the economic or institutional capacity for undertaking a grassroots based solution to the problem, so reservations remain the only practical solution for social antidiscrimination
- People who support reservations keenly invite all the anti-reservationists to lead the life of a backward class citizen and live within the means that they have for themselves. It is their contention that in a experimental setup like this the differences in achievement/performance would disappear or reduce down to experimental errors/random error. Underlying idea being that everyone is born equal but into an unequal circumstances. And when the circumstances have been a result of a social system then the system either needs to be abandoned orreformed.
- Reservations are a political necessity in India because vast influential parts of voting population see reservations as beneficial to themselves. All governments have supported maintaining and/or increasing reservations. Reservations are legal and binding. As shown by Gujjar agitations (Rajasthan, 2007-2008), increasing reservations is also essential for peacekeeping in India.
- Reservations will go a long way in capacity building with regard to the human resource of the country. In the long run, it has tremendous economic benefits as it will raise the productivity of the majority of the potential workforce of the country
- The government of India, is bound and empowered by the constitution of the country to secure for all citizens equality in social, economic and political sphere.

A VISIONARY'S PLANS

B. R. Ambedkar is well known as the principal architect of the Indian Constitution, a social reformer and an emancipator of the poor and the deprived. Having studied bar at the Gray's Inn in UK, he had established himself as a legal luminary. He was a great scholar and a prolific writer in diverse areas like sociology, anthropology, history, economics, politics, law and religion.

However, what is not so well known is the fact that he was also an eminent economist. His academic achievements in economics include a Ph.D. degree from Columbia University, Master of Science in Economics from the London School of Economics and Doctor of Science in Economics from the University of London. He contributed a great deal to the formulation of India's postwar economic development plan in general and planning and development of water resources and electric power in particular.

In his book, Abraham elaborates on Ambedkar's economic philosophy and seeks to trace the relevance of his ideas on economic planning and development to the present day problems of the economy. Evidently, Ambedkar's views on Centre-State financial relations, fiscal deficit, necessity to reduce non-plan expenditure, Government's responsibility towards the weaker sections of society, necessity of land reforms, transfer of surplus labour from agriculture to industry etc. are of contemporary relevance.

Ambedkar enunciated the principles of Centre-State financial relations in the Constitution of India keeping in view the need for a strong Centre and proximity of state governments to the people based on his analysis of 'The evolution of Provincial Finances in British India'. No less important is his contribution to incorporate in the Constitution the provision for the appointment of a Finance Commission every five years to decide on the sharing of the tax kitty between the Centre and States.

The crucial importance of this provision can be seen from the fact that even after five decades, and 10 Finance Commissions, the financial relations between the Centre and States remain somewhat strained. During the discussion on the functions of the Comptroller and Auditor General at the time of framing the Constitution in 1949, Ambedkar enunciated that the Governments should spend the resources mobilised from the public not only as per rules and regulations but should also ensure that 'faithfulness, wisdom and economy' have gone into the acts of expenditure by public authorities. Ambedkar's initiative to ensure that electricity is listed in the 'Concurrent List' in the VII Schedule of the Constitution enabled the Centre to take positive steps for intensified growth of the power sector in subsequent years. The subsequent creation of the Central Electricity Authority (CEA) has been singularly instrumental in planning, developing and nurturing the mammoth system of generation, transmission and distribution facilities that span the length and breadth of the country today.

Thanks to Ambedkar's initiatives during pre-independence years, the need to generate more power at a faster pace for accelerating the country's all round development was recognised since the inception of planning process in 1950. In successive Five Year Plans, power development was accorded a very high priority.

Ambedkar had clearly visualised that India should exploit not only the hydropower resources but also all natural resources such as coal and petroleum. The book clearly brings out Ambedkar's significant contribution to economic planning and development and his emphasis on the need for land reforms, infrastructure development and industrialisation in order to eradicate poverty and improving the standard of living of the people. The author also highlights his vision and agenda for the social and economic emancipation of the Dalits and other weaker sections of the Indian society.

While fighting relentlessly against inequalities, Ambedkar felt that even in a democracy, leaving economic and social matters to be determined exclusively by a political majority could lead to the dictatorship of the 'haves' and perpetuation of age-long tyranny. He, therefore, saw to it that the economic and social objectives were enshrined in the Constitution itself as Directive Principles of State Policy.

Ambedkar also influenced the country's labour policy. His tenure as Labour Member in the Viceroy's Council during 1942-46 was a watershed in the history of labour legislation and labour welfare in India. According to Ambedkar, unemployment and underemployment were the greatest enemies of labour. Hence he tried to formulate a full employment policy for labour and a state supported labour welfare system.

He adopted a multi-pronged approach in the formulation of labour policy with provisions for: providing safeguard and social security measures for workers; giving equal opportunity to workers and employers to participate in the formulation of labour policy; and establishing a machinery for enforcing labour laws and settling disputes.

Abraham has made a commendable effort in piecing together the scatter information from Ambedkar's speeches and writings as also from articles and contributions of eminent political personalities, legal experts and social scientists. His book will be a source of inspiration to the younger generation.

5

'Ambedkar' as Thinker

Dalits are never tired of projecting Ambedkar as the greatest of all the leaders. That unfortunately smacks of sectarian attitude and of their blind devotion to him. They need to understand that the measure of greatness of any person could only be her / his contribution to better the human situation, in terms of correct understanding of its ailment and contribution to cure it. What Ambedkar did could be seen in relation to the broad five currents in Indian politics of his times:

- o The Reformists current that wanted to bring about development on the western pattern, possibly with the support of British imperialism,
- o Congress, that represented Indian capital and which demanded self-rule under the domination of British imperialism,
- o The Terrorist Nationalists who had taken up arms in their fight for freedom against British imperialism,
- o The Communists who were trying to implant Bolshevik revolution in India, and
- o The Muslim League which opened up a separatist front of Muslims.

All of them scarcely reflected an understanding of the Indian situation. For instance, none showed even a cursory concern about the problems of one fourth of their countrymen who were forced to live worse than animals as ordained by their decadent religion. It was indeed surprising that although all craved for self-rule from the British, none concerned with the caste-system which basically was responsible in pushing the country repeatedly into slavery. None seemed to attempt an objective analysis of either the history or the present of this country. It could circumstantially be said that their motivations came from their narrow class-caste interests. These movements were motivated by the desire of an abstract freedom for country and a refusal to see the concrete slavery of their own people. Granted that the problems before the country were really intricate, still no one would dare say that the need for democratisation was in anyway subordinate.

The real people's movement in the country was required to wage simultaneous war against imperialism, internal compradore bourgeoisie, landlords and Brahminism. It was only Ambedkar who clearly indicated this requirement. In this light, he was certainly ahead of all others. His own bitter experiences with untouchability had stood him in good stead in seeing this more clearly than any other. He strove to build his movement along this understanding but unfortunately it was neither in his power to deal comprehensively with all the issues, nor was there an ideological and programmatic clarity required therefore. He inevitably had to focus his attention on dalits who were the worst victims of this multifaceted oppression. It was the misfortune of Indian history that this struggle progressed in a constricted manner and eventually got dissolved into regressive statist politics. It reflected both the limitation of Ambedkar as well the situational compulsion on him.

The anti-caste movements before Ambedkar were mainly welfare oriented. Some wanted a higher rank for their own caste in the caste hierarchy and some taking the inferior culture of their caste to be the reason for their suffering, aimed at improving the same. Mahatma Phuley's movement was an exception to this trend insofar as it attempted to unite the Sudra and Atı-Sudra castes against the exploitation by the parasitic castes of Shetjis (capitalists) and Bhatjis (priests). While Ambedkar accepted the lineage/inheritance of this movement and held Phuley in greatest esteem as his one of the three Gurus, he went beyond to declare annihilation of caste to be the object of his movement in the direction of the goal of 'liberty, equality and fraternity'. In the historical context it certainly was a radical step. He rightly diagnosed that the caste system is basically sustained by the peculiar economic constitution of the Indian village of which the land relations were the main features. Towards breaking this link he toyed with an idea of separate settlement for dalits at one time and at another exhorted them to leave villages for cities.

He had clearly understood that castes stood on multiple props, viz., the religio-cultural relations, feudal relations in village setting of which land relations constituted the crux and the sociopolitical nexus with the State. Annihilation of castes thus needed destruction of all of them. He soon realised the necessity of political power for this multi-fronged attack. Even to bring about the residual change in the belief system either through the cultural or religious route, he stressed the necessity of political power. In this way, for the first time he brought the problem of untouchability and caste out of the confines of culture to the political agenda. Unfortunately, this political agenda got lost into the maze of parliamentary politics that soon became be-all-end-all with Dalit leaders. Even during Ambedkar's times the economic aspects of the problem remained largely untouched giving the impression to his followers as though they did not count. In the overall context it can be seen that they could not be as easily dealt with as the religio-cultural and political aspects of the problem. Moreover, it meant direct confrontation with the State for which Ambedkar was certainly not prepared. Alternately, the feudal relations in villages could be destroyed only if the private ownership of land is abolished and co-operativisation of farming is introduced. He thought, this structural change could be effected through the Constitution. It was a folly that he would soon realise when even as the 'chief architect' of the Constitution he failed so much as to bring this point on the agenda of the Constituent Assembly.

CONCEPTION OF AN IDEAL

Babasaheb Ambedkar envisioned his ideal in the famous three principles: liberty, equality and fraternity. They were the basis for the ideal society of his conception. He denied that he had adopted them from the French Revolution. He said he had derived them from the teachings of Buddha. These principles were the clarion call of the French Revolution but later became the ideological props of the liberal bourgeoisie in Europe. Since Marx had ridiculed these principles as the fantasy of the bourgeois society, many people tended to stereotype Ambedkar as the petty-bourgeois liberal democrat. As according to Ambedkar the source of these principles is different from the French Revolution, familiar to Marx, there is a prima facie scope to argue that Marx's ridicule does not apply to him. His conception of these principles is indeed substantially different from that associated with the liberal bourgeoisie. Actually, what Marx refers to are the slogans of liberty and equality of the bourgeois parliamentary democracy.

There, 'liberty' is the liberty to contract and 'equality' refers to equality in market. Ambedkar insists that the conception of the ideal society ought to have them all the three together. Absence of any would not be acceptable to him. The ideal society of his dream could only be seen within a kind of spiritual frame. It would be interesting to compare this society with the communist society of Marx's conception. Marx reached his inference following the dialectical track of historical materialism. In Ambedkar' case it was just his vision. Inevitably, he had to attribute the origin of them to some spiritual source.

For Ambedkar they meant to denote the State of society sans exploitation and with an emotive ambience of fellow feeling. It was beyond him to describe this State further in concrete terms and much so to indicate the forms of struggle to reach it. Known for his obsession with pragmatism and belief that any definitive laws could not bind the flow of human history, he would avoid the speculative construction of this distant stage of human society.

Not even Marx could describe what his dream communist society would be like beyond that it would be freed of the familiar contradictions. It essentially reflected a contradiction between human desire and material reality. It would be disaster to derive the meaning of this ideal State of Ambedkar's conception from what he did. He left that to posterity to decide as per their circumstances. But, rationally there could be little doubt that the vision of Ambedkar can only be realised in the communist society of Marx's conception where most (not all) of the contradictions in human society would have been resolved.

Dalits ought to internalise this vision and strive for its realisation. Ambedkar had a radical enough interpretation of his principles of liberty, equality and fraternity so as to feel inadequacy even in Marxism. He said that Marxism supported only equality. He was in need of a body of thought that would give equal importance to all these three principles. He met it with a convenient conceptualisation of religion. It is paradoxical that a person who is rational enough not to bind the posterity with his vision volitionally binds himself with what is said more than 25 centuries before.

It is natural to find ideals better articulated in spiritual spheres but it is equally true that these dream worlds are incapable to provide any clue for their realisation on the earth except for their pet prescription to ignore the material reality and imagine it happened in the mind. They run away from the fact that the evil humans suffer from are the attributes of the divisions in human society, and their abolition essentially calls for struggles by the sufferers against those who perpetrate sufferings. Howsoever, inherently rational the religion may be or radical its interpretation may be it cannot fully escape these limitations.

It can be seen in relation to Buddhism handed down by Babasaheb Ambedkar with his radical interpretation. Notwithstanding the familiar quibbling around the Dhamma and Dhamma among dalits, what remained of Buddhism with them is what would happen to any religion. It is a different question whether Marxism embodied Ambedkar's ideals or not but it is certain that they are neither realisable neither through any kind of constitutional acrobatics nor through any religious practice.

STATE

Ambedkar's conception of State reflects some amount of autonomy from the hegemony of the ruling classes. It is why he expected it to act as per the constitutional structure and endeavoured to incorporate the pro-Dalit bias into the Constitution. He must have realised the true nature of it, the boundaries of the autonomy and basic class bias of the State, when he actually reached not only the Constituent Assembly but also became the chairman of its Drafting Committee.

In his anxiety to secure some provisions in favour of dalits, he accepted to be the 'hack' to write what was acceptable to the ruling caste-class representatives. He must have thought that within the given constraints he had done a good job of making the Constitution responsive to the needs of the downtrodden people. Indeed, many of the provisions in the directive principles and elsewhere apparently bear clear imprint of his zeal and owe their existence to him. But, even they had to be within the strategic space provided by the rulers. His realisation of the folly was near complete when he had to burst out in utter dejection at its ineffectual implementation, that he would be the first man to burn the Constitution as it was of no good to any one. He was inaccurate, as the Constitution had proved good enough to the upper caste-class combine who had hegemonised complete political space in post-1947 India. He attributed it to the 'devils' in the Congressmen who had occupied the constitutional 'temple' he and others had built.

Ambedkar could not reach the point of understanding that the State is a mere instrument in the hands of the ruling classes to coerce the ruled ones into submission to their interests. Until the downtrodden themselves become the ruling class, they cannot expect the State to do good to them. Whatever good that appears to come to their share, in ultimate balance accrues to the other side in multiple measure.

The post-1947 State, which has never tired of propagandising its concern for dalits and poor, has in fact been singularly instrumental in aggravating the caste problem with its policies. Even the apparently progressive policies in the form of Land Ceiling Act, Green Revolution, Programme of Removal of Poverty, Reservations to Dalits in Services and Mandal Commission etc. have resulted against their professed objectives. The effect of the Land Ceiling Act, has been in creating a layer of the middle castes farmers which could be consolidated in caste terms to constitute a formidable constituency. In its new incarnation, this group that has traditionally been the immediate upper caste layer to dalits, assumed virtual custody of Brahminism in order to coerce Dalit landless labourers to serve their socioeconomic interests and suppress their assertive expression in the bud. The Green Revolution was the main instrument to introduce capitalisation in agrarian sector.

It reinforced the innate hunger of the landlords and big farmers for land as this State sponsored revolution produced huge surplus for them. It resulted in creating geographical imbalance and promoting unequal terms of trade in favour of urban areas. Its resultant impact on dalits has been far more excruciating than that of the Land Ceiling Act. The much publicised programme for Removal of Poverty has aggravated the gap between the heightened hopes and aspirations of dalits on one hand and the feelings of depravation among the poorer sections of non-dalits in the context of the special programmes especially launched for upliftment of dalits. The tension that ensued culminated in increasingly strengthening the caste-based demands and further aggravating the caste-divide. The reservations in services for dalits, notwithstanding its benefits, have caused incalculable damage in political terms. Reservations created hope, notional stake in the system and thus dampened the alienation; those who availed of its benefit got politically emasculated and in course consciously or unconsciously served as the props of the system. The context of scarcity of jobs provided ample opportunity to reactionary forces to divide the youth along caste lines. Mandal Commission, that enthused many progressive parties and people to upheld its extension of reservation to the backward castes, has greatly contributed to strengthen the caste identities of people. Inasmuch as it empowers the backward castes, actually their richer sections, it is bound to worsen the relative standing of dalits in villages.

Thus, the State, its welfare mask notwithstanding, has viciously and consistently acted against dalits and poor people. It is a complete contra-evidence to hopes of Ambedkar who strove to maximise and make use of the autonomous space of the State for the benefits of the have-nots, particularly dalits. It is one thing to assume autonomous space but quite another to equate it with caste-class neutrality. Unfortunately, the Dalit political behaviour always reflected this erroneous notion of caste-class neutrality of the State. It has already caused great damage to the Dalit interests. The radical Ambedkar might have strategy to use State for Dalit cause but would never see it as caste-class neutral.

SOCIALISM

Despite his ambivalence and reservations about the emphasis on the economic dimension in socialism, Ambedkar broadly remained a socialist. Some scholars do find little scope for suspecting his socialist credentials because of his disapproval of Russell's criticism of property, his non-acceptance of Marxian formulations and his placement of social issues higher than the economic and political issues. He called the complaint against love of money as 'philosophy of sour grapes' and ridiculed materialism as 'the ideology of pigs'. This impression is moreover strengthened by his reservations to accept the economic interpretation of history. But, in all fairness it may be said that what he appears to mean is the integrative consideration of all the factors that are needed for any society to be based on liberty, equality and fraternity. Notwithstanding his variant conception, there should not be any doubt about his socialistic antecedents. His conception of socialism also underwent evolution. Once he had stated that there was hardly any difference between his socialism and communism. As such, his disagreement with the communists was about the means and not about the aim. He warns the communists that the classless society can emerge only after the emergence of a casteless society. It implies that his quarrel with the then communists was over the stages of revolution. In the 1920s and 30s, these people had borrowed the communist dogma and parroted class struggle in utter disregard of the reality.

Ambedkar, on the contrary, was firmly rooted in it. They believed that the soviet Russian model of revolution was importable for bringing about a socialist revolution into India whereas Ambedkar realistically postulated that unless the consciousness of the working class was congenial for revolution, there was no question of it materializing. And, unless the caste system is destroyed, creation of the pro-revolution consciousness was out of question. His annoyance with the Bombay communists was largely because of their dogmatic behaviour. It is unfortunate that the ideal of classlessness that was latent in his agenda never really surfaced during his lifetime.

Ambedkar relies on the concept of 'State' for materialisation of his conception of socialism. His conception of State is largely idealist. He wanted the State to intervene in the economic structure and its monitoring. He wanted to constitutionalise this State intervention so that it would not be subject to change any time with the whims of simple majority vote in the legislation.

Ambedkar who taught, "The lost rights cannot be regained by making appeals or requests to the robbers; it needs struggles"; did not say anything on how the oppressed people will get such strength as to create the constitutional provisions, that would put the class structure upside down. On behalf of his party-Scheduled Caste Federation, he had submitted a draft for the future constitution to the Constituent Assembly for the independent India. It was published later as "States and Minorities". This book has really aided students in understanding some aspects of his conception of socialism.

Nevertheless, one cannot afford to forget the constraints placed by the context in which it was written. The context was that he had failed to get into the Constituent Assembly and was therefore anxious to strike a feasible and still radical note that could find the support of the vast majority of the have-nots which might then create some pressure either for its inclusion in the Constitution or for his entry into the Constituent Assembly. For some years, during the preceding turbulence of negotiations for transfer of power, he found himself totally marginalised. Notwithstanding the probable limitations of this draft, its provisions in operational terms were still very radical. The main provisions are:

- o All important industries and services shall belong to the nation.
- o Insurance industry shall be in public sector and insurance will be compulsory for every citizen.
- o Private sector and entrepreneurs shall have a role in the economy but it shall not be dominating.
- o Nationalisation of land and promotion of cooperative farming on a collective principle.

These provisions, if implemented, would have gone a long way towards supporting democratic revolution in the country. It would have limited inequality and exploitation in the economic and political sphere. Politically, it would have had far-reaching impact. Ambedkar till the end could not completely remove the Fabian influence (which he might have gathered while in England) on him. In his times, particularly before World War II, few people in India were well versed in Marxist philosophy. The knowledge of Marxism seldom exceeded some broad principles and 'Stalin's dictatorship' painted by imperialists or the 'revolt of the workers, the insurgency of the poor. Ambedkar also does not seem to have gone very far from this point. Without indulging into the debate of ifs and buts, there should not be any iota of doubt that the ideal society of his conception could materialise only through socialism.

DEMOCRACY

Ambedkar had unshakeable faith in democracy. In his conception of an exploitation-less society, democracy has an extraordinary role. Democracy means 'one person, one vote'; and 'one vote, one value'. Democracy means empowerment of any person for participating in the process of decision-making relating to her/him, democracy means liberty, equality and fraternity-Ambedkar's definition of democracy had such a tone. Because he presided over making of the Constitution and is being projected as its chief architect, there is a misunderstanding that parliamentary democracy is what he wanted. But nothing could be farther from the truth than this. He himself spoke against parliamentary democracy. For instance, he defined parliamentary democracy as "voting by the people in favour of their owners and handing over the rights of ruling over themselves". This provides a glimpse of the expanse of his ideal, which certainly was much beyond the Indian Constitution or any common place understanding about him.

His conception of democracy appears to be purely people oriented. He showed that the bookish concepts of equality are detrimental to the disabled sections of society in the prevailing social setting and proposed a fundamental change in the concept of equality. It envisaged complete abolition of inequality. His principle of positive discrimination is based on this very concept of equality. But the operational aspects of this concept involved the need for some kind of autonomous institution, which was met by 'State' and 'religion'. It is necessary to stress that his greatness lies in the radicality of his conceptions, his vision of a human society sans any kind of exploitation; not in the remedies or apparatus he proposed in the circumstances prevailing in his time.

ASPECTS OF THE STRATEGY AND TACTICS

In the context of strategy, some of Ambedkar's contributions are really noteworthy. He brought the struggle against Brahminism into the political battlefield. He inferred that without political power the social and religious structures will collapse and motivated his followers to capture political power. But his conception of political power being acutely constrained by the parliamentary framework where bargaining is the predominant medium of securing political power, inevitably it made way for all kinds of aberrations and perversities to creep in. The prevailing politics being the game of possibilities, he was soon sucked into its vortex. Politics came to dominate the other aspects of his personality. Slowly, the impact of politics started becoming visible everywhere. This phase significantly contributed to multiplication of his inconsistencies out of tactical imperatives. Dalits have taken this legacy of parliamentary politics very seriously, almost as the be all and end all of their political being. It may be, interesting to probe how much damage this kind of political orientation inflicted on the Dalit movement.

It is altogether a different question whether Ambedkar had any other alternative to parliamentary politics for political practice. It may be argued that in the context of his resources, adversarial environment and to some extent his personal limitations, he had none. Even if it is taken as correct, it should not be forgotten that it was a matter of strategy and tactic that presuppose contextual variables: it cannot be taken as the lasting value.

The fundamental source of most of Ambedkar's political thoughts and action is his conception of State and religion, that he had adopted as the extraneous instruments to reconcile the state of flux of things and the necessity of order in them. It is necessary to understand that both, the State as well as religion, are the products of the evolutionary process of the human society. There is nothing inevitable about them. Marx took State as the instrument of coercion in the hands of ruling classes and religion as the opium of the masses. Dalits have a long experience of nearly five decades with the so-called welfare State of Ambedkar's design. What does it say? Does the State side with them in their conflict with the landlords? Does it come to their rescue when every day three or four of their daughters are raped?

Does it come to save the shame of their women when they are paraded naked in the streets? Does it take their side when they come in conflict with landlords, moneylenders in villages or with management in the modern settings? Does it really ensure they get their dues as provided in the Constitution or punish the defaulting management for noncompliance? To all of such questions the answer could only be in the negative. It is not a matter of 'devils occupying the temples' as Ambedkar lamented seeing the people occupying the Constitutional positions. The State possesses the characteristics of its master class. In India the upper caste capitalists, landlords, top bureaucrats, etc. being the ruling class, the State can never have saints who would favour dalits. It is a fact that even the government by a Dalit party like the BSP could not transform it into a Dalit State.

Religion, in Ambedkar's conception is necessary to maintain the moral order of the society. It may be interesting to examine to what extent it conforms to this idealistic expectation. Buddhism, which undoubtedly is the most rational of all the religions, does not have any evidence of having created over its near millennium long tenure in India such an order of the society which could claim liberty, equality and fraternity of Ambedkar's conception. Ambedkar's argument that the Bhikku Sangha in Buddhism was the prototype of this kind of society becomes invalid once we call into question the role of Sangha in the production process.

Before that, the order that envisaged nostalgically to recreate the value of the vanishing Gana Rajya in microcosm against the evil of rising monarchies, cannot just sublimate to the era of capitalism without being an alley of exploiters unless it transforms itself in some way as a catalyst for the revolution. The moral tenets of Buddhism likewise cannot submerge the lure of surplus extraction, that is its dominating ethos. If at all, it may help it become more pronounced by weakening the resistance of the exploited masses. As we empirically see, the Buddhism of his conception could not produce even a trace of morality in its adherents. On the contrary, for the masses it presents the distorted, if not inverted, worldview; it orients them to look inwards for their misery and be blind to the reality that some one exploits him. He could certainly derive mental peace and pleasure but it is a state of an intoxicated mind. Keeping in mind the causal links in Ambedkar's adoption of these instruments, the redefinition project needs to address these issues afresh.

The strategy of the ruling class always stresses on diversion of peoples' attention from their real problems and their disarmament-both in physical and ideological terms. They invariably have a multilayered strategy in place for this purpose. The vanguard parties of the ruling classes open up sentimental fronts and attempt to divert the attention of people as their real problems get aggravated. Secondly, their time-tested methods of adulterating radical ideas with the masses are always in operation. Towards this end, we see all the ruling parties vying with each other in co-opting Ambedkar. 'Ambedkar' represents a potentially dangerous ideological weapon in the hands of the Indian proletariat and so the ruling class will be hell bent on blunting its edge. They will do everything to eulogise him not only for wooing dalits for their immediate electoral gains but also to neutralise him as the radical ideological force by propagandising a distorted version of the latter. Dalits will have to exercise vigil over their ideological assets even after redefining Ambedkar.

AMBEDKAR'S THINKING OF CASTE

Although Indian society is fragmented into castes, there has been some change due to the movement of Dr. Ambedkar and other reformers. Some of his followers have benefited in terms of education and wealth due to his efforts. However, the change is not striking, and many are still subjected to hatred and perish in poverty. Caste-based violence continues to be an all pervading phenomenon. Even after the abolition of untouchability by law, practices, such as inhuman treatment, raping untouchable women and so forth, still occur in India. The situation at the time of Dr. Ambedkar was worse, and he personally experienced the caste system in its most inhuman form, being born into and brought up in an untouchable family.

A few seminal experiences awakened him to reality of the caste system. The first took place in Goregaon when Dr. Ambedkar was a boy of nine. He was to visit his father along with his brother. The location of his father's work place was far from the railway station, and no cart man was willing to take them on a bullock cart. One cart man agreed with the condition that the boys would have to drive the cart while he would sit behind. Throughout this escapade which lasted through the night, the boys went hungry because they could not get pure water to drink, even though they had plenty of food. Their inability to get water was of course due to the fact that untouchables were barred from using public wells. This incident had a very important place in Dr. Ambedkar's life and it left an indelible impression on his mind.

His worst experience of the caste system took place in Baroda when he was to become the Military Secretary to the Baroda State. He could not get accommodation in Baroda because he was an untouchable, though highly educated. He found a quarter in a Parsi boarding house and assumed a Parsi name. At work, the Brahman clerks and subordinates kept their distance and threw files and papers on him to avoid his touch. Even in the club, he was only allowed to sit in the corner and was not allowed to take part in games. No clear assignment was given to him, though he was a Military Secretary.

When the Parsis discovered his identity, they besieged his boarding house and threatened to beat him. Eventually, the owner expelled him and he had to leave Baroda.

The third seminal experience took place in Chalisgaon, where no horse carriage driver was willing to take Dr. Ambedkar from the railway station to the place where a meeting was to be held. After a long wait, a carriage was finally brought. The driver and he were the only two occupants of the carriage. The carriage had not gone 200 paces when there was almost a collision with a motor car. Dr. Ambedkar was surprised that the driver, who was paid for hire every day, should have been so inexperienced. The accident was averted only because of the loud shout of a policeman. They somehow arrived at the culvert on a river. Around it there were no walls as there are on a bridge.

The carriage was thrown down on the stone pavement of the culvert, and the horse and the carriage fell down from the culvert into the river. So heavy was the fall that Dr. Ambedkar was knocked senseless. As a result of this he received several injuries. His leg was fractured and he was disabled for several days. On inquiry, Dr. Ambedkar was told the real facts. The delay at the railway station was due to the fact that the carriage drivers were not prepared to drive with a passenger who was an untouchable. They felt it was beneath their dignity. The Mahar untouchables could not tolerate that their leader should walk to their quarters. A compromise was therefore arrived at: the owner of a carriage would give it on hire but not drive. Although they could not find someone to drive it, the Mahars thought this to be a happy solution, evidently forgetting that the safety of the passenger was more important than the maintenance of his dignity. It was then that Dr. Ambedkar learned that even a menial Hindu carriage driver looked upon himself as superior to any untouchable even if that person be a barrister-at-law like Dr. Ambedkar.

There are many more incidences such as these from Dr. Ambedkar's life. These few, however, are sufficient for any person to understand the suffering experienced due to the practice of untouchability and caste. Many people in contemporary India still suffer from this system of graded inequality. They are living the life of degraded human beings.

Dr. Ambedkar's Analysis of Caste: Understanding the origin, genesis and mechanism of caste in India is a very complex problem. Many able minds have tried to penetrate it, including Dr. Ambedkar who began work on this issue as early as 1916. He attempted to link the many chains in the history of India in order to show how the caste system evolved. In Dr. Ambedkar's understanding, the prime factor responsible for the evolution of the system of untouchability was the religious persecution of Buddhists, while other social-psychological factors are secondary. The existence of caste in India is due to the notion of inequality imposed by religion, which gives rise to social and cultural practices and prejudices. If these social and cultural practices cease, caste could be annihilated. This is a simple formulation of the quite complex issue of caste.

The life and work of the Buddha marks the flowering of the axial period in India in the sixth century BC. This period was one of great turmoil as smaller tribal societies were transforming into larger settled ones and eventually mighty empires. It has been shown that these smaller, pre-imperial societies were not based on a graded system of inequality or caste. This is not to say that there was no class system. Further, these societies often exhibited unethical and immoral aspects, like incest, alcoholism, war mongering, and the savage practice of ritual sacrifice. Thus the revolutionary role of the Buddha was in first clearly proclaiming that the happiness of humans and society lies in ethics and not in rituals. Dr. Ambedkar understood the Buddha's awakening under the bodhi tree as a true revolution. "It was as great a revolution as the French Revolution. Though it began as a religious revolution, it became more than a religious revolution. It became a social and political revolution."

The Buddha's revolution which culminated in the emergence of the mighty empire of Ashoka (r. 270-232 B. C.) further strengthened the Buddhist world view based on liberty, equality, and fraternity; a universal message that went beyond the Indian subcontinent. Under Ashoka, equality of punishment irrespective of the social standing of the criminal emerged. The priestly class was given the same treatment as that of the common people. Although Ashoka prevented worship of clan deities (kula devata) which served as the basis of income for the Brahmins, he was ecumenical and promoted inter-religious tolerance. He did not persecute the Brahmins, yet the Brahmans lost their social prestige as the majority of the people abandoned the animal sacrifices that the Brahmans officiated. The rule of law was established, and even animals received good treatment, as noted by the famous Chinese pilgrim, Hsuan Tsang.

In Revolution and Counter revolution in Ancient India, Dr. Ambedkar described that after the establishment of the rule of law, the Brahmins lived as a depressed class for the nearly 140 years of the Mauryan Empire. Pushyamitra Sunga of the Samvedi Brahmin clan then conspired to destroy Buddhism as the state religion and to make the Brahmins the sovereign rulers of India with the political power of the state behind it through murdering Ashoka's grandson, Emperor Brhadratha, in 185 B.C. After his accession, Pushyamitra launched a violent and virulent campaign of persecution against Buddhists and Buddhism. Thus, the counter-revolution against Buddhism began with the emergence of the Brahmins under the Sunga Dynasty.

At the same time, various major Brahmanical texts were written in order to counter Buddhism. According to Dr. Ambedkar, these texts are the true sources of inequality and were largely post-Mauryan developments. For example, Dr. Ambedkar showed that the Code of Manu (Manusmriti) was written by Sumati Bharagava after Psuhyamitra's revolt in 185 B.C. The Code of Manu, which served as the law of inequality, was drafted and enforced with the newly acquired state power by the Brahmins, while the myth of the first cosmic being Purusha, which tells of the divine origin of caste, was interpolated into the Rig-Veda. According to Dr. Ambedkar, the Manusmriti, the Bhagavad Gita, Shankaracharya's Vedanta, the Mahabharata, the Ramayana and the Puranas are all post-Mauryan texts which serve as sources of inequality.

It should be noted, however, that the Buddhists of ancient India did not accept this worldview all at once-perhaps they never did as is evident from the continuous struggle between the Brahmans and the untouchables (former Buddhists) of modern India. The hatred and contempt preached by the Brahmins was directed against Buddhists in particular and not against other groups. After the Mauryan Period, most Indians who had upheld Buddhism slipped back into Brahmanised Hinduism.

Other Indians who did not became untouchables, like the "Broken Men." The "Broken Men", according to Dr. Ambedkar, were the remaining peoples of broken and defeated tribal groups of ancient India. Dr. Ambedkar wrote about this concept of "Broken Men" and how they came into being when the primitive societies were breaking up and transforming into the larger settled societies of imperial India. Brahmanism never tried to absorb these Buddhists into the caste system but rather shut them right out of it by making them untouchables and all that they stood for, like no education, no means of economic development, etc. Untouchability was thus only born sometime around 400 A.D., as these "Broken Men" were not able to abandon beef eating when cow killing was made a capital offence by the Gupta kings. In this way, the cow politics of present day India has its roots in the counter-revolution of the Brahmans against the Buddhists. Untouchability was thus born out of the struggle for supremacy between Buddhism and Brahmanism on a variety of levels from political power to social convention.

This is not to say that Buddhism was destroyed all at once. The struggle went on until the Muslim invasion in 1200 C.E. The Muslim invasions played a decisive role as the Muslim invaders killed Buddhist monks or caused them to flee India. According to Dr. Ambedkar, "Religion like any other ideology can be attained only by propaganda. If propaganda fails, religion must disappear. The priestly class, however detestable it may be, is necessary to the sustenance of religion. For it is by its propaganda that religion is kept up.

Without the priestly class religion must disappear." Due to this onslaught, the Buddhist Sangha in India underwent a great change in its composition. A disorganized system of married clergy with families who were called aryas developed.

They took the place of the bhikkhus and began to cater to the religious needs of the general community. They eventually attained the status of bhikkhus through the performance of some sacraments. They officiated at religious ceremonies, but at the same time, in addition to their profession of priesthood, they earned their livelihood through such avocations as masonry, painting, sculpting, gold smithing, and carpentry. These artisan-priests, who were in later times larger in number than the bhikkhus, became the religious guides of the people. Their avocations left them little time and desire for the acquisition of learning, for deep thinking, or for devotion to meditation and other spiritual exercises. They could not be expected to raise Buddhism to a higher position through their endeavours, nor could they check its course towards ruin through the introduction of salutary reforms. It is obvious that this new Buddhist priesthood had neither prestige nor learning and was a poor match for the rival Brahmins.

The upheaval caused by the Muslim invaders in the Buddhist Community lasted for a while. However, the Muslims did not destroy or challenge its principles or doctrines, which governed the spiritual life of the people. On the other hand, the Brahmanic invasion changed the principles which Buddhism had preached for centuries as universal ones of a spiritual life. According to Dr. Ambedkar, the Brahmanic invasion of Buddhist India is significant but usually neglected by the historians of India. Buddhist India is not a myth or construction of Dr. Ambedkar. This is supported by material evidence (Rhys Davids 1903). However, the concept of Vedic India or the Golden Vedic Age is truly a construction of recent times by Hindu Nationalists. The neo-Brahmanism of the post-Mauryan period brought the real changes in the political and social structure.

Through the medieval and colonial periods, the struggle against Brahmanism continued, though it was very much weakened due to the forces of time. The saint-poets of the 14th century onwards, such as Kabir, Nanadnar, Chokamela, and Tukaram, came from untouchable castes or backward classes and reflect "Buddhist" sentiments. Their teaching is marked with anti-caste and anti-Brahmanistic ideas. They ridiculed the Vedas and the religious texts of the Brahminism. They praised the ideals of liberty, equality and fraternity. This influenced Untouchables in south India who also realized in the beginning of the twentieth century that they were Buddhists and began their now well documented movement (G. Aloysius, 2004).

This deep-seated caste based hatred is responsible for most of the problems and evils in India today, including the degradation of women. The creative energy of the country is imprisoned in the caste system. The life and mission of Dr. Ambedkar was to annihilate caste and create a new society based on the principles of liberty, equality, and fraternity. He also knew that the solution lies in making people aware of their social history and why they are condemned to such a life. He wanted to usher India into an era of enlightenment, or "Right Enlightenment". (Nanda, 2002). This enlightened vision is the preface and key to everything else in conquering ignorance (the origin of suffering) and in the higher life (the end of suffering). For developing this enlightened vision, Dr. Ambedkar felt one needs to realize and understand the law of causality (paticca samuppada) or dhamma, "This is, that is; with the arising of this, that arises. This is not, that is not. With the cessation of this, that ceases."

NATURE OF CASTE

Before launching into our field of enquiry, it is better to advise ourselves regarding the nature of a caste. I will therefore draw upon a few of the best students of caste for their definitions of it:

1. Mr. Nesfield defines a caste as "a class of the community which disowns any connection with any other class and can neither intermarry nor eat nor drink with any but persons of their own community".
2. Mr. Senart, a French authority, defines a caste as "a close corporation, in theory at any rate rigorously hereditary: equipped with a certain traditional and independent organisation, including a chief and a council, meeting on occasion in assemblies of more or less plenary authority and joining together at certain festivals: bound together by common occupations, which relate more particularly to marriage and to food and to questions of ceremonial pollution, and ruling its members by the exercise of jurisdiction, the extent of which varies, but which succeeds in making the authority of the community more felt by the sanction of detrain penalties and, above all, by final irrevocable exclusion from the group".
3. Dr. Ketkar defines caste as "a social group having two characteristics: (i) membership is confined to those who are born of members and includes all persons so born; (ii) the members are forbidden by an inexorable social law to marry outside the group".
4. According to Sir H. Risley, "a caste may be defined as a collection of families or groups of families bearing a common name which usually denotes or is associated with specific occupation, claiming common descent from a mythical ancestor, human *or* divine, professing to

follow the same professional callings and are regarded by those who are competent to give an opinion as forming a single homogeneous community".

To review these definitions is of great importance for our purpose. It will be noticed that taken individually the definitions of three of the writers include too much or too little: none is complete or correct by itself and all have missed the central point in the mechanism of the Caste system. Their mistake lies in trying to define caste as an isolated unit by itself, and not as a group within, and with definite relations to, the system of caste as a whole. Yet collectively all of them are complementary to one another, each one emphasising what has been obscured in the other. By way of criticism, therefore, *I* will take only those points common to all Castes in each of the above definitions which are regarded as peculiarities of Caste and evaluate them as such. To start with Mr. Senart.

He draws attention to the "idea of pollution" as a characteristic of Caste. With regard to this point it may be safely said that it is by no means a peculiarity of Caste as such. It usually originates in priestly ceremonialism and is a particular case of the general belief in purity. Consequently its necessary connection with Caste may be completely denied without damaging the working of Caste. The "idea of pollution" has been attached to the institution of Caste, only because the Caste that enjoys the highest rank is the priestly Caste: while we know that priest and purity are old associates. We may therefore conclude that the "idea of pollution" is a characteristic of Caste only in so far as Caste has a religious flavour. Mr. Nesfield in his way dwells on the absence of messing with those outside the Caste as one of its characteristics. In spite of the newness of the point we must say that Mr. Nesfield has mistaken the effect for the cause. Caste, being a self-enclosed unit naturally limits social intercourse, including messing etc. to members within it. Consequently this absence of messing with outsiders is not due to positive prohibition, but is a natural result of Caste, *i.e.* exclusiveness. No doubt this absence of messing originally due to exclusiveness, acquired the prohibitory character of a religious injunction, but it may be regarded as a later growth. Sir H. Risley, makes no new point deserving of special attention. We now pass on to the definition of Dr. Ketkar who has done much for the elucidation of the subject. Not only is he a native, but he has also brought a critical acumen and an open mind to bear on his study of Caste. His definition merits consideration, for he has defined Caste in its relation to a system of Castes, and has concentrated his attention only on those characteristics which are absolutely necessary for the existence of a Caste within a system, rightly excluding all others as being secondary or derivative in character. With respect to his definition it must, however, be said that in it there is a slight confusion of thought, lucid and clear as otherwise it is. He speaks of *Prohibition of Intermarriage* and *Membership by Autogeny* as the two characteristics of Caste. I submit that these are but two aspects of one and the same thing, and not two different things as Dr. Ketkar supposes them to be. If you prohibit intermarriage the result is that you limit membership to those born within the group.

Thus the two are the obverse and the reverse sides of the same medal. This critical evaluation of the various characteristics of Caste leave no doubt that prohibition, or rather the absence of intermarriage—endogamy, to be concise—is the only one that can be called the essence of Caste when rightly understood. But some may deny this on abstract anthropological grounds, for there exist endogamous groups without giving rise to the problem of Caste. In a general way this may be true, as endogamous societies, culturally different, making their abode in localities more or less removed, and having little to do with each other are a physical reality.

The Negroes and the Whites and the various tribal groups that go by name of American Indians in the United States may be cited as more or less appropriate illustrations in support of this view. But we must not confuse matters, for in India the situation is different. As pointed out before, the peoples of India form a homogeneous whole. The various races of India occupying definite territories have more or less fused into one another and do possess cultural unity, which is the only criterion of a homogeneous population. Given this homogeneity as a basis, Caste becomes a problem altogether new in character and wholly absent in the situation constituted by the mere propinquity of endogamous social or tribal groups. Caste in India means an artificial chopping off of the population into fixed and definite units, each one prevented from fusing into another through the custom of endogamy.

Thus the conclusion is inevitable that *Endogamy is the only characteristic that is peculiar to caste,* and if we succeed in showing how endogamy is maintained, we shall practically have proved the genesis and also the mechanism of Caste. It may not be quite easy for you to anticipate why I regard endogamy as a key to the mystery of the Caste system. Not to strain your imagination too much, I will proceed to give you my reasons for it. It may not also be out of place to emphasize at this moment that no civilized society of today presents more survivals of primitive times than does the Indian society. Its religion is essentially primitive and its tribal code, in spite of the advance of time and civilization, operates in all its pristine vigour even today. One of these primitive survivals, to which I wish particularly to draw your attention, is the *Custom of Exogamy.*

The prevalence of exogamy in the primitive worlds is a fact too well-known to need any explanation. With the growth of history, however, exogamy has lost its efficacy, and excepting the nearest blood-kins, there is usually no social bar restricting the field of marriage. But regarding the peoples of India the law of exogamy is a positive injunction even today. Indian society still savours of the clan system, even though there are no clans; and this can be easily seen from the law of matrimony which centres round the principle of exogamy, for it is not that *Sapindas* (blood-kins) cannot marry, but a marriage even between *Sagotras* (of the same class) is regarded as a sacrilege. Nothing is therefore more important for you to remember than the fact that endogamy is foreign to the people of India.

The various *Gotras* of India are and have been exogamous: so are the other groups with totemic organization. It is no exaggeration to say that with the people of India exogamy is a creed and none dare infringe it, so much so that, in spite of the endogamy of the Castes within them, exogamy is strictly observed and that there are more rigorous penalties for violating exogamy than there are for violating endogamy. You will, therefore, readily see that with exogamy as the rule there could be no Caste, for exogamy means fusion. But we have castes; consequently in the final analysis creation of Castes, so far as India is concerned, means the superposition of endogamy on exogamy. However, in an originally exogamous population an easy working out of endogamy (which is equivalent to the creation of Caste) is a grave problem, and it is in the consideration of the means utilized for the preservation of endogamy against exogamy that we may hope to find the solution of our problem.

Thus the superposition of endogamy on exogamy means the creation of caste. But this is not an easy affair. Let us take an imaginary group that desires to make itself into a Caste and analyse what means it will have to adopt to make itself endogamous. If a group desires to make itself endogamous a formal injunction against intermarriage with outside groups will be of no avail, especially if prior to the introduction of endogamy, exogamy had been the rule in all matrimonial relations. Again, there is a tendency in all groups lying in close contact with one another to assimilate and amalgamate, and thus consolidate into a homogeneous society. If this tendency is to be strongly counteracted in the interest of Caste formation, it is absolutely necessary to circumscribe a circle outside which people should not contract marriages. Nevertheless, this encircling to prevent marriages from without creates problems from within which are not very easy of solution.

Roughly speaking, in a normal group the two sexes are more or less evenly distributed, and generally speaking there is an equality between those of the same age. The equality is, however, never quite realized in actual societies. At the same time to the group that is desirous of making itself into a caste the maintenance of equality between the sexes becomes the ultimate goal, for without it endogamy can no longer subsist. In other words, if endogamy is to be preserved conjugal rights from within have to be provided for, otherwise members of the group will be driven out of the circle to take care of themselves in any way they can. But in order that the conjugal rights be provided for from within, it is absolutely necessary to maintain a numerical equality between the marriageable units of the two sexes within the group desirous of making itself into a Caste. It is only through the maintenance of such an equality that the necessary endogamy of the group can be kept intact, and a very large disparity is sure to break it.

The problem of Caste, then, ultimately resolves itself into one of repairing the disparity between the marriageable units of the two sexes within it. Left to nature, the much needed parity between the units can be realized only when a couple dies simultaneously. But this is a rare contingency. The husband may die before the wife and create a *surplus woman,* who must be disposed of; else through intermarriage she will violate the endogamy of the group. In like manner the husband may survive his wife and be *surplus man,* whom the group, while it may sympathise with him for the sad bereavement, has to dispose of, else he will marry outside the Caste and will break the endogamy. Thus both the *surplus man* and the *surplus woman* constitute a menace to the Caste if not taken care of, for not finding suitable partners inside their prescribed circle (and left to themselves they cannot find any, for if the matter be not regulated there can only be just enough pairs to go round) very likely they will transgress the boundary, marry outside and import offspring that is foreign to the Caste. Let us see what our imaginary group is likely to do with this *surplus man* and *surplus woman.*

We will first take up the case of the *surplus woman.* She can be disposed of in two different ways so as to preserve the endogamy of the Caste.

First: burn her on the funeral pyre of her deceased husband and get rid of her. This, however, is rather an impracticable way of solving the problem of sex disparity. In some cases it may work, in others it may not. Consequently every surplus woman cannot thus be disposed of, because it is an easy solution but a hard realization. And so the *surplus woman* (= widow), if not disposed of, remains in the group: but in her very existence lies a double danger. She may marry outside the Caste and violate endogamy, or she may marry within the Caste and through competition encroach upon the chances of marriage that must be reserved for the potential brides in the Caste. She is therefore a menace in any case, and something must be done to her if she cannot be burned along with her deceased husband. The second remedy is to enforce widowhood on her for the rest of her life. So far as the objective results are concerned, burning is a better solution than enforcing widowhood. Burning the widow eliminates all the three evils that a *surplus woman* is fraught with. Being dead and gone she creates no problem of remarriage either inside or outside the Caste. But compulsory widowhood is superior to burning because it is more practicable. Besides being comparatively humane it also guards against the evils of remarriage as does burning; but it fails to guard the morals of the group. No doubt under compulsory widowhood the woman remains, and just because she is deprived of her natural right of being a legitimate wife in future, the incentive to immoral conduct is increased. But this is by no means an insuperable difficulty. She can be degraded to a condition in which she is no longer a source of allurement.

The problem of *surplus man* (= widower) is much more important and much more difficult than that of the *surplus woman* in a group that desires to make itself into a Caste. From time immemorial man as compared with woman has had the upper hand. He is a dominant figure in every group and of the two sexes has greater prestige. With this traditional superiority of man over woman his wishes have always been consulted. Woman, on the other hand, has been an easy prey to all kinds of iniquitous injunctions, religious, social or economic. But man as a maker of injunctions is most often above them all. Such being the case, you cannot accord the same kind of treatment to a *surplus man* as you can to a *surplus woman in* a Caste.

The project of burning him with his deceased wife is hazardous in two ways: first of all it cannot be done, simply because he is a man. Secondly, if done, a sturdy soul is lost to the Caste. There remain then only two solutions which can conveniently dispose of him. I say conveniently, because he is an asset to the group. Important as he is to the group, endogamy is still more important, and the solution must assure both these ends. Under these circumstances he may be forced or I should say induced, after the manner of the widow, to remain a widower for the rest of his life. This solution is not altogether difficult, for without any compulsion some are so disposed as to enjoy self-imposed celibacy, or even to take a further step of their own accord and renounce the world and its joys. But, given human nature as it is, this solution can hardly be expected to be realized. On the other hand, as is very likely to be the case, if the *surplus man* remains in the group as an active participator in group activities, he is a danger to the morals of the group.

Looked at from different point of view celibacy, though easy in cases where it succeeds, is not so advantageous even then to the material prospects of the Caste. If he observes genuine celibacy and renounces the world, he would not be a menace to the preservation of Caste endogamy or Caste morals as he undoubtedly would be if he remained a secular person. But as an ascetic celibate he is as good as burned, so far as the material well-being of his Caste is concerned. A Caste, in order that it may be large enough to afford a vigorous communal life, must be maintained at a certain numerical strength. But to hope for this and to proclaim celibacy is the same as trying to cure atrophy by bleeding.

Imposing celibacy on the *surplus man* in the group, therefore, fails both theoretically and practically. It is in the interest of the Caste to keep him as a *Grahastha* (one who raises a family), to use a Sanskrit technical term. But the problem is to provide him with a wife from within the Caste. At the outset this is not possible, for the ruling ratio in a caste has to be one man to one woman and none can have two chances of marriage, for in a Caste thoroughly self-enclosed there are always just enough marriageable women to go round for the marriageable men. Under these circumstances the *surplus man* can be provided with a wife only by recruiting a bride from the ranks of those not yet marriageable in order to tie him down to the group. This is certainly the best of the possible solutions in the case of the *surplus man*. By this, he is kept within the Caste. By this means numerical depletion through constant outflow is guarded against, and by this endogamy morals are preserved. It will now be seen that the four means by which numerical disparity between the two sexes is conveniently maintained are: (1) burning the widow with her deceased husband; (2) compulsory widowhood—a milder form of burning; (3) imposing celibacy on the widower and (4) wedding him to a girl not yet marriageable. Though, as I said above, burning the widow and imposing celibacy on the widower are of doubtful service to the group in its endeavour to preserve its endogamy, all of them operate as *means*. But means, as forces, when liberated or set in motion create an end. What then is the end that these means create? They create and perpetuate endogamy, while caste and endogamy, according to our analysis of the various definitions of caste, are one and the same thing. Thus the existence of these means is identical with caste and caste involves these means. This, in my opinion, is the general mechanism of a caste in a system of castes.

Let us now turn from these high generalities to the castes in Hindu Society and inquire into their mechanism. I need hardly premise that there are a great many pitfalls in the path of those who try to unfold the past, and caste in India to be sure is a very ancient institution. This is especially true where there exist no authentic or written records or where the people, like the Hindus, are so constituted that to them writing history is a folly, for the world is an illusion. But institutions do live, though for a long time they may remain unrecorded and as often as not customs and morals are like fossils that tell their own history. If this is true, our task will be amply rewarded if we scrutinize the solution the Hindus arrived at to meet the problems of the *surplus man* and *surplus woman.*

DHARMA IN ORTHODOX HINDU CASTE SOCIETY

According to one view, the Caste system shows how strongly many have felt about each person following his or her dharma, or destined path. A perversion, according to many Hindus, of dharma's true meaning, caste still plays a significant role in Hindu society; however, post Independence, caste is rapidly losing favour in India and caste-based discrimination has been illegitimised. The British Raj and the subsequent governments have used the caste based politics effectively to divide and conquer for their own personal political gains.

The Vedas do not condone discrimination of any sort. The four 'varna's (literally, 'colour') or castes, were based upon the duties to society and worked together towards the welfare of the society. They had equal standing in the society. However over a period of time this division of labour was misunderstood and exploited. This became more ingrained over centuries until social mobility all but became a thing of the past. In spite of centuries of numerous reform movements, notably within Vedanta, bhakti yoga and Hindu streams of Tantra, and reformers, with recent stalwarts like Swami Vivekananda and Mahatma Gandhi, caste is so deeply ensconced in the Indian consciousness that even Christian converts have been known to separate church meetings for different castes. A number of Muslim communities have retained caste practices as well. What was first an injunction to living one's dharma in surrender to God became an oppressive mandate to surrender to Man.

THE SIX VEDIC SCHOOLS OF THOUGHT

Six Schools: The six Astika or orthodox (accepting the authority of the Vedas) schools of Hindu philosophy are Nyaya, Vaisheshika, Samkhya, Yoga, Purva Mimamsa (also called just 'Mimamsa'), and Uttara Mimamsa (also called 'Vedanta'). The non-Vedic schools are called Nastika, or heterodox, and refer to Buddhism, Jainism and Lokayata. The schools that continue to affect Hinduism today are Purva Mimamsa, Yoga, and Vedanta.

Purva Mimamsa: The main objective of the Purva ("earlier") Mimamsa school was to establish the authority of the Vedas. Consequently this school's most valuable contribution to Hinduism was its formulation of the rules of Vedic interpretation. Its adherents believed that revelation must be proved by reasoning, that it should not be accepted blindly as dogma. This empirical and eminently sensible manner of religious application is key to the Sanatana/ Hindu Dharma and was especially championed by rationalists like Adi Shankara and Swami Vivekananda.

Yoga: Sadhus (Hindu ascetic) are often seen meditating in padmasana (lotus pose). The Yoga system is generally considered to have arisen from the Samkhya philosophy. The yoga referred to here, however, is specifically Raja Yoga (or meditational union). It is based on the sage Patanjali's extremely influential text entitled the Yoga Sutra, which is essentially a compilation and systematization of meditational Yoga philosophy that came before. Upanishads and Bhagwad Gita are also indispensable literature in the study of Yoga. The most significant difference from Samkhya is that the Yoga school not only incorporates the concept of Ishvara (a personal God) into its metaphysical worldview but also that it holds Ishvara as the ideal upon which to meditate. This is because Ishvara is the only aspect of purusha (the infinite Divine Ground) that has not become entangled with prakrti (the temporal creative forces). It also utilizes the Brahman/Atman terminology and concepts that are found in depth in the Upanishads, adopting Vedantic monist concepts. Realization of the goal of Yoga is known as moksha or samadhi. It, like the Upanishads, seeks realization of the Atman as being nothing other than the infinite Brahman through ethical (mind), physical (body) and meditational (soul) practices of one-pointedness on the 'one supreme truth.'

Uttara Mimamsa: The Three Schools of Vedanta: The Uttara ("later") Mimamsa school is perhaps one of the cornerstone movements of Hinduism and certainly was responsible for a new wave of philosophical and meditative inquiry, renewal of faith, and cultural reform. Primarily associated with the Upanishads and their commentary by Badarayana, the Vedanta Sutras, Vedanta thought split into three groups, initiated by the thinking and writing of Adi Shankara. Most Hindu thought today in some way relates to changes affected by Vedantic thought, which focused on meditation, morality and centeredness on the one Self rather than on rituals and societal distinctions like caste. The great debate between followers among the major Hindu philosophical school, Vedanta, from followers of Advaita philosophy on one hand and the strict theistic schools such as those of Ramanuja and Madhva on the other, focused on the true nature of Brahman, on whether Brahman was essentially attributeless or with attributes, *i.e.*, a personal Supreme Being.

PURE MONISM: ADVAITA

Advaita literally means "not two"; thus this is what we refer to as a monistic (or non-dualistic) system, which emphasises oneness. Its consolidator was Shankara (788?-820?). Shankara expounded his theories largely based on previous teachings of the Upanishads and his own guru Govinda Bhagwadpada. By analysis of experiential consciousness, he exposed the relative nature of the world and established the non-dual reality of Brahman in which Atman (the individual soul) and Brahman (the ultimate reality) are identified absolutely. It is not merely philosophy, but a conscious system of applied ethics and meditation, all geared towards attaining peace and understanding of truth. Adi Shankara denounced caste and meaningless ritual as foolish, and in his own charismatic manner, exhorted the true devotee to meditate on God's love and apprehend truth. To Advaitists (nondualists) Ultimate Truth is best expressed as Nirguna Brahman, or God without form, or God without personal attributes; indeed, some might go so far as to say it is not 'God' but something beyond.

However, even that definition can be limiting. Nirguna Brahman can never be described as that as It transcends all definitions. All personal forms of God such as Vishnu or Shiva are different aspects of God in personal form or God with attributes, Saguna Brahman. God's energy is personified as Devi, the Divine Mother. For Vaishnvaites who follow Ramanuja's philosophy, Devi is Lakshmi, who is the Mother of all and who pleads with Vishnu for mankind who is entrenched in sin. For Shaivites, Devi is Parvati. For Shaktas, who worship Devi, Devi is the personal form of God to attain the impersonal Absolute, God, *i.e.*, Shiva. For them, Shiva is personified as God without attributes.

DR. AMBEDKAR'S "AWAKENED" VISION

The New Buddhism: Dr. Ambedkar likened Indian society to an orange. If one removes the artificial rind of Hinduism, what remains is a fragmented society with mutually conflicting groups called the castes that run into 6000 in kind. Ambedkar did not strive for positional change in the whole system of graded inequality. He wanted to bring structural change to Indian society. He concluded that the contemporary state of degradation in India was due to the triumph of Brahmanism over Buddhism-the victory of a world view which sanctifies a graded inequality amongst living beings over one which prizes ethical conduct towards all such beings. David Brazier in his thought-provoking book, The New Buddhism, raises some very important points by questioning what the real project of the Buddha was after his enlightenment. He stresses that the Buddha had a vision of an ideal society which he shared with his disciples and thus awakened them to the reality of the world. This vision he termed as bodhi, that is, awakened vision. This vision of an awakened society moved the Buddha to turn the wheel of the Dhamma and to express his enlightenment experience to others to make this awakened society a reality.

Dr. Ambedkar also challenged traditional Buddhist positions and views. While he accepted that the Buddha was centrally concerned with suffering and the end of suffering, he did not define suffering based on the traditional eight types of suffering. His set of sufferings includes suffering due to humans' own wrongdoing and suffering due to inequality to other humans. In The Buddha and His Dhamma, he reformulates the life and teachings of the Buddha so that they can speak to contemporary Indian society and modern world. For him, the function of the Dhamma is two fold. That is to purify one's mind and to reconstruct world. In short, the purpose of the Dhamma is to transform an individual into a Buddha and to transform the world into a sangha. In the preface to The Buddha and His Dhamma, Dr. Ambedkar speaks of the purpose of the Dhamma as the creation of Dhamma Rajya, an ideal society based on liberty, equality and fraternity. It is clear that Dr. Ambedkar was trying to revive the Buddha's original project of the reconstruction of world. He called this vision Navayana or the "New Buddhism," which is a universal model applicable to all societies.

Steps Towards an Awakened Society: In the early years, Dr. Ambedkar was still struggling with his spirituality and slowly defining for himself this awakened vision. Therefore, most of his work for the liberation of his people came within a framework of activism concerning laws, committees, and commissions in the British India. For example, he gave evidence before the Southborough Committee for franchise and representation to the Indian legislatures in 1919. This was his first successful campaign without any mandate from his people. He successfully gained representation for depressed classes in the legislative assembly in Bombay. He was invited to participate in the Round Table Conference during 1932-1934 in order to discuss the future constitution of India, which he subsequently drafted. At this conference, he clashed with Gandhi, who denied the independent political rights of untouchables by deliberately trying to keep them in the fold of Hinduism. He also submitted a memorandum to the Cabinet Mission Plan in 1946 on behalf of the All India Scheduled Caste Federation (AISCF) in order to guarantee civil and political rights for them in free India.

The limited effect of such work within the system led Dr. Ambedkar to increasingly work outside of it as well. He began initiating mass protest movements, such as the Mahad Water Tank Movement (1927), and the Kalaram Temple Entry Movement (1934). He consciously created conditions for the illiterate people around him to become aware of the reality of the caste system. These conditions included writing books addressing various issues, editing several newspapers, launching political parties, and forming social organizations.

After clashing with Gandhi on the issue of the political empowerment of untouchables, Dr. Ambedkar realized the futility of changing the minds of the high caste Hindus. Although Gandhi outwardly showed his commitment to the untouchables, his real purpose appears to have been political. He wanted to ensure numerical power to Hindus (i.e. high-caste Hindus) vis-a-vis Muslims. These events led Ambedkar to renounce the systemic container of Hinduism. On May 30-31, 1936 at Dadar in Mumbai, he delivered a lengthy speech entitled "What way Liberty?" In this historic speech, he detailed the path leading towards liberty and gave a call to conversion. He did not make it clear as to which religion he was going to convert. However, at the end of this speech, he gave a clarion call to his people, which echoed the teaching of the Buddha, to "be your own light and refuge":

While thinking over what message should I give you on this occasion, I recollected the message given by the Lord Buddha to his Bhikkhu Sangha just before his mahaparinirvana and which has been quoted in Mahaparinibbana Sutta:

> *"Once the Bhagwan, after having recovered from illness, was resting on a seat under a tree and his disciple venerable Ananda went to the Buddha. Having saluted, he sat beside him and said, 'I have seen the Lord in illness as well as in happiness. But from the present illness of the Lord, my body has become heavy like lead, my mind is not is peace. I cannot concentrate on the Dhamma, but I feel consolation and satisfaction that the Lord will not attain the parinibbana until a message is given to the Sangha.'"*
>
> *"Then the Lord replied, 'Ananda! What does the Sangha expect from me? Ananda, I have preached the Dhamma with an open heart, without concealing anything. The Tathagata has not kept anything concealed as some other teachers do. So Ananda, what more can the Tathagata tell the Bhikkhu Sangha. So Ananda, be self illuminating like the sun. Do not be dependent for light like the Earth. Believe in yourself, do not be dependent on others. Be truthful. Always take refuge in the truth and do not surrender to anyone.'"*

I also take refuge in the words of the Buddha to be your own guide. Take refuge in your own reason. Do not listen to the advice of others. Do not succumb to others. Be truthful and take refuge in the truth. Never surrender to anything. If you keep in mind this message of Lord Buddha at this juncture, I am sure, your decision will not be wrong.

In order to realize an awakened society, Dr. Ambedkar saw than an inner revolution among his people needed to take place in tandem with the social and political work of gaining equal rights for untouchables. This internal revolution he found in the act of conversion from the dependency and subservience of being an untouchable in Hinduism to the independence and empowerment of a Buddhist identity and complete development as a human being. In this way, Dr. Ambedkar began to develop a vision for his people in order to make them realize the importance of the Buddha Dhamma. He saw that religious reformation is often a precursor to political emancipation. In his Annihilation of Caste, he cited such examples in the revolutions of Protestant Europe, the first Mauryan ruler Chandragupta, and the contemporary revolution of Guru Nanak and the Sikhs in Punjab. He concluded that the emancipation of the mind is a necessary preliminary for the political emancipation of the people.

DOES HINDUISM RECOGNISE FRATERNITY?

There are two forces prevalent in Society. Individualism and Fraternity. Individualism is ever present. Every individual is ever asking "I and my neighbours, are we all brothers, are we even fiftieth cousins, am I their keeper, why should I do right to them" and under the pressure of his own particular interests acting as though he was an end to himself, thereby developing a non-social and even an antisocial self. Fraternity is a force of opposite character. Fraternity is another name for fellow feeling. It consists in a sentiment which leads an individual to identify himself with the good of others whereby "the good of others becomes to him a thing naturally and necessarily to be attended to like any of the physical conditions of our existence". It is because of this sentiment of fraternity that the individual does not "bring himself to think of the rest of his fellow-creatures as struggling rivals with him for the means of happiness, whom he must desire to see defeated in their object in order that he may succeed in his own." Individualism would produce anarchy. It is only fraternity, which prevents it and helps to sustain the moral order among men. Of this there can be no doubt.

How does this sentiment of Fraternity of fellow feeling arise? J. S. Mill says that this sentiment is a natural sentiment.

> *"The social state is at once so natural, so necessary, and so habitual to man, that, except in some unusual circumstances or by an effort of voluntary abstraction he never conceives himself otherwise than as a member of a body; and this association is riveted more and more, as mankind are further removed from the state of savage independence. Any condition, therefore, which is essential to a state of society, becomes more and more an inseparable part of every person's conception of the state of things which he is born into, and which is the destiny of a human being.*

Now, society between human beings, except in the relation of master and slave, is manifestly impossible on any other footing than that the interests of all are to be consulted. Society between equals can only exist on the understanding that the interests of all are to be regarded equally. And since in all states of civilisation, every person, except an absolute monarch, has equals, every one is obliged to live on these terms with some body; and in every age some advance is made towards a state in which it will be impossible to live permanently on other terms with any body. In this way people grow up unable to conceive as possible to them a state of total disregard of other people's interests."

Does this sentiment of fellow feeling find a place among the Hindus? The following facts throw a flood of light on this question.

The first fact that strikes one is the number of castes. No body has made an exact computation of their number. But it is estimated that total is not less than 2000. It might be 3000. This is not the only distressing aspect of this fact. There are others. Castes are divided into sub-castes. Their number is legion. The total population of the Brahmin Caste is about core and a half. But there are 1886 sub-castes of the Brahmin Caste. In the Punjab alone the Saraswat Brahmins of the Province of Punjab are divided into 469 sub-castes. The Kayasthas of Punjab are divided into 590 sub-castes. One could go on giving figures to show this infinite process of splitting social life into small fragments.

The third aspect of this splitting process is the infinitely small fragments into which the Castes are split. Some of the Baniya sub-castes can count no more than 100 families. They are so inter related they find extremely difficult to marry within their castes without transgressing the rules of consanguinity. It is noteworthy what small excuses suffice to bring about this splitting. Equally noteworthy is the hierarchical character of the Caste System. Castes form an hierarchy in which one caste is at the top and is the highest, another at the bottom and it is the lowest and in between there are castes every one of which is at once above some castes and below some castes. The caste system is a system of gradation in which every caste except the highest and the lowest has a priority and precedence over some other castes.

How is this precedence or this superiority determined? This order of superiority and inferiority or this insubordination is determined by rules: (1) which are connected with religious rites and (2) which are connected with commensuality.

Religion as a basis of Rules of precedence manifests itself in three ways. Firstly through religious ceremonies, secondly through incantations that accompany the religious ceremonies and thirdly through the position of the priest.

Beginning with the ceremonies as a source of rules of precedence it should be noted that the Hindu Scriptures prescribe sixteen religious ceremonies. Although those are Hindu ceremonies every Hindu Caste cannot by right claim to perform all the sixteen ceremonies. Few can claim the right to perform all. Some are allowed to perform certain ceremonies; some are not allowed to perform certain of the ceremonies. For instance take the ceremony of Upanayan, wearing of the sacred thread. Some castes can't. Precedence follows this distinction in the matter of right to perform the ceremonies. A caste which can claim to perform all the ceremonies is higher in status than the caste which has a right to perform a few.

Turning to the Mantras, it is another source for rules of precedence. According to the Hindu Religion the same ceremony can be performed in two different ways: (1) Vedokta and (2) Puranokta. In the Vedokta form the ceremonies are performed with Mantras (incantations) from the Vedas. In the Puranokta form the ceremony is performed with Mantras (incantations) from the Puranas. Hindu Religious Scriptures fall into two distinct categories: (1) The Vedas which are four, and (2) the Puranas which are eighteen. Although they are all respected as scriptures they do not all have the same sanctity. The Vedas have the highest sanctity and the Puranas have the lowest sanctity. The way the Mantras give rise to social precedence will be obvious if it is borne in mind that not every caste is entitled to have the ceremony performed in the Vedokta form.

Three castes may well claim the right to the performance of one of the sixteen ceremonies. But it will be that one of it is entitled to perform it in the Vedokta form, another in the Puranokta form. Precedence goes with the kind of Mantra that a caste is entitled to use in the performance of a religious ceremony. A caste which is entitled to use Vedic Mantras is superior to a caste which is entitled to use only Puranokta Mantras.

Taking the priest as a second source of precedence connected with Religion, Hinduism requires the instrumentality of a priest for the derivation of the full benefit from the performance of a religious ceremony. The priest appointed by the scripture is the Brahmin. A Brahmin therefore is indispensable. But the scriptures do not require-that a Brahmin shall accept the invitation of any and every Hindu irrespective of his caste to officiate at a religious ceremony. The invitation of which caste he will accept and of which he will refuse is a matter left to the wishes of the Brahmin. By long and well-established custom it is now settled at which caste he will officiate and at which caste he will not. This fact has become the basis of precedence as between castes. The caste at which a Brahmin will officiate is held as superior to a caste at whose religious functions a Brahmin will not officiate.

There is no sharing among Hindus of joys and sorrows involved in the vital facts of life. Everything is separate and exclusive. The Hindu is separate and exclusive all through his life. A foreigner coming to India will not find men crying Hindu Pani (water for Hindus) and Musalman Pani (water for Musalmans). He will find Brahmin Coffee

This view of the caste is due to taking the separate aspects of caste separately. One must take them in conjunction. The resultant social utility or distillate of caste can be ascertained only by putting together the separate aspects of caste and judge them in their combination. Following this line of attacking the problem, the following conclusions follow:

(1) Caste divides Labourers
(2) Caste disassociates work from interest
(3) Caste disconnects intelligence from manual labour
(4) Caste devitalises by denying to him the right to cultivate vital interest and
(5) Caste prevents mobilisation. Caste System is not merely division of labour.

Civilised society undoubtedly needs division of labour. But in no civilised society is division of labour accompanied by this unnatural division of labourers into watertight compartments. Caste System is not merely a division of labourers, which is quite different from division of labour it is an hierarchy in which the divisions of labourers are graded one above the other. In no other country is the division of labour accompanied by this gradation of labourers. There is also a third point of criticism against this view of the Caste System. This division of labour is not spontaneous, it is not based on natural aptitudes. Social and individual efficiency requires us to develop the capacity of an individual to the point of competency to chose and to make his own career. This principle is violated in the Caste System in so far as it involves an attempt to appoint tasks to individuals in advance, selected not on the basis of trained original capacities, but on that of the social status of the parents.

Looked at from another point of view this stratification of occupations which is the result of the Caste System is positively pernicious. Industry is never static. It undergoes rapid and abrupt changes. With such changes an individual must be free to change his occupations. Without such freedom to adjust himself to changing circumstances it would be impossible for him to gain his livelihood. Now the Caste System will not allow Hindus to take occupations where they are wanted if they do not belong to them by heredity. If a Hindu is seen to starve rather than take to new occupations not assigned to his Caste, the reason is to be found in the Caste System. By not permitting readjustment of occupations, caste becomes a direct cause of much of the unemployment we see in the country. As a form of division of labour the Caste System suffers from another serious defect. The division of labour brought about by the Caste System is not a division based on choice. Individual sentiment, individual preference has no place in it. It is based on the dogma of predestination. Considerations of social efficiency would compel us to recognise that the greatest evil in the industrial system is not so much poverty and the suffering that it involves, as the fact that so many persons have callings which make no appeal to those who are engaged in them.

Such callings constantly provoke one to aversion, ill will and the desire to evade. There are many occupations in India which on account of the fact that they are regarded as degraded by the Hindus provoke those who are engaged in it to aversion. There is a constant desire to evade and escape from such occupations which arises solely because of the blighting effect which they produce upon those who follow them owing to the slight and stigma cast upon them by the Hindu religion.

The second mischief it dose is to dissociate intelligence from work and create contempt for labour. The theory of the Caste is that a Brahmin who is permitted to cultivate his intellect is not permitted to labour, indeed is taught to look down upon labour. While the Sudra who is required to labour is not permitted to cultivate his intelligence. The disastrous consequences of this have been well portrayed by Mr. R.C.Dutt. Wealth without education and wealth is brutal. Each is necessary to every one. They are necessary for the growth of a man.

That the Brahmin should cultivate knowledge, Kshatriya should bear arms, the Vaishya should trade and that the Sudra should serve is presented as a theory of mutual interdependence found in the family. It is asked why should the Sudra need trouble to acquire wealth when the three Varnas are there to support him; Why need the Sudra bother to take to education when the Brahmin to whom he can go when the occasion for reading or writing arises; Why need the Sudra worry to arm himself because there is the Kshatriya to protect him?

The theory of Chaturvarnya understood in this sense may be said to look upon the Sudra as the ward and the three Varnas as his guardians. Thus interpreted it is a simple and alluring theory. Assuming this to be the correct view of the underlying conception of Chaturvarnya it seems to me that the system is neither foolproof nor knave-proof. What is to happen if the Brahmins, Vaishyas and Kshatriyas fail to pursue knowledge, to engage in economic enterprises and to be efficient soldiers which are their respective functions? Contrary-wise, suppose that they discharge their functions but flout their duty to the Sudra or to one another? What is to happen to the Sudra if the three classes refuse to support him on fair terms or combine to keep him down? Who is to safeguard the interests of the Sudra or for the matter of that of the Vaishya and Kshatriya when the person who is trying to take advantage of his ignorance is the Brahmin? Who is to defend the liberty of the Sudra or that of the Brahmin and the Vaishya, when the person who is robbing him of is the Kshatriya?

Interdependence of one class on another class is inevitable. Even dependence of one class upon another may sometimes become allowable. But why make one person depend upon another in the matter of his vital needs? Education every one must have. Means of defence every one must have. These are the paramount requirements of every man for his self-preservation. How can the fact that his neighbour is educated and armed, help a man who is uneducated and disarmed. The whole theory is absurd. These are the questions which the defenders of Chaturvarnya do not seem to be troubled about. But they are very pertinent questions. Assuming their conception of Chaturvarnya that the relationship between the different classes is that of ward and guardian is the real conception underlying Chaturvarnya, it must be admitted that it makes no provision to safeguard the interests of the ward from the misdeeds of the guardian.

Whether the relationship of guardian and ward was the real underlying conception on which Chaturvarnya was based there is no doubt that in practice the relation was that of master and servant. The three classes, Brahmins, Kshatriyas and Vaishyas although not very happy in their mutual relationship managed to work by compromise. The Brahmin flattered the Kshatriya and both let the Vaishya live in order to be able to live upon him. But the three agreed to beat down the Sudra. He was not allowed to acquire wealth lest he should be independent of the three Varnas. He was prohibited from acquiring knowledge lest he should keep a steady vigil regarding his interests. He was prohibited from bearing arms lest he should have the means to rebel against their authority. That this is how the Sudras were treated by the Trayavarnikas is evidenced by the Laws of Manu. There is no code of laws more infamous regarding social rights than the Laws of Manu.

Any instance from anywhere of social injustice must pale before it. Why have the mass of people tolerated the social evils to which they have been subjected? There have been social revolutions in other countries of the world. Why have there not been social revolutions in India is a question which has incessantly troubled many. There is only one answer, it is that the lower classes of Hindus have been completely disabled for direct action on account of this wretched system of Chaturvarnya. They could not bear arms and without arms they could not rebel. They were all ploughmen or rather condemned to be ploughmen and they were not allowed to convert their ploughshares into swords. They had no bayonets and therefore everyone who chose ploughs did sit upon them. On account of the Chaturvarnya they could receive no education. They could not think out or know the way to their salvation. They were condemned to be lowly and not knowing the way of escape and not having the means of escape, they became reconciled to eternal servitude which they accepted as their inescapable fate.

It is true that even in Europe the strong has not shrunk from the exploitation, nay the spoliation of the weak but in Europe, the strong have never contrived to make the weak helpless against exploitation so shamelessly as was the case in India among the Hindus. Social war has been raging between the strong and the weak far more violently in Europe than it has ever been in India. Yet the weak in Europe has had in him freedom of military service his physical weapon, in suffrage his political weapon and in education his moral weapon. Three weapons for emancipation were never withheld by the strong from the weak in Europe. All these weapons were however denied to the masses in India by Chaturvarnya.

There cannot be a more degrading system of social organisation than Chaturvarnya. It is the system, which deadens, paralyses and cripples the people from helpful activity. This is no exaggeration. History bears ample evidence. There is only one period in Indian history, which is a period of freedom, greatness and glory. That is the period of the Maurya Empire. At all other times the country suffered from defeat and darkness. But the Maurya period was a period when Chaturvarnya was completely annihilated, when the Sudras, who constituted the mass of the people came into their own and became the rulers of the country. The period of defeat and darkness is the period when Chaturvarnya flourished to the damnation of the greater part of the people of the country.

Caste prevents mobilisation. Occasions arise when society must mobilise all its resources to one end in order to save itself from a catastrophe. To take a catastrophe like war, Society must mobilise all its resources for militarization. Every one must do war. Every one must be a soldier. Is this possible under the theory of caste? Obviously not. Indeed the destiny of a defeat which has been the lot of India throughout history is due to caste. Caste prevented general mobilisation. Or the extent of mobilisation was of a very limited character. Only the Kshatriyas were expected to fight. The rest the Brahmins and the Vaishyas were not armed and the Sudras who formed the large majority of the country were disarmed. The result was that once the small class of Kshatriyas were defeated by a foreign foe, the whole country fell at his feet. It could offer no resistance. It was not capable of resistance. Indian wars have been mostly wars of single battles or single campaigns. This was due to the fact that once the Kshatriyas fell everything fell. Why? Simply because there was no general mobilisation and the theory deeply imbedded in the psychology of the people.

If these conclusions are sound, how can a philosophy which dissects society in fragments, which dissociates work from interest, which disconnects intelligence from labour, which expropriates the rights of man to interests vital to life and which prevented society from mobilising resources for common action in the hour of danger, be said to satisfy the test of Social Utility.

The Philosophy of Hinduism therefore neither satisfies the test of social utility nor does it satisfy the test of individual justice.

The result of this analysis is so odd that it will surprise many. Astonished some may even say that if the conclusions are so odd then there must be something wrong in the analysis of the philosophy of Hinduism. To those who refuse to accept this analysis because they do not have a correct notion what is central in the philosophy of Hinduism. If they do they will feel no surprise at the conclusions.

This matter is so important that it needs to be explained. It may be recalled that the foregoing analysis of the religious revolution showed that religious ideals as forms of divine governance for human Society fall into two classes, one in which Society is the centre and the other in which the Individual is the centre. The same analysis showed that for the former the appropriate test of what is good and what is right i.e. the test of the moral order is utility while for the latter the test is justice.

Now the reason why the philosophy of Hinduism does not answer the test either of utility or of justice is because the religious ideal of Hinduism for divine governance of human society is an ideal, which falls into a separate class by itself. It is an ideal in which the individual is not the centre. The centre of the ideal is neither individual nor society. It is a class-the class of Supermen called Brahmins.

Those who will bear the dominant and devastating fact in mind will understand why the philosophy of Hinduism is not founded on individual justice or social utility. The philosophy of Hinduism is founded on a totally different principle.

To the question what is right and what is good the answer, which the philosophy of Hinduism gives, is remarkable. It holds that to be right and good the act must serve the interest of this class of supermen, namely, the Brahmins. Oscar Wilde said that to be intelligible is to be found out. Manu is neither afraid nor ashamed of being found out. Indeed Manu does not leave it to be found out. He expresses his view in resonant and majestic notes as who are the Supermen and anything which serves the interest of the Supermen is alone entitled to be called right and good.

THE HINDU AND HIS BELIEF IN CASTE

Among the Hindu social reformers there is a moderate section. This section holds that untouchability is separate from the caste system. Following this ideology they hold that it is possible to remove untouchability without attacking the caste system. The religious minded Hindu is as opposed to the removal of untouchability as he is to the removal of the caste system. He is as opposed to dealing with social reform in two stages as he is in dealing with it in one stage. But the politically minded Hindu is tremendously fond of the idea. That is obviously for two reasons. In the first place, it gives the Hindu the chance of showing himself in international world as a better specimen of democracy than he really is. Secondly, by leaving caste alone there is no risk of the caste Hindus forsaking the Congress.

Those who propose to deal with untouchability without damaging the caste system, rest their case on verse 4 of Chapter X of the Manusmriti. In the verse, Manu says that there are only four varnas and that there is no fifth varna. This verse is interpreted to mean that the untouchables are included in the fourth varna, that they are part of the Sudras and as there is no objection to touching the Sudras there could be no objection to touching the Untouchables. However pleasing this construction may be to the politically minded Hindu, it does accord with the intention of what Manu wanted to convey. The verse is open to another construction. It may mean that Manu was not prepared to enlarge the Chaturvarnya and make it a Panchavarnya by recognising these communities which were outside the four varnas as constituting the fifth varna.

In saying that there is no fifth varna what he means to suggest is that he did not want to incorporate those outside the four varnas into the Hindu society by making the Hindu society consist of five varnas instead of four. That he wanted to convey the latter intention is abundantly clear by speaking of a category of people as Bahyas or Varna Bahyas which means those outside the varna system. If Manu wanted to include all persons within the four varnas there was no reason for speaking of some people as varna Bahyas. Indeed, he recognises two sub-divisions within the class of Varna Bahyas. He calls them Hinas and Antayevasins . Given these facts, it is obvious that the construction sought to be placed in the verse in the Manusmriti will not deceive the orthodox Hindu into accepting that the maintenance of untouchability is contrary to the Manusmriti and that its abolition is not therefore contrary to the tenets of the Hindu religion.

The argument based on the interpretation of Manu's text is too intellectual for the ordinary uneducated Hindu. He knows only two things. One thing he knows is that there are three barriers in the matter of social intercourse which he must observe. They are (1) prohibition against inter-dining, (2) prohibition against inter-marriage, while in untouchability there is third barrier added and (3) prohibition against physically touching certain class of people. The first two barriers make up the caste. The third forms untouchability. The caste Hindu does not bother about the number of barriers. He is particular about the observance of the barrier. When he is asked not to observe, he turns round and asks why not? His argument is that, if I am free to observe the first two barriers, what is wrong if I observe the third? Psychologically, caste and untouchability are one integral system based on one and the same principle. If the caste Hindus observe untouchability it is because they believe in caste.

Looked at from this point of view, the idea of hoping to remove untouchability without destroying the caste system is an utter futility. The underlying idea that caste and untouchability are two different things is founded on a fallacy. The two are one and are inseparable. Untouchability is only an extension of the caste system. There can be no severance between the two. The two stand together and will fall together.

There is another reason why untouchability cannot disappear by a stratagem, legal or rational. As has already been pointed out, the Hindu social order is based on the principle of graded inequality. It may not bean exaggeration to say that not many people understand the significance of this principle. The social system based on inequality stands on a different footing from a social system based on graded, inequality. The former is a weak system which is not capable of self-I preservation. The latter on the other hand, is capable of self-preservation. In a social system based on inequality, the low orders can combine to overthrow the system. None of them have any interest to preserve it. In a social system based on graded inequality the possibility of a general common attack by the aggrieved parties is nonexistent. In a system of graded inequality, the aggrieved parties are not on a common level.

This can happen only when they are only high and low. In the system of graded inequality there are the highest (the Brahmins). Below the highest are the higher (the Kshatriyas). Below the higher are those who are high (Vaishya). Below the high are the low (Sudra) and below the low are those who are lower (the Untouchables). All have a grievance against the highest and would like to bring about their down fall. But they will not combine. The higher is anxious to get rid of the highest but does not wish to combine with the high, the low and the lower lest they should reach his level and be his equal. The high wants to overthrow the higher who is above him but does not want to join hands with the low and the lower, lest they should rise to his status and become equal to him in rank.

The low is anxious to pull down the highest, the higher and the high but he would not make a common cause with the lower for fear of the lower gaining a higher status and becoming his equal in the system of graded inequality there is no such class as completely unprivileged class except the one which is at the base of the social pyramid. The privileges of the rest are graded. Even the low is a privileged class as compared with the lower. Each class being privileged, every class is interested in maintaining the social system.

Untouchability may be a misfortune to the Untouchables. But there is no doubt that it is a good fortune to the Hindus. It gives them a class which they can look down upon. The Hindus do not want a system in which nobody will be anybody. They also do not want a system in which everybody may be somebody. They want a system in which they will be some bodies and others will be nobodies. The Untouchables are nobodies. This makes the Hindus some bodies. The system of untouchability sustains the natural pride of the Hindus and make them feel as well as look big. This is an additional reason why the Hindus are not likely to give up untouchability particularly those large majority who are small men.

Untouchability will vanish only when the whole of the Hindu Social Order, particularly the caste system will be dissolved. Is this possible? Every institution is sustained by some sort of a sanction. There are three kinds of sanction, which supply life force to an institution. They are legal, social and religious. The vitality of the institution depends upon the nature of the sanction. What is the nature of the sanction behind the caste system? Unfortunately, the sanction behind the caste system is the religious sanction, for, the caste as a new form of the Varna system derives its sanction from the Vedas which form the sacred book of the Hindu religion and which are infallible. I say unfortunately because anything which has a religious sanction becomes by virtue of it sacred and eternal. To the Hindu, caste is sacred and caste is eternal. If caste cannot vanish what hope is there for untouchability to disappear?

6

Ambedkar as Political Thinker

POONA PACT

(1) There shall be seats reserved for the Depressed Classes out of the general electorate seats in the Provincial Legislatures as follows:

Madras	30
Bombay with Sindh	15
Punjab	8
Bihar and Orissa	18
Central Provinces	20
Assam	7
United Provinces	20
Total	148

These figures are based on the total strength of the Provincial Councils, announced in the Prime Minister's decision.

(2) Election to these seats shall be by joint electorates subject, however, to the following procedure:
All the members of the Depressed Classes registered in the fengral electoral roll in a constituency will form an electoral college, which will elect a panel of four candidates belonging to the Depressed Classes for each of such reserved seats, by the method of the single vote; the four persons getting the highest number of votes in such primary election, shall be candidates for election by the general electorate.

(3) Representation of the Depressed Classes in the Central Legislature shall likewise be on the principal of joint electorates and reserved seats by the method of primary election in the manner provided for in Clause two above, for their representation in the Provincial Legislatures.

(4) In the Central Legislatures, eighteen per cent of the seats allotted to the general electorate for British India in the said legislature shall be reserved for the Depressed Classes.

(5) The system of primary election to a panel of candidates for election to the Central and Provincial Legislatures, as here in before mentioned, shall come to an end after the first ten years, unless terminated sooner by mutual agreement under the provision of Clause six below.

(6) The system of representation of the Depressed Classes by reserved seats in the Provincial and Central Legislature as provided *for* in Clauses I and 4 shall continue until determined by mutual agreement between the communities concerned in the settlement.

(7) Franchise for the Central and Provincial Legislatures for the Depressed Classes shall be as indicated in the Lothian Committee Report.

(8) There shall be no disabilities attaching to any one on the ground of his being a member of the Depressed Classes in regard to any elections to local bodies or appointment to the Public Services. Every endeavour shall be made to secure fair representation of the Depressed Classes in these respects, subject to such educational qualifications as may be laid down for appointment to the Public Services.

(9) In every province out of the educational grant, an adequate sum shall be earmarked for providing educational facilities to the members of the Depressed Classes.

This pact forms the charter of the political liberty of the Untouchables. The first election.......

SPEECH ON ROUND TABLE CONFERENCES

Dr. B. R. Ambedkar: Mr. Chairman, my purpose in rising to address this conference is principally to place before it the point of view of the depressed classes, whom I and my colleague, Rao Bahadur Srinivasan, have the honour to represent, regarding the question of constitutional reform. It is a point of view of 43,000,000 people, or one-fifth of the total population of British India.

The depressed classes form a group by themselves, which is distinct and separate from the Mohammedans, and, although they are included among the Hindus, they in no sense form an integral part of that community. Not only have they a separate existence, but they have also assigned to them a statute which is invidiously distinct from the status occupied by any other community in India. There are communities in India, which occupy a lower and subordinate position; but the position assigned to the depressed classes is totally different.

It is one which is midway between that of the serf and the slave, and which may, for convenience, be called servile with this difference, that the serf and the slave were permitted to have physical contact, from which the Depressed Classes are debarred. What is worse that this enforced servility and bar to human intercourse, due to their untouchability, involves, not merely the possibility of discrimination in public life, but actually works out as a positive denial of all equality of opportunity and the denial of those most elementary of civic rights on which all human existence depends. I am sure that the point of view of such a community, as large as the population of England or of France, and so heavily handicapped in the struggle for existence, cannot but have some bearing on the right sort of solution of the political problem, and I am anxious that this Conference should be placed in possession of that point of view at the very start.

The point of view I will try to put as briefly as I can. It is this that the bureaucratic form of Government in India should be replaced by a Government, which will be a Government of the people, by the people, and for the people. This statement of the view of the depressed classes I am sure will be received with some surprise in certain quarters. The tie that bounds the Depressed Classes to the British has been of a unique character. The Depressed Classes welcomed the British as their deliverers from age long tyranny and oppression by the orthodox Hindus. They fought their battles against the Hindus, the Mussalmans and the Sikhs and won for them this great Empire of India.

The British, on their side, assumed the role of trustees for the depressed classes. In view of such an intimate relationship between the parties, this change in the attitude of the depressed classes towards British Rule in India is undoubtedly a most momentous phenomenon. But the reasons for this change of attitude are not far to seek. We have not taken this decision simply because we wish to throw in our lot with the majority. Indeed, as you know, there is not much love lost between the majority and the particular minority I represent. Ours is an independent decision. We have judged of the existing administration solely in the light of our own circumstances and we have found it wanting in some of the most essential elements of a good Government.

When we compare our present position with the one, which it was our lot to bear in Indian society of the pre-British days, we find that, instead of marching on, we are only marking time. Before the British, we were in the loathsome condition due to our untouchability. Has the British Government done anything to remove it? Before the British, we could not enter the temple. Can we enter now? Before the British, we were denied entry into the Police Force. Does the British Government admit us in the Force? Before the British, we were not allowed to serve in the Military. Is that career now open to us?

To none of these questions can we give an affirmative answer. That the British, who have held so large a sway over us for such a long time, have done some good we cheerfully acknowledge. But there is certainly no fundamental change in our position. Indeed, so far as we were concerned, the British Government has accepted the social arrangements as it found them, and has preserved them faithfully in the manner of the Chinese tailor who, when given an old coat as a pattern, produced with pride an exact replica, rents, patches and all. Our wrongs have remained as open sores and they have not been righted, although 150 years of British rule have rolled away.

We do not accuse the British of indifference or want of sympathy. What we do find is that they are quite incompetent to tackle our problems. If the case was one of indifference only it would have been a matter of small moment, and it would not have made such a profound change in our attitude. But what we have come to realise on a deeper analysis of the situation is that it is not merely a case of indifference, rather it is a case of sheer incompetence to undertake the task. The depressed classes find that the British Government in India suffers from two very serious limitations.

There is first of all an internal limitation, which arises from the character, motives, and interests of those who are in power. It is not because they cannot help us in these things but because it is against their character, motives and interests to do so. The second consideration that limits its authority is the mortal fear it has of external resistance. The Government of India does realise the necessity of removing the social evils which are eating into the vitals of Indian society and which have blighted the lives of the downtrodden classes for so many years.

The Government of India does realise that the landlords are squeezing the masses dry, and the capitalists are not giving the labourers a living wage and decent conditions of work. Yet it is most painful thing that it has not dared to touch any of these evils. Why? Is it because it has no legal powers to remove them? No. The reason why it does not intervene is because it is afraid that its intervention to amend the existing code of social and economic life will give rise to resistance. Of what good is such a Government to anybody? Under a Government, paralysed between two such limitations, much that goes to make life good must remain held up. We must have a Government in which the men in power will give their undivided allegiance to the best interest of the country. We must have a Government in which men in power, knowing where obedience will end and resistance will begin, will not be afraid to amend the social and economic code of life which the dictates of justice and expediency so urgently call for. This role the British Government will never be able to play, It is only a Government which is of the people, for the people and by the people that will make this possible. These are some of the questions raised by the Depressed Classes and the answers which in their view these questions seem to carry. This is therefore the inevitable conclusion which the Depressed Classes have come to: namely, that the bureaucratic Government of India, with the best of motives, will remain powerless to effect any change so far as our particular grievances are concerned. We feel that nobody can remove our grievances as well as we can, and we cannot remove them unless we get political power in our own hands. No share of this political power can evidently come to us so long as the British Government remains as it is. It is only in a Swaraj constitution that we stand any chance of getting the political power into our own hands, without which we cannot bring salvation to our people.

There is one thing, Sir, to which I wish to draw your particular attention. It is this, I have not used the expression Dominion Status in placing before you the point of view of the Depressed Classes. I have avoided using it, not because I do not understand its implications nor does the omission mean that the depressed classes object to India's attaining Dominion Status. My chief ground for not using it is that it does not convey the full content of what the Depressed Classes stand for. The Depressed Classes, while they stand for Dominion Status with safeguards, wish to lay all the emphasis they can on one question and one question alone. And that question is, how will Dominion India function? Where will the centre of political power be? Who will have it? Will the Depressed Classes be heirs to it?

These are the questions that form their chief concern. The Depressed Classes feel that they will get no shred of the political power unless the political machinery for the new constitution is of a special make. In the construction of that machine certain hard facts of Indian social life must not be lost sight of. It must be recognised that Indian Society is a gradation of Castes forming an ascending scale of reverence and a descending scale of contempt-a system which gives no scope for the growth of that sentiment of equality and fraternity so essential for a democratic form of Government. It must also be recognised that while the intelligentsia is a very important part of Indian society, it is drawn from its upper strata and although it speaks in the name of the country and leads the political movement, it has not shed the narrow particularism of the class from which it is drawn. In other words what the Depressed Classes wish to urge is that the political mechanism must take account of and must have a definite relation to the psychology of the society for which it is devised. Otherwise you are likely to produce a constitution which, however symmetrical, will be truncated one and a total misfit to the society for which it is designed.

There is one point with which I should like to deal before I close this matter. We are often reminded that the problem of the Depressed Classes is a social problem and that its solution lies elsewhere than in politics. We take strong exception to this view. We hold that the problem of the Depressed Classes will never be solved unless they get political power in their own hands. If this is true, and I do not think that the contrary can be maintained, then problem of Depressed Classes is I submit eminently a political problem and must be treated as such. We know that political power is passing from the British into the hands of those who wield such tremendous economic, social and religious sway over our existence.

We are willing that it may happen, though the idea of Swaraj recalls to the mind of many of us the tyrannies, oppressions and injustices practised upon us in the past and fear of their recurrence under Swaraj. We are prepared to take the inevitable risk of the situation in the hope that we shall be installed, in adequate proportion, as the political sovereigns of the country along with our fellow countrymen. But we will consent to that on one condition and that is that the settlement of our problems is not left to time. I am afraid the Depressed Classes have waited too long for time to work its miracle. At every successive step taken by the British Government to widen the scope of representative Government the Depressed Classes have been systematically left out. No thought has been given to their claim for political power. I protest with all the emphasis I can that we will not stand this any longer. The settlement of our problem must be a part of the general political settlement and must not be left over to the shifting sands of the sympathy and goodwill of the rulers of the future. The reasons why the Depressed Classes insist upon it are obvious. Every one of us knows that the man in possession is more powerful than the man who is out of possession.

Everyone of us also knows that those in possession of power seldom abdicate in favour of those who are out of it. We cannot therefore hope for the effectuation of the settlement of our social problem. If we allow power to slip into the hands of those who stand to lose by settlement unless we are to have another revolution to dethrone those, whom we today help to ascend the throne of power and prestige. We prefer being despised for too anxious apprehensions, than ruined by too confident a security, and I think it would be just and proper for us to insist that the best guarantee for the settlement of our problem is the adjustment of the political machine itself so as to give us a hold on it, and not the will of those who are contriving to be left in unfettered control of that machine.

What adjustments of the political machine the Depressed Classes want for their safety and protection I will place before the Conference at the proper time. All I will say at the present moment is that, although we want responsible Government, we do not want a Government that will only mean a change of masters. Let the Legislature be fully and really representative if your Executive is going to be fully responsible.

I am sorry Mr. President. I had to speak in such plain words. But I saw no help. The Depressed Classes have had no friend. The Government has all along used them only as an excuse for its continued existence. The Hindus claim them only to deny them or, better still, to appropriate rights. The Mohammedans refuse to recognise their separate existence, because they fear that their privileges may be curtailed by the admission of a rival. Depressed by the Government, suppressed by the Hindu and disregarded by the Muslim, we are left in a most intolerable position of utter helplessness to which I am sure there is no parallel and to which I was bound to call attention.

Regarding the other question, which is set down for discussion, I am sorry it was decided to tag it on to a general debate. Its importance deserved a session for itself. No justice can be done to it in a passing reference. The subject is one in which the Depressed Classes are deeply concerned and they regard it as a very vital question. As members of a minority, we look to the Central Government to act as a powerful curb on the provincial majority to save the minorities from the misrule of the majority. As an Indian, interested in the growth of Indian nationalism, I must make it plain that I am a strong believer in the Unitary form of Government and the thought of disturbing it I must confess does not please me very much. This Unitary Government has been the most potent influence in the building up of the Indian nation. That process of unification, which has been the result of a unified system of Government, has not been completed and I should be loathed to withdraw this most powerful stimulus in the formative period and before it has worked out its end.

However, the question in the form in which it is placed is only an academic question and I shall be prepared to consider a federal form, if it can be shown that in it local autonomy is not inconsistent with central unity. Sir, all that I, as a representative of the depressed classes, need say on their behalf I have said. May I crave your indulgence to permit me as an Indian to say a word or two generally on the situation, which we have to meet. So much has been said regarding its gravity that I shall not venture to add a word more to it, although I am no silent spectator of the movement.

What I am anxious about is to feel whether we are proceeding on right lines in evolving our solution. What that solution should be rests entirely upon the view that British delegates choose to take. Addressing myself to them I will say, whether you will meet the situation by conciliation or by applying the iron heel must be a matter for your judgement for the responsibility is entirely yours. To such of you as are particular to the use of force and believe that a regime of Letters de Cachet and the Bastille will ease the situation, let me recall the memorable words of the greatest teacher of political philosophy, Edmund Burke. This is what he said to the British nation when it was faced with the problem of dealing with the American colonies:

> *"The use of force alone is but temporary. It may endure for a moment, but it does not remove the necessity of subduing again; a nation is not governed which is perpetually to be conquered. The next objection to force is its uncertainty. Terror is not always the effect of force, and an armament is not a victory. If you do not succeed, you are without resource; for conciliation failing, force remains, but force failing, no further hope of reconciliation is left. Power and authority are sometimes bought by kindness, but they can never be begged as alms by an impoverished and defeated violence. A further objection to force is that you impair the object by your very endeavours to preserve it. The thing you fought for (to wit the loyalty of the people) is not the thing you recover but depreciated, sunk, wasted and consumed in the contest."*

The worth and efficacy of this advice you all knew. You did not listen to it and you lost the great continent of America. You followed it to the lasting good of yourself and the rest of the Dominions that are with you. To such of you as are willing to adopt a policy of conciliation I should like to say one thing. There seems to be prevalent an impression that the Delegates are called here to argue for and against a case for Dominion Status and that the grant of Dominion Status will be dependent upon which side is the victor in this battle of wits.

With due deference to all who are sharpening their wits, I submit that there can be no greater mistake than to make the formula of logic govern so live an issue. I have no quarrel with logic and logicians. But I warn them against the disaster that is bound to follow if they are not careful in the selection of the premises they choose to adopt for their deductions.

It is all a matter of temper whether you will abide by the fall of your logic, or whether you will refute it, as Dr. Johnson did the paradoxes of Berkeley by trampling them under his feet. I am afraid it is not sufficiently realised that in the present temper of the country, no constitution will be workable which is not acceptable to the majority of the people.

The time when you were to choose and India was to accept is gone, never to return. Let the consent of the people and not the accident of logic be the touchstone of your new constitution, if you desire that it should be worked.

ROUND TABLE CONFERENCES AND GANDHI

Meanwhile, the Indian Freedom Movement had gained momentum under the leadership of Mahatma Gandhi. In 1930, a Round Table Conference was held by the British Government in London to decide the future of India. Baba Saheb represented the 'untouchables'. He said there:-The Depressed Classes of India also join in the demand for replacing the British Government by a Government of the people and by the people... Our wrongs have remained as open sores and have not been righted although 150 years of British rule have rolled away. Of what good is such a Government to anybody?" The British had done nothing to alleviate the status of the depressed classes. He declared that India must have a minimum of Dominion Status. He pressed for a separate electorate for the depressed classes. Soon a second conference was held, which Mahatma Gandhi attended representing the Congress Party.

Baba Saheb met Gandhi in Bombay before they went to London. Gandhi told him that he had read what Baba Saheb said at the first conference. Gandhi told Baba Saheb he knew him to be a real Indian patriot. At the Second Conference, Baba Saheb asked for a separate electorate for the Depressed Classes-Hinduism, "he said-has given us only insults, misery, and humiliation." A separate electorate would mean that the 'untouchables' would vote for their own candidates and be allotted their votes separate from the Hindu majority. Baba Saheb was made a hero by thousands of his followers on his return from Bombay-even though he always said that people should not idolise him.

News came that separate electorates had been granted. Gandhi felt that separate electorates would separate the Harijans from the Hindus. The thought that the Hindus would be divided pained him grievously. He started a fast, saying that he would fast unto death. The Mahatma's Fast: Gandhiji felt that separate electrorates would only separate the Harijans from the Hindus. The very thought that the Hindu would be divided pained him much. He started a fast against separate electorates. He said he would fast unto death in necessary. There was anxiety in the country because of Gandhiji's fast. Many Congress leaders went to Ambedkar to save Gandhiji.

"Muslims, Christians and Sikhs have obtained the right of separate electorates. Gandhiji did not fast to oppose them. Why should Gandhiji fast to oppose Harijans getting separate electorates?" questioned Ambedkar. "If you are unwilling to give the 'untouchables' separate electorates, what other solution is there? It is essential to save Gandhiji. But just to save him I am not prepared to give up the interests of the backward classes," he declared. He said, reserve a larger number of seats for the untouchables' than the British have given; then I will give up the claim for separate electorates." Only Baba Saheb could save Gandhi's life-by withdrawing the demand for separate electorates. At first he refused, saying it was his duty to do the best he could for his people-no matter what. Later he visited Gandhi, who was at that time in Yeravda jail. Gandhi persuaded Baba Saheb that Hinduism would change and leave its bad practices behind. Finally Baba Saheb agreed to sign the Poona Pact with Gandhi in 1932. Instead of separate electorates, more representation was to be given to the Depressed Classes. However, it later became obvious that this did not amount to anything concrete.

In the Prime of His Life: Baba Saheb had by this time collected a library of over 50,000 books, and had a house named Rajgriha built at Dadar in north Bombay to hold it. In 1935 his beloved wife Ramabai died. The same year he was made Principal of the Government Law College, Bombay. Also in 1935 a conference of Dalits was held at Yeola. Baba Saheb told the conference:-We have not been able to secure the barest of human rights... I am born a Hindu. I couldn't help it, but I solemnly assure you that I will not die a Hindu." This was the first time that Baba Saheb stressed the importance of conversion from Hinduism for his people-for they were only known as 'untouchables' within the fold of Hinduism.

During the Second World War, Baba Saheb was appointed Labour Minister by the Viceroy. Yet he never lost contact with his roots-he never became corrupt or crooked. He said that he had been born of the poor and had lived the life of the poor, he would remain absolutely unchanged in his attitudes to his friends and to the rest of the world. The All-India Scheduled Castes Federation was formed in 1942 to gather all 'untouchables' into a united political party.

Architect of the Constitution

After the war Baba Saheb was elected to the Constituent Assembly to decide the way that India-a country of millions of people-should be ruled. How should elections take place? What are the rights of the people? How are laws to be made? Such important matters had to be decided and laws had to be made. The Constitution answers all such questions and lays down rules. When India became independent in August 1947, Baba Saheb Ambedkar became First Law Minister of Independent India. The Constituent Assembly made him chairman of the committee appointed to draft the constitution for the world's largest democracy. All his study of law, economics, and politics made him the best qualified person for this task.

A study of the Constitutions of many countries, a deep knowledge of law, a knowledge of the history of India and of Indian Society-all these were essential. In fact, he carried the whole burden alone. He alone could complete this huge task. On July 15, 1947, the British Parliament passed the act of Indian

Independence and on August 15, 1947, India became free. The Constituent Assemble of Independent India appointed a Drafting Committee with Dr. Ambedkar as its Chairman to draft the Constitution of India. Dr. Ambedkar was also invited to join the Cabinet as the Minister of Law. Ambedkar toiled over the Constitution while he took care of his ministry. In February 1948, Dr. Ambedkar presented the Draft Constitution before the people of India. After completing the Draft Constitution, Baba Saheb fell ill.

At a nursing home in Bombay he met Dr. Sharda Kabir and married her in April 1948. On November 4, 1948 he presented the Draft Constitution to the Constituent Assembly, and on November 26, 1949 it was adopted in the name of the people of India. On that date he said: I appeal to all Indians to be a nation by discarding castes, which have brought separation in social life and created jealousy and hatred." Later Life-Buddhist Conversion: In 1950, he went to a Buddhist conference in Sri Lanka. On his return he spoke in Bombay at the Buddhist Temple. In order to end their hardships, people should embrace Buddhism. I am going to devote the rest of my life to the revival and spread of Buddhism in India." Why did he choose Buddhism?: Ambedkar told his friend Dattopant Thengadi: "I am in the evening of my life. There is an onslaught of ideas on our people from different countries from the four corners of the world. In this flood our people may be confused. There are strong attempts to separate the people struggling hard, from the main life-stream of this country and to attract them towards other countries. This tendency is fast growing. Even some of my colleagues who are disgusted with 'untouchability', poverty and inequality are ready to be washed away by this flood. What about the others? They should not move away from the main stream of the nation's life; and I must show them the way. At the same time, we have to make some changes in the economic and political life. That is way I have decided to follow Buddhism." There is a way of life which has come down as a steady stream in India for thousand of years. Buddhism is not opposed to it. The backward people must rebel against the injustice done to them; they must wipe it out. But 'untouchability' is a problem of the Hindu Society. To solve this, a path which does not harm the culture and the history of Bharat must be followed. This is the basis of his resolution.

He did not believe in the theory that Aryans came from a different land and that they defeated the Dasyus' (the Dravidians) of this country. There is no foundation for this in the Vedas. The word 'Arya' appears some 33 or 34 times in the Vedas. The word has been used as an adjective meaning 'the noble' or 'the elder'. It is said in the Mahabharata that 'Dasyus' can be found in all 'varnas' (castes) and 'ashramas' (stage of life). In this way Ambedkar used to support this view. On 14th October 1956 at a big function in Nagpur, Ambedkar, with his wife, embraced Buddhism. In May 1956, on Buddha's Anniversary,

Dr. Ambedkar announced that on October 14 he would embrace Buddhism. With him his wife and some three lakh followers also converted to the faith. When asked why, Dr. Ambedkar replied, "Why can't you ask this question to yourself and... your forefathers...?"

For the next five years Baba Saheb carried on a relentless fight against social evils and superstitions. On October 14, 1956 at Nagpur he embraced Buddhism. He led a huge gathering in a ceremony converting over half a million people to Buddhism. He knew that Buddhism was a true part of Indian history and that to revive it was to continue India's best tradition. 'Untouchability' is a product only of Hinduism. Bhim was an average student.

He became fond of gardening and, whenever he could, he bought saplings and with great devotion nurtured them to full growth. While studying in Satara, many of his classmates left for good jobs in Bombay. He too wanted to go to Bombay and get a job and become independent. He realized that if he ever were to be successful, he would have to concentrate more on his studies. He became interested in reading. He read not just the prescribed books in school but any book in general. His father was too pleased when he digressed from school books but he never said "no" when Bhim wanted a book.

Fight against Untouchability

As a leading Dalit scholar, Ambedkar had been invited to testify before the Southborough Committee, which was preparing the Government of India Act 1919. At this hearing, Ambedkar argued for creating separate electorates and reservations for Dalits and different religious communities. In 1920, he began the publication of the weekly Mooknayak (Leader of the Dumb) in Mumbai. Attaining popularity, Ambedkar used this journal to criticize orthodox Hindu politicians and a perceived reticence in the Indian political community to fight caste discrimination. His speech at a Depressed Classes Conference in Kolhapur impressed the local state ruler Shahu IV, who shocked orthodox society by dining with Ambedkar and his untouchable colleagues. Ambedkar exhorted his Mahar community to abandon the idea of sub-castes, and held a joint communal dinner in which the principle of segregation was abandoned. Upon his return from Europe, Ambedkar established a successful legal practise, and also organised the Bahishkrit Hitakarini Sabha (Group for the Wellbeing of the Excluded) to promote education and socioeconomic upliftment of the depressed classes. In the same vein, he was highly critical of the practice of untouchability in Indian Muslim Society, lending credence to the view that he was not exclusively against Hindus or Hinduism, but was speaking of reforming social evils.

In his illustrious publication "Pakistan and the Partition of India", he writes that, while Islam speaks of "brotherhood", the practice of slavery and caste discrimination were rampant in Muslim society in South Asia, such as the Ashraf/Ajlaf caste divide and the severe discrimination against the Arzal castes or Dalit Muslim untouchables. With the help of Shahu Maharaj of Kolhapur, a sympathizer of the cause for the upliftment of the depressed classes, Bhimrao started a fortnightly newspaper, the Mooknayak (Leader of the Dumb) on January 31, 1920. The Maharaj also convened many meeting and conferences of the "untouchables" which Bhimrao addressed. Impressed by Ambedkar, the Maharaj declared at a meeting, "You have found your saviour in Ambedkar. I am confident he will break your shackles." In July 1924, Ambedkar founded the Bahishkrut Hitkarini Sabha.

The aim of the Sabha was to uplift the downtrodden socially and politically and bring them to the level of the others in the Indian society. The Sabha aimed at scrapping the caste system from the Hindu religion. The Sabha started free school for the young and the old and ran reading rooms and libraries. Dr. Ambedkar took the grievances of the "untouchables" to court and gave them justice. Soon he became a father-figure to the poor and downtrodden and was respectfully called "Baba Saheb." On March 19-20, 1927 a conference of the depressed classes was held at Mahad. Ten thousand delegates attended, workers and leaders attended. Baba Saheb condemned the British for banning the recruitment of "untouchables" into the military.

He declared: "No lasting progress can achieved unless we put ourselves through a threefold process of purification. We must improve the general tone of our demeanour, re-tone our pronunciation and revitalize our thoughts. I, therefore, ask you now to take a vow to renounce eating carrion, the... flesh of... animals, from this moment....Make an unflinching resolve not to eat the thrown away crumbs. We will attain self-elevation only if we learn self-help, regain our self respect and gain self-knowledge."

On December 25 of the same year, thousands responded to Ambedkar's call. Speaker after speaker spoke, passions rose and the vast gathering waited for the satyagraha to begin with intense anticipation. The satyagraha was deferred when the matter was referred to the court. At the end of conference, a copy of the Manusmruti, the age-old code of the Hindus that gave rise to the caste system, was ceremoniously burnt. In a thundering voice, Ambedkar demanded in its place a new smruti, devoid of all social stratification. This act sent shockwaves through the nation. On October 13, 1935, at a conference at Nasik, Dr. Ambedkar reviewed the progress made on the condition of the "untouchables" in the decade since Ambedkar started his agitation. Ambedkar declared that their efforts had not borne the kind of results he had expected.

He then made a fantastic appeal to the "untouchables." He encouraged them to forsake the Hindu religion and convert to a religion where they would be treated with equality.

The nation was shocked. The British Government agreed to hold elections on the provincial level in 1937. The Congress, Muslim League and Hindu Mahasabha started gearing up for the elections. Dr. Ambedkar set up the Independent Labour Party in August 1936 to contest the elections in the Bombay province. On February 17, 1937, Ambedkar and many of his candidates won this a thumping majority. Around the same time, the Chavdar Taley water dispute which was referred to the Bombay High Court in 1927 finally handed down its verdict in favour of the depressed classes.

The Constituent Assemble adopted the Draft Constitution as the Constitution of India on November 26, 1949 with all its 356 Articles and eight Schedules and Article 11 which abolished untouchability in all forms. A Legacy Marking Indian Sociopolitical History: Ambedkar's legacy, as a sociopolitical reformer, has been long-lasting on modern India. In post independence India his sociopolitical thought has acquired respect across political spectrum and influenced various spheres of life like socioeconomic, education and Government policies of affirmative action by socioeconomic and legal incentives. Ambedkar organized untouchable political parties and social organizations, and served in the legislative councils of British India.

He would intensify his criticism of orthodox Hindu society, as well as his criticism of slavery and exclusivism in Islam. Despite this, his reputation as a scholar led to his appointment as free India's first law minister, and chairman of the committee responsible to draft a constitution. Ambedkar's work would guarantee political, economic and social freedoms for untouchables and other ethnic, social and religious communities of India. His polemical condemnation of Hinduism and attacks on Islam would make him unpopular and controversial, although his conversion to Buddhism sparked a revival in interest of Buddhist philosophy in India. In 1926, he became a nominated member of the Bombay Legislative Council. By 1927 Dr. Ambedkar decided to launch active movements against untouchability. He did begin with public movements and marches to open up & share public drinking water resources to which until then untouchable communities had no access; also he put up a struggle for entry in Hindu Temples which was not allowed by upper caste communities.

Poona Pact

Ambedkar had become one of the most prominent untouchable political figures of the time. He had grown increasingly critical of mainstream Indian political parties for their perceived lack of emphasis for the elimination of the caste system. Ambedkar criticized the Indian National Congress and its leader Mahatma Gandhi, whom he accused of reducing the untouchable community to a figure of pathos. Ambedkar was also dissatisfied with the failures of British rule, and advocated a political identity for untouchables separate from both the Congress and the British. At a Depressed Classes Conference on August 8, 1930 Ambedkar outlined his political vision: "...Safety of the Depressed Classes hinged on their being independent of the Government and the Congress" both: "We must shape our course ourselves and by ourselves... Political power cannot be a panacea for the ills of the Depressed Classes. Their salvation lies in their social elevation. They must cleanse their evil habits. They must improve their bad ways of living.... They must be educated.... There is a great necessity to disturb their pathetic contentment and to instill into them that divine discontent which is the spring of all elevation."

Born in a class considered low and outcast. Dr. Ambedkar fought untiringly for the downtrodden. The boy who suffered bitter humiliation became the first Minister for Law in free India, and shaped the country's Constitution. A determined fighter, a deep scholar, human to the tips of his fingers. We Need Dharma-But Casteism Should Go: 'Undouchablity' is a branch of casteism; until casteism is wiped out 'untouchability' will not go-this was Ambedkar's firm belief.

He argued that to wipe out casteism, political power was very necessary. He believed that Dharma was essential for men. But he revolted against those who, in the name of Dharma, treated some of their fellowmen like animals. Many people criticised him. Some newspapers also wrote against him. There were many occasions when his life was in danger. Also, Ambedkar knew from his own experience that even a bright man could not come up in life vacuse of casteism. People give his cast importance and make him powerless. Ambedkar fought casteism. He was disgusted to find how difficult it was to secure justice and to find how many men were still narrow-minded. He even said that it would be better to give up the Hindu Dharma itself. Muslim and Christian priest and missionaries learnt about this declaration; they tried very hard to attract Ambedkar. They met and assured him that the 'untouchables' who changed their religion would be given equal status in their society.

Bibliography

Agarawal, S.: *Dr. B.R. Ambedkar: The Man and his Message: A Commemorative Volume*, Prentice-Hall of India, New Delhi, 1991.

Aggarwal, L. B.: *The Harijans in Rebellion*, Taraporewala and Sons, Bombay, 1934.

Bakshi, S. R.: B.R. *Ambedkar: His Political and Social Ideology*. New Delhi: Deep & deep publications, 2000.

Barill, C.: *Social and Political Ideas of B.R. Ambedkar*, Aalekh Publishers, Jaipur, 1977.

Benjamin, Joseph: *Scheduled Castes in Indian Politics and Society*, Ess Ess Publications, New Delhi, 1989.

Chatterjee, Partha: *Caste and Subaltern Consciousness*, Oxford University Press, Delhi, 1994.

Desai, I. P.: *Anti-reservation Agitation and Struggle of Gujarat Society*, Adjanta Publications, Delhi, 1985.

Dubois, Abbe: *Hindu Manners, Customs and Ceremonies*, AES, New Delhi, 1983.

Engineer, Asghar Ali.: *Mandal Commission Controversy*, Ajanta Publications, Delhi, 1991.

Epstein, T. S.: *Economic Development and Social Change in South India*, Manchester University Press, Manchester, 1962.

Gorhe, Neelam: *Social Development and Dalit Women*, Gyan Pub. House, New Delhi, 1995.

Hardgrave, Robert L. Jr.: *The Dravidian Movement*, Popular Book Depot, Bombay, 1965.

Hocart, A. M.: *Caste*, Mathew and Co., London, 1950.

Ishwaran, K.: *Shivpur: A South Indian Village*, Routledge, London, 1968.

Juergensmeyer, Mark: *Religion as Social Vision: The Movement Against Untouchability in 20th Century Punjab*, University of California Press, Berkeley, 1979.

Kamble, J. R.: *Rise and Awakening of Depressed Classes in India*, National Publishers, New Delhi, 1979.

Khairmode, C.B.: *Dr. Bhimrao Ramji Ambedkar*, Pratap, Bombay, 1978.

Khare, R. S.: *The Untouchable as Himself: Ideology, Identity and Pragmatism Among the Lucknow Chamars*, Cambridge University Press, London, 1984.

Kshirsagar, R. K.: *Dalit Movement in India and Its Leaders (1857-1956)*, MD Pub. Pvt. Ltd., New Delhi, 1994.

Kuber, W.N.: *Dr. Ambedkar: A Critical Study*, People's Publishing House, New Delhi, 1973.

Lal, Shyam: *Caste and Political Mobilisation: The Bhangis*, Panchsheel Prakashan, Jaipur, 1981.

Lobo, C.H.J.J.: *Dr B.R. Ambedkar: The Champion of Social Democracy in India*, Hilerina Publishers, Bangalore, 1984.

Mahar, Michael J.: *The Untouchables in Contemporary India*, University of Arizona Press, Arizona, 1972.

Mallik, Suneila: *Social Integration of the Scheduled Castes*. Abhinav, New Delhi, 1979.

Mann, K.: *Tribal Women in a Changing Society*, Mittal Publications, Delhi, 1987.

Paranjpe, A. C.: *Caste, Prejudice and the Individual*, Lalvani Publishing House, New Delhi, 1970.

Parmaji, S.: *Caste Reservations and Performance*, Mamata Publications, Warangal, 1985.

Punekar, S.M.: *Harijan Contribution to Medieval Thought*, Prasaranga, Bangalore University, Bangalore, 1991.

Rajasekharaiah, A.M.: *B.R. Ambedkar: the Politics of Emancipation*, Sindhu Publications, Bombay, 1971.

Raju, G.G.: *The Life of B.R. Ambedkar*, Babasaheb Dr. Ambedkar Memorial Society, Hyderabad, 1979.

Ram, Jagivan: *Caste Challenge in India*, Vision Books, New Delhi, 1980.

Rege, Sharmila: *Sati: A Critical Analysis*, University of Poona, Poona, 1989.

Sarkar, J.: *Caste, Occupation and Change*, B. R. Publishing Co., Delhi, 1984.

Sharma, G. S.: *Legislation and Cases of Untouchability and Scheduled Castes in India*, Allied Publishers, Bombay, 1975.

Shashi B.R.: *Ambedkar and Human Rights*, KK Publishers, New Delhi, 1981.

Silverberg, James: *Social Mobility in the Caste System in India*, Mouton Publishers, The Hague, 1968.

Singh, K. K.: *Patterns of Caste Tensions*, Asia Publishing House, Bombay, 1967.

Srinivas, M. N.: *Caste in Modern India and Other Essays*, Asia Publishing House, Bombay, 1962.

Thorat, S.: *Ambedkar's Contribution to Water Resource Development*, Central Water Commission, New Delhi, 1993.

Tope, T.K.: *Dr. B.R. Ambedkar, A Symbol of Social Revolt*, Maharashtra Information Centre, New Delhi, 1964.

Venkateshwarlu, D.: *Harijan-Upper Class Conflicts*, Discovery, New Delhi, 1990.

Webster, John: *The Christian Dalits: A History*, Indian Society for Promoting Christian Knowledge (ISPCK), Delhi, 1994.

Yogesh, A.: *The Changing Frontiers of Caste*, National Publishing House, Delhi, 1968.

Zelliot, Eleanor: *From Untouchable to Dalit: Essays on the Ambedkar Movement*, Manohar, New Delhi, 1992.

Index

❑❑❑